D1068511

BIG APPLE GANGSTERS

BIG APPLE GANGSTERS
The Rise and Decline of the Mob in New York

Jeffrey Sussman

ROWMAN & LITTLEFIELD
Lanham • Boulder • New York • London

Published by Rowman & Littlefield
An imprint of The Rowman & Littlefield Publishing Group, Inc.
4501 Forbes Boulevard, Suite 200, Lanham, Maryland 20706
www.rowman.com

6 Tinworth Street, London SE11 5AL, United Kingdom

British Library Cataloguing in Publication Information Available

Library of Congress Cataloging-in-Publication Data

Names: Sussman, Jeffrey, author.
Title: Big apple gangsters : the rise and decline of the mob in New York /
   Jeffrey Sussman.
Description: Lanham : Rowman & Littlefield, [2020] | Includes
   bibliographical references and index. | Summary: "Through profiles of
   the most colorful and powerful crime bosses, gang members, corrupt cops,
   and numerous mob associates as well as pivotal events in the history of
   organized crime, Big Apple Gangsters reveals just how influential the
   mob has been in controlling large numbers of businesses not just in New
   York, but also in other cities"—Provided by publisher.
Identifiers: LCCN 2020007481 (print) | LCCN 2020007482 (ebook) | ISBN
   9781538134047 (cloth) | ISBN 9781538134054 (epub)
Subjects: LCSH: Organized crime—New York (State)—New York. |
   Gangsters—New York (State)—New York. | Mafia—New York (State)—New
   York.
Classification: LCC HV6441 .S87 2020 (print) | LCC HV6441 (ebook) | DDC
   364.1092/27471—dc23
LC record available at https://lccn.loc.gov/2020007481
LC ebook record available at https://lccn.loc.gov/2020007482

To my wife and best friend, Barbara

Contents

Acknowledgments

I AM GRATEFUL TO ALL THOSE named here for their time, expertise, and assistance.

Retired New York Detective Anthony Celano proved to be an excellent resource, not only for introducing me to numerous people with information about the Mob but also for letting me know about his own participation in investigating Mob activities.

Former criminal defense attorney Joseph Giannini told me about numerous mobsters he had defended during court proceedings.

Retired New York Detective Tommy Dades gave me valuable insights into the Mafia Cop case and witness Burton Kaplan.

Former prosecutor Michael Vecchione also provided information about the Mafia Cop case and insights into the current activities of the Mafia.

Former prosecutor Robert Santucci also provided valuable insights into the current activities of the Mafia.

Attorney Jay Goldberg, author of *The Courtroom Is My Theater*, told me about his defense of numerous high-level Mafioso and relayed personal information about Gregory Scarpa.

Attorney S. M. Chris Franzblau provided valuable information and insights about organized crime.

As in my previous books, Steven Spataro, East Hampton Chief Reference Librarian, was able to provide numerous research materials and photos that were essential for the writing of this book.

New York detectives Ralph Salerno and Remo Fanceschini (both deceased) provided me with valuable information about numerous New York gangsters from the 1920s through the 1990s.

My wife, Barbara, read the entire manuscript and offered helpful suggestions, and she has a better grasp of correct spelling than do computer programs.

Editor Kathryn Knigge and Editorial Assistant Charlotte Gosnell were especially helpful.

In addition, I thank all the people who spoke to me off the record about organized crime in New York.

Introduction

A LONG WITH MY 12-YEAR-OLD PALS, I loved baseball and idolized players on the Brooklyn Dodgers, such as Jackie Robinson, Duke Snider, and Gil Hodges, but—unlike my pals—I became fascinated by gangsters, too. Introduced to guest after guest at my Bar Mitzvah reception in the Grand Ballroom of the Commodore Hotel (now the Grand Hyatt), I met a man who—when he shook my hand—said, "I'm your Uncle Irving." "Nice to meet you," I replied. He handed me a $100 bill accompanied by a wink. He was the only one to hand me a large single denomination bill. Other guests gave me US Savings Bonds or checks. One man gave me a pair of 18-karat gold cufflinks. I had never seen a $100 bill before, and its presence in my hand excited me. Later that night I asked my father who Uncle Irving was. I never knew I had an Uncle Irving and was surprised when he had handed me money. My father told me,

"Actually, he's my uncle by marriage to my aunt Cele. He married her after his first wife died, and he had met her while smuggling liquor across the Canadian border during Prohibition."

"So he was a bootlegger," I said.

"That's right, and he was in fierce competition with another bootlegger named Dutch Schultz, known as the 'Beer Baron of the Bronx.' When the Dutchman was assassinated in Newark, Irv was one of several people rounded up by the cops. He was indicted for the murder but never tried. Even though Prohibition was over, the DA thought he was involved because he and the Dutchman had been enemies. However, a man named Charlie "the Bug" Workman took the rap and was sentenced for the murder. Bootlegging made Irv very rich. He had a mansion in upstate New York on property adjacent to the governor's mansion, but his base of operations was in New York City. He had a multifloor warehouse on 125th Street in Harlem. From that location, his truckers delivered hard liquor and beer to speakeasies throughout the city. His partner during Prohibition was a man named Abner 'Longy' Zwillman, who is the organized crime boss of New Jersey."

Years later, I learned that Zwillman was either murdered or committed suicide. He worked with a gangster named Willie Moretti, the godfather of Frank Sinatra's career. Moretti was shot in the face and killed by his Mafia cohorts, who feared that Moretti's worsening dementia and garrulousness in front of a Senate investigatory committee would result in him revealing gangland secrets to investigators. Better to shut him up—Mafia style.

My next meeting with a mobster was with my mother's cousin Joe (whose last name I shall not reveal because I see no point in embarrassing his daughters and grandchildren). Joe and his brother had operated an Italian grocery store in the Corona section of Queens in New York City during the 1930s. While one brother went to law school, the other brother ran the grocery, and they took turns until they received their respective law degrees. As owners of a store patronized by recently arrived immigrants from Italy, they learned to speak Italian. Their customers worked paycheck to paycheck and often had to purchase food on credit. Many of those customers also borrowed money from Joe and his brother. Some of them borrowed several thousand dollars to use as down payments on modest homes. That practice eventually grew into a mortgage company, which—in turn—grew into a title company. Along the way, the brothers associated with low-level members of the Mafia, who also provided money to customers of the grocery. Rather than compete, the brothers and the mobsters worked together. Some of those Mafioso eventually rose to positions of importance in the Mob and helped to fund various real-estate deals for the brothers. In the mid-1950s, Joe was retained to torch a warehouse in the Bronx in which he had a partial interest. The insurance settlement would be worth more than the warehouse generated in rental income. Joe was caught and his picture appeared on the front page of a tabloid newspaper, *The Daily Mirror*. My father paid his bail. Following Joe's trial that ended in probation and a fine, his law license was revoked. Some of his partners installed him as a manager of a Mob-owned restaurant, and he also became a private detective. I never understood how a disbarred lawyer could obtain a license as a private investigator, but in the 1950s, judicial corruption was rife and mobsters were able to bribe whoever had a hand out.

When Joe would visit us, I would ask him to take out his snub-nosed .38-caliber revolver from his shoulder holster and let me hold it; he would unload the bullets from the cylinder and then hand me the gun. It was black metal and had a brown hand grip. I held the gun in my hand as if it were a talisman. The trigger was easy to pull, and the hammer clicked impotently. I was always regretful that I had to return the gun to Joe before he left our house.

My father, always a good friend to Joe, made the mistake of inviting him to a weekly pinochle card game. One night, Joe was losing hand after hand, and he pulled out his gun and said he wanted to win the next hand. My father's friends were furious and refused to play again if Joe was going to be present. My father had to explain to Joe why he could no longer attend. But Joe had bigger ventures to attend to. While he maintained his private detective practice, he gave up restaurant management and opened a private airport for small planes. With his brother, he continued to invest in real estate, and they opened several shopping malls on Long Island. Having become quite wealthy, he went back to college and earned a PhD in clinical psychology. He became a tenured professor of psychology at a local college. He retired after several years and moved with his wife into a stunningly modernistic mansion in Fort Lauderdale, Florida. I never knew the full nature of his criminality, but one of my relatives had told me when I was in college that if I invested $10,000 with Joe, I would receive $20,000 in 6 months. Apparently Joe never abandoned his loan-sharking practice from his days operating an Italian grocery.

Another event served to arouse my interest in mobsters: When I was a teenager, I worked for my father on Saturday mornings. He owned and operated two dress-manufacturing companies one in Queens and one in Brooklyn. I worked in the Queens factory. In addition to sweeping floors, I was often charged with carrying 50-pound bolts of cloth from the basement to the cutter's table. There, on a table about 30 feet long, the bolt would be unrolled, and the cutter would place paper patterns of dresses on the cloth and cut out the pieces that would become dresses when sewed together. One day, while carrying a bolt of cloth up from the basement, I heard my father and another man yelling at one another. At the top of the stairs, I was able to see both men, who looked as if they would come to blows. Spittle sprung from my father's mouth, and his fists were clenched as if ready to throw punches. When he was a young man, he had been an amateur boxer, so an exchange of fists would not have been surprising. My father's antagonist called him a Jew bastard, and I thought for sure that would lead to violence. Instead my father told him to "get the fuck out!" His antagonist didn't budge, but pointed his index finger at him and said, "We'll get you! You son of a bitch!" With that, the stranger made the symbol of a pistol with his right hand, flexed his right index finger as if pulling a trigger, and left. I didn't say anything at that moment because I was too stunned to talk. But in my father's car on the way home I asked about it. My father told me that the man was a gangster named

Johnny Dio, who ran an illegal union and a trucking company. He wanted my father to let his union organize my father's workers, and he wanted my father to use his trucking company. The workers had voted down union membership because they would have earned less than my father was paying them. The trucking deal was another matter. My father continued to resist the threats that arrived almost daily via telephone. Two weeks later, while my parents had taken me out for a dinner to celebrate my graduation from the eighth grade, our house was burglarized. Nothing was taken, but the kitchen had been wrecked. The contents of the refrigerator had been dumped on the floor and thrown against walls: a smashed melon dribbled down one wall; sour cream was spread like a bas-relief against another wall; red grapes had been trampled on the floor; a gargoyle of peanut butter hung from the ceiling; broken bottles littered the counter tops; a mixture of juices, milk, and soda had been poured over the stove and sink; honey was smeared over the burners on the stove; apple sauce was poured over the kitchen chairs. A message had been delivered: this is just the beginning. Things will get worse if you don't cooperate. The next day, my father visited the president of the trucking company that he had retained for years and explained what was going on. The man said, "Bob, you'll have to go with their trucking company. Otherwise, their guys will kill you and your family. I hate to lose your business, but you have no choice."

Joe, the family friend and private detective, was called on, and he was able to negotiate a deal with the trucking company. It would not have been what my father wanted, but it was better than the original offer. Two years later, my father died of cancer. His partner was no match for the Mob's trucking company, which repeatedly raised its rates to the point where it cost more to have merchandise shipped than the merchandise was worth. To satisfy the debt it was owed, the Mob grabbed pieces of the business, and in a few years, they took it over. The Mob then operated the business for a year, never paid its creditors, sold merchandise at steep discounts, and then incinerated the factory for the insurance settlement. It was known as a classic Mob bust out.

My interest in the Mob was given further impetus as a result of a friendship with a man who helped me when I was on the balls of my ass. I had recently been divorced, gave up my interest in a company that I had operated with my wife, and was looking around for a new way to make a living. I had known Tom for a number of years but had never relied on him for help. When he learned of my circumstances and of my intention to start my own PR/marketing company, he was able to get a number of clients for me. I spent a lot of time talking with Tom, and our friendship grew. I wanted to learn more about this man who had been so generous in helping me. He was one of the most empathetic men I had been fortunate to have as a friend. His story is not one that would necessarily lead to empathy and generosity. Tom was the son of a professional gambler, a member of the Mafia, who controlled a number of gambling venues for Frank Costello, known as the Prime Minister of the Underworld. Tom's mother was a seamstress. His parents had divorced when Tom was a young boy. His father lived in the penthouse of the luxurious Sherry-Netherland Hotel on Fifth Avenue, while his mother lived in a modest apartment in Brooklyn. Costello was Tom's godfather, not in the Mafia sense but in the religious one. Tom and his brother lived with their mother but would periodically spend weekends with their father. He was not a demonstratively loving man; instead, he would give his sons several hundred dollars and tell them to have a good time. Tom felt sorry for his mother who made little money as a seamstress and resented his father who never contributed to his former wife's welfare. That resentment led Tom to embrace the goals of communism. Yet, he still enjoyed the privileges that his father's wealth and position provided. When Tom was in high school, his father and Costello picked him up in a large elegant Cadillac and drove to Saratoga for the races. There, Tom was introduced to Meyer Lansky, the brains and financial wizard of the Mob. Tom was given several hundred dollars to bet on the races. He lost it all. He thought of how that money would have been useful for his mother, and he cursed his foolishness. However, it didn't stop him from calling on Costello when he needed a favor. When Tom graduated from high school, he wanted to take his prom date to the Copacabana, so he called Costello, who owned the nightclub, and asked for a reservation. When Tom and his date arrived, they were escorted to a table right in front of the stage. Their dinner and champagne were served on the house. When Tom offered to pay, he was told that there would be no charge. Through his father and Costello, Tom was given an opportunity to join the Mafia but chose not to. (It's interesting that one is told that only Italians whose parents are also Italian can be made members of the Mafia, but Tom's mother was Jewish, as was Costello's wife.)

Tom told me numerous stories about the Mob as well as admitting that one of his cousins was a captain in the Mafia. He said he would never permit the guy into his house because he thought he was a psychopath. Yet, he found many mobsters to be more complicated than they were made out to be in popular movies and novels.

Tom's sympathy for communism naturally led him to be strongly antifascist, and in 1940 he joined the Canadian infantry to fight the Nazis. When the United States entered the war in 1941, Tom enlisted in the US infantry and was later wounded in the Battle of the Bulge. He carried shrapnel in one thigh for the rest of his life. He died in 2015. When I attended his memorial service, I was not surprised that hundreds of people turned out to honor him.

One final anecdote: in1990, I was hired to write a documentary tentatively titled *Sucked into the Mob*. For the project, I interviewed a former detective whose focus had been Mob investigations. He told me the following story:

> I had grown up in a neighborhood where mobsters were prevalent. You either became a mobster, a cop, or a priest. My father guided me into becoming a cop. After five years on the job, I was asked to join an organized crime strike force, since I was familiar with the mob. One day, I was assigned to arrest a man I had grown up with. We had been friends in high school. Now he was a made man. He had lured a member of his crew to their social club late at night. Once inside, my old friend shot his crew member in the back of the head. He left the body there and drove home, where he had dinner with his wife and two daughters. Nobody said anything about the blood spatter on his white shirt. Imagine, he didn't even put on a clean shirt before sitting down to have dinner with his family. These guys are able to lead two lives; they can separate their criminal lives from their home lives, and the two never meet. It's like a form of schizophrenia.

In thinking about those experiences and others, I decided to investigate the lives of the most notorious gangsters of the Big Apple, especially the ones who not only dominated the underworld during the 20th century but who also controlled much of the commerce and political life in the richest city in the world. In so doing, I also investigated the role of organized crime in the life of the city.

Although there were gangs in New York after the Civil War, gangs did not become organized until Arnold Rothstein mentored four young gangsters who would help to create the National Crime Syndicate. They were Lucky Luciano, Meyer Lansky, Frank Costello, and Ben "Bugsy" Siegel; also coming along for the ride were Vito Genovese and Joseph Bonanno. Others who became associated with the syndicate included Louis "Lepke" Buchalter, Albert "Mad Hatter" Anastasia, Jacob "Gurrah" Shapiro, and the members of Murder Inc. Following the outset of Prohibition in 1920, the biggest gangsters in New York were making millions of dollars a year from bootlegging. Following the end of Prohibition, the gangsters expanded their already existing ventures in prostitution, drug dealing, fixed boxing matches, labor racketeering, gambling, trucking, and various other illegal activities. The Big Apple gangsters wielded significant control of the city and continued to do so right up through the 1990s. Their power was diminished incrementally by ambitious crusading prosecutors who went on to have high-profile political careers, beginning with Thomas Dewey, extending into Senate investigation committees headed by Senators Estes Kefauver and John L. McClellan, and finally leading to Attorney General Robert Kennedy prosecuting more than 300 mobsters and US Attorney Rudolph Giuliani going after the Mafia Commission members and winning convictions that led to long prison terms. Although organized crime is still woven into the fabric of New York City, there are fewer strands, and those that exist are less colorful than the ones that defined the fabric of New York for decades. This book will not only provide portraits of the most colorful and significant gangsters of New York, but it will also trace their rise and decline and the resulting contraction of power of organized crime in the Big Apple.

Chapters need not be read in sequence because each chapter is a self-contained biographical portrait of an individual gangster; hence, there is some overlap of material when more than one gangster was involved in a particular crime.

1

The Master

ARNOLD ROTHSTEIN, in addition to being a venture capitalist of organized crime, was a one-man Harvard Business School for the criminal underworld. His brilliant student criminals included Meyer Lansky, Lucky Luciano, Ben "Bugsy" Siegel, and Frank Costello. He taught them how to organize their criminal activities, develop top-down corporate structures of governance, and shield themselves from the grip of law enforcement through bribery and political favors. (That lesson didn't take hold in the case of Lucky Luciano, who was given a 50-year prison sentence for running prostitution rings and pimping.)

Rothstein proved his confidence in his students' abilities to provide substantial returns on his investments because he advanced them thousands of dollars to finance their operations and made many hundreds of thousands of dollars in return. By the time his students had graduated into big-time criminal activities, they had organized a growing National Crime Syndicate that would become the most powerful criminal enterprise in the United States, its financial wherewithal as great as a *Fortune 500* company. Had it been listed on the New York Stock Exchange, its price would have multiplied over the decades. Alas, membership in the syndicate was limited, and its stock was not publicly traded.

Though Rothstein is often credited with fixing the 1919 World Series, a stupendous accomplishment that fired the imaginations of novelists, journalists, and filmmakers, he should also be known as the father of organized crime. Yet, that's rarely the case. Even the brilliant novelist of *The Great Gatsby*, F. Scott Fitzgerald, couldn't help creating a character, Meyer Wolfsheim, based on Rothstein, describing him as the man who fixed the 1919 World Series between the Chicago White Sox and the Cincinnati Reds.

"He's quite a character around New York—a denizen of Broadway."

"Who is he, anyhow? An actor?"

"No."

"A dentist?"

"Meyer Wolfsheim? No he's a gambler." Gatsby hesitated, then added coolly, "He's the man who fixed the World Series back in 1919."

"Fixed the World Series?" I repeated.

The idea staggered me. I remembered, of course, that the World Series had been fixed in 1919, but if I had thought of it at all I would have thought of it as a thing that merely happened at the end of some inevitable chain. It never occurred to me that one man could start to play with the faith of 50 million people—with the single-mindedness of a burglar blowing a safe.

"How did he happen to do that?" I asked after a minute.

"He just saw the opportunity."

"Why isn't he in jail?"

"They can't get him, old sport. He's a smart man."[1]

And Damon Runyon, in *Guys and Dolls*, based a more colorful kind of gambler on Rothstein: Nathan Detroit, a character whose portrayal in movies and on the stage has entertained audiences for decades. (On stage, Detroit has been played by Alan King, Bob Hoskins, and Nathan Lane, among various others; in the movie of *Guys and Dolls*, Frank Sinatra played the part.) In the movie *Eight Men Out*, the slim and attractive Rothstein is portrayed as a portly, cold-hearted schemer who ruined the lives of some magnificent baseball players (such as Shoeless Joe Jackson) in the infamous Black Sox Scandal. Rothstein, as the father of organized crime, was so much more than those portrayals, which—of course—come close to being caricatures of a complex, many-sided scoundrel.

Though the fix of the 1919 World Series is the source of Rothstein's notoriety, it was a minor accomplishment compared to the breadth and depth of his manifold criminal endeavors. From bankrolling many Prohibition activities and drug deals to fixing horse races and boxing matches, from running gambling casinos to shylocking, from paying off judges and politicians to paying thugs to rough up recalcitrant debtors, from operating insurance companies to owning and managing office buildings, Rothstein was a combination of J. P. Morgan and Morgan the Pirate.

Although members of the demimonde comprised his long list of customers, he also financed legitimate business, though legitimacy bored him. That which was legal was as dull as a puddle of water in a gutter. Illegality, however, was like a drug that got his adrenaline shooting through his veins and arteries. It was voltaic; it aroused his passions and riveted his attention. Yet, he preferred operating quietly in the shadows: a puppet master pulling the strings of all the marionettes on his various illicit merchant banking stages.

Though a brilliant mentor, Rothstein was not known for kindness and generosity. If he gave with one hand, he took back much more with the other. If, for example, one wanted to borrow money from him, that person would have to be prepared to accept onerous financing charges, often as high as 48 percent. In addition, he might insist on siphoning a percentage of the income from a borrower's business during the life of the loan and for some time thereafter. If a payment was late, the interest rate increased, as did Rothstein's ownership position in the borrower's business. If his borrowers had insufficient collateral to cover their loans, they had to take out insurance policies with Rothstein's insurance company. The premiums were exorbitant, and the policies could not be cancelled by the insured. In addition to the financial leverage he had, Rothstein might also resort to strong-arm tactics to convince recalcitrant borrowers that their sense of responsibility for paying off their debts was insufficient. A little discipline would curb their deviations. Often a pair of thugs, armed with brass knuckles, blackjacks, and baseball bats provided inescapable solutions and so were rarely required to make second visits.

Though he owned office buildings and had ostensibly legitimate offices for his insurance and real-estate companies, Rothstein preferred to operate from his reserved table in a popular Broadway restaurant named Lindy's. (When Rothstein was absent from the restaurant, no one was permitted to sit at his table.) Lindy's was located at 1626 Broadway, between 49th and 50th Streets. The restaurant, known for its delicious cheesecake, was celebrated as Mindy's by Damon Runyon in *Guys and Dolls*. From his Broadway hangout, Rothstein did business, lending money and collecting money and betting on fixed horse races and boxing matches. There, he accepted the respect of underlings and clients; runners for bookies were continually rushing in and rushing out, dropping off betting slips on Rothstein's table. The obsequious maitre d' took phone messages for Rothstein, who was like a king in his castle.

From what depths did this king of the underworld rise up to have such power? Rothstein was not born into gangland royalty nor was he born into immigrant poverty as were the gangsters he mentored. He began life on July

17, 1882, in New York City; he was the son of affluent German Jews, Esther and Abraham. His father was considered so honest and trustworthy that he was known as Abe the Just. Abe was admired as a man who never broke a promise. His word was his bond, as solid as a notarized contract. He was so judicious that he was often called on to negotiate disagreements between litigants, for all sides trusted his impartiality. Yet, young Arnold disliked his father, disliked what he considered to be his father's priggish prudery and sense of self-righteousness. He also believed that his parents favored their older son, Harry, whom Arnold grew to despise. When Esther traveled away from home, she often took Harry with her and left Arnold at home with his father. Angry at his mother not choosing to take him, young Arnold retreated into a darkened closet and cried; his father heard his son sobbing, opened the closet door, and discovered Arnold curled up in a fetal position. When asked what was wrong, Arnold moaned that his parents hated him. Abe attempted to console his son and convince him that his parents loved him as much as they loved Harry. The boys were equal in the hearts of their parents. Arnold would have none of it. He thought his father was a liar. If he could not be the center of his parents' attention by being good, then he decided he would be bad. From that date onward, Arnold's behavior consisted of one rebellious act after another. In time, he discovered the game of shooting craps; it was a game for which his father had contempt because he thought it was a game for hoodlums and truants. Aha! Arnold had found an important means of being bad, of angering his father, and gaining his disapproval; it was better to be the focus of his disapproval than not be noticed. Though Abe was furious, he could not keep his son from dice games; besides, Arnold was winning, so why should he quit? That attitude further angered his father. Arnold was having a good time, and he enjoyed the company of gamblers and hustlers. And Arnold's new pals were impressed by his natural abilities: his risk taking and his quick mind for quickly figuring out percentages. Though he was a poor student at school, bored by his lessons and lectures and rarely in attendance, he was excellent at mathematics and could do complex computations in his head.

Arnold was making money from dice games and hustling pool games. When his bankroll was beginning to make a bulge in his pants, his father noticed and told him that gambling was not for respected members of society. That suited Arnold. The more Abe criticized his son's gambling, the more Arnold spent time not only shooting dice but also playing poker and pool.

In his biography of Rothstein, Leo Katcher writes, "What did he need of schools when there was such places as gambling houses, pool rooms, and the prop room of Hammerstein's Victoria Theatre on the corner of 42nd Street and Seventh Avenue? There was a dice game in the prop room every Monday."[2]

From the age of 16, Rothstein found the kind of people that he would associate with for the rest of his life. In *Boxing and the Mob*, the author wrote,

> He wandered into a seedy pool hall on the Bowery populated by gamblers, hustlers, pimps petty thieves, and the women who were attracted to them. Some of the women lived off the earnings of the thieves and hustlers. Many others, in thrall to pimps, supported their servitude by prostitution. Arnold watched them with fascination and guiltless pleasure as low stakes pool hustlers fleeced tourists and young men from uptown who had been out for a night of excitement and slumming among the demimonde. Arnold had found his métier, the sawdust on the floor, the aroma of cheap booze in the air, and the implied lawlessness of the place. These were to be Arnold's people; they would become his tutors and—when he became a master of their world—they would become his employees.[3]

The pool halls and gambling casinos provided Rothstein with his undergraduate education, and he learned with an alacrity that impressed bookies and gambling entrepreneurs. One of those whom he impressed was Big Tim Sullivan, the political boss of the Lower East Side and the Bowery. Sullivan took an almost paternal interest in Rothstein; he realized that Rothstein could greatly increase the income of his own gambling casinos, so he mentored Rothstein in the basic operations of a casino. Sullivan owned several gambling casinos and believed that Rothstein was the man who could increase earnings through the manipulation of games of chance. He would provide Rothstein with his postgraduate education in not only gambling but also loan sharking, fencing, blackmail, extortion, arson, and financing of an assortment of illegal activities. Rothstein was no longer rebelling against the rules and regulations of his father's straight-arrow world; he was traveling rapidly, following a route to wealth and power that Sullivan had mapped out for him. Rothstein would always honor Sullivan as the man who had helped to navigate his entry into the world of sophisticated gamblers. Instructed by Sullivan, Rothstein was committed to gambling only on sure things, except when it came to card games. In such instances, he trusted his instincts to be the best player in the game.

In addition to educating Rothstein in the ways of the sophisticated gambler, Sullivan helped him raise money to buy his own casino on the west side of Manhattan; Rothstein also purchased interests in saloons, brothels, and theaters. Operating beyond the borders of legality required that Rothstein not be arrested and put in jail, so Sullivan also taught Rothstein the benefits of bribing policemen, judges, and local politicians, for they would become Rothstein's partners and permit him to operate undisturbed and without the intrusion of competitors.

Rothstein was rapidly rising to the top of a criminal pyramid; and on his way up, he began to realize that the gangs of New York were disorganized, fighting one another for small rewards, and often suffering physical damage and prison sentences. He believed that so much more could be gained if the gangs were organized. For that to happen, Rothstein would need students as eager as he had been to learn the ropes of a successful criminal enterprise. The existing gangs were too entrenched in their old ways to undertake a radical reevaluation.

It was more than kismet that Rothstein attracted the young aspiring gangsters Luciano, Lansky, Costello, and Siegel. His reputation among young aspiring criminals was that of a great teacher, the man with the Midas touch. From him, one could learn all one needed to know to earn a fortune from the rackets and remain out of the clutches of law enforcement.

To begin, he taught them that there was no benefit to warring gangs fighting with one another. Monk Eastman, the Hudson Dusters, the Gophers, and the Plug Uglies were all destined for self-destruction. Modern gangs could each be profitable if they neatly divided their territories, settled disputes through a board of directors, and controlled the prices of contraband, such as heroin, so one gang would not be underselling another. Although price fixing is illegal in the world of corporate America, organized criminals operate in their own world where all goods come with fixed prices. The gangs envisioned by Rothstein would combine the attributes of oligarchy, plutocracy, and totalitarianism. Its governing body would brook no protests and no deviation by its members to agreed-upon rules. The ultimate sanction for disobedience would be death. Rothstein emphasized that an organized criminal organization, including its illegal enterprises and sanctions, would function like a large corporation. And its profits could be as great, if not greater, than that of any major US corporation. In addition, one could hardly declare income to the IRS for money earned from bootlegging, smuggling, robbery, etc. Of course, that was how the government finally caught up with Al Capone. Although most mobsters were sensible enough not to live beyond their apparent means, many were foolish enough to flaunt their wealth, and so attracted the attention of the government.

Rothstein's answer was to take control of brokerage houses, insurance companies, garment manufacturers, trucking companies, and private banks, all of which could be used to prove legitimate sources of income. For an extra layer of protection, Rothstein advised his students on the essential value of bribing judges, prosecutors, police, and politicians. The bribery was simply a valuable and necessary cost of doing business.

As Rothstein was growing in power and wealth, his own mentor and protector Sullivan was spiraling downward: his mind was turning to mush as he deteriorated through the final stage of tertiary syphilis. He had made Rothstein a beneficiary of his knowledge and power. Now Rothstein was on his own and thriving, and his businesses were generating streams of money that he poured into foreign corporate real-estate holdings, into Swiss bank accounts, and into his own Caribbean banks.

Rothstein's money came from any opportunity that he could control. As a master of the world of gambling, Rothstein fixed horse races and boxing matches and won huge sums of money. It was not unusual for him to win from $100,000 to $800,000 on the outcomes of sports events he was able to fix. On one horse race, he managed to win $1,350,000. So as not to alter the odds in a way that would reduce his winnings, Rothstein was highly secretive about placing bets. And to throw people off his intentions, he would not only have front men place bets for him in cities across the country, but he would also bet small amounts on losers and let others know he had placed those bets. Not all sporting events that Rothstein had a hand in went smoothly or without controversy. The Black Sox scandal, of course, was one such event, but so was a controversial boxing match between Jack Dempsey and Gene Tunney on September 23, 1926. Rothstein, who claimed he only bet on sure things, won $500,000 on the match. Was it fixed? There is evidence that it was: on the morning of the fight, Dempsey drank a small glass of olive oil to aid his digestion. It was a practice in which he regularly indulged before a fight. The glass of olive oil was given to him by Mike Dent, a Dempsey bodyguard. Shortly thereafter, Dempsey began having stomach cramps, which lasted throughout the day. He wasn't sure he would get into the ring, but his determination not to give into the malady, which he believed was short-lived, was important to Dempsey's image as a tough, fists-like-bricks slugger. Such a fierce fighter as Dempsey would not use a stomach ache as an excuse to avoid his pugilistic responsibilities. Nevertheless, Dempsey consulted his doctor, who believed that some noxious substance had been added to the olive oil that caused pain followed by diarrhea. Dempsey accepted the diagnosis and then let it be known he would be going into the ring. When word of Dempsey's condition spread, so did the rumors that gamblers had paid Dent to taint Dempsey's olive oil. That rumor led to another that the ever-resourceful and nefarious Rothstein had paid Dent to make Dempsey sick with food poisoning. Rothstein, who would never sacrifice large sums of money on a hunch or a whim, bet $125,000 on Tunney to win. The odds were four to one in Rothstein's favor, and he grinned broadly at the end of the fight. David Pietrusza writes in his biography of Rothstein, "We also knew that Abe Attell and Arnold Rothstein were on the scene, among the handful of observers predicting a Tunney victory. A. R. prominent at ringside, won a fortune on the long shot, Tunney. Attell was everywhere."[4]

Although Rothstein fixed horse races and boxing matches, he rarely attempted to fix card games. The only ways of doing so were either to use decks of marked cards or to have an observer who could surreptitiously report on what another player held in his hand. Instead of those methods, Rothstein relied on what he considered his superior ability to outwit opponents in poker and other card games. He also thought that his mathematical skills gave him an edge over players who were less sophisticated. As he did in dice games, he often won at card games. His self-confidence was not illusory. On the rare occasions when he did lose, he suspected he had been cheated. In the fall of 1928, Rothstein played in a 3-day poker game in a suite at the Penn Central Hotel. He played and bet like a man possessed, an obsessive compulsive gambler, so unlike the man who only bet on sure things. He was losing big time and his anger was rising to a boil. He hated losing, and nothing he tried was working. He cursed in frustration. At the end of that last day of play, he was down $320,000. He was so furious that he declared the game had been fixed, and he refused to pay. The hell with it. When the winners still demanded he pay, he reiterated his refusal to pay, again claiming the game had been fixed. To the winners, this was an example that Rothstein was indeed as bad as his reputation: he was known as a welcher. Though he was quick to collect debts by means fair or foul, he was at best reluctant to pay his own debts, especially if the debts accrued as a result of his gambling. Seeing that his comments about being cheated had only angered the other players, Rothstein attempted to cool their tempers. He said he would pay them, but he had to wait until after the upcoming elections: he was temporarily short of cash but would have more than $500,000 following the electoral wins of Herbert Hoover as president and Franklin Roosevelt as governor but that was not good enough. No one trusted Rothstein to pay up. Up and down Broadway he owed money to gamblers and bookies and avoided paying them. It was no wonder that Rothstein finally took a bullet in his gut. Two of the winning card players, Nigger Nate Raymond and Titanic Thompson, were thought to be responsible for the shooting, but there was no evidence to support that claim. George "Hump" McManus was next to be blamed because he was the one who supposedly pulled out a revolver and shot Rothstein. Then, as Rothstein clutched his side, McManus allegedly tossed the revolver out of the window, landing on Seventh Avenue, where a taxi driver picked it up. There were no fingerprints, other than the taxi driver's, on the gun. With a bullet in his gut, Rothstein staggered out of the room, made his way down a flight of stairs, muttered to a hotel employee that he had been shot, and asked that an ambulance be called. He continued bleeding profusely as a siren-screaming ambulance sped him to Stuyvesant Polyclinic Hospital. When cops placed him on an operating table, Rothstein was asked by cops if he knew who had shot him. He responded that "you stick to your trade, I'll stick to mine." He maintained the gangster tradition of omerta, of never ratting, even on an enemy—not even when you're dying. Rothstein died 2 days after the shooting, and McManus was indicted for murder. Thompson testified that it was not McManus who shot Rothstein, but he didn't know who the shooter was; McManus was later acquitted.

Rothstein, age 46, was buried in Ridgewood's Union Field Cemetery. His business interests were taken over by his protégés, Lansky and Luciano, while his heirs, including a girlfriend, spent years and wasted money fighting over his dwindling estate.

While Lansky, Luciano, and Costello are often regarded as the wily fathers of organized crime in the 20th century, their rise to power was built on the wisdom, chicanery, and organizational skills of Arnold Rothstein, the man who did more than fix the 1919 World Series.

2

Don't Ever Call Him Bugsy

WHEN ANGRY AT SOMEONE, Ben Siegel would shoot a hard, murderous glare in that person's direction, and his pale blue eyes would turn steely gray. Violence might be seconds away. His outbursts of rage could happen as unexpectedly and as quickly as a sudden bolt of lightning. But if you were a friend who had mistakenly said something that had angered the handsome gangster, you could cool the hot fury in his eyes with a soft compliment. "I didn't mean it. Hey, baby blue eyes. You know I wouldn't do anything to hurt you." And he would set you at ease with a disarming smile.

He was a vain man and as handsome as a movie star, tall, leanly muscled, and elegantly draped in a blue pinstriped suit. He was a fitness buff, who regularly worked out in a YMCA gym; when gangster pal Mickey Cohen saw Siegel in a bathing suit, sauntering around his Holmby Hills swimming pool, Cohen suggested that Siegel should be offered a contract to model bathing suits. Siegel laughed, said no, and waved off the compliment with a long cigar in his right hand, but he was nevertheless flattered. He took pride in his lean, muscular body, his perpetually tanned face, and slicked black hair. Instead of modeling, he would have liked to have been a movie star like his boyhood pal, George Raft (né Ranft), who had been a protégé of Prohibition gangster Owney Madden. In fact, Siegel prevailed on Raft to get him a screen test. Yet, he was too proud to have a casting director view it and possibly reject his efforts. Siegel was not willing to accept rejection or failure in anything he undertook. For a tough gangster, he was surprisingly thin-skinned. Yet, had he not invested himself in the criminal life and not been so vulnerable to rejection, he very well may have succeeded as a star of the silver screen, even a minor star. His friends, such as Raft, Cary Grant, Ava Gardner, and Lana Turner, all thought he had the makings of a star: he was charming, seductive, and self-assured. Many actors who met him at swank Hollywood parties were drawn to him and thought he could have joined their ranks. Instead, as a behind-the-scenes boss of various movie-industry unions, he had his front men blackmail production heads to avoid strikes. Hundreds of thousands of dollars in cash were passed in envelopes to Siegel. When he wasn't being a thug, he could be seen in the company of gorgeous stars, such as Turner, Gardner, Betty Grable, and Marie McDonald, all of whom he seduced with his charm, good looks, and radiant power.

He may have been the most charming, elegant, and handsome gangster of all time, a Lothario in a bespoke suit—but never call him "Bugsy." He hated the nickname, derived from the expression, "crazy as a bedbug." A bug is an insect, Siegel would heatedly explain, and not a human being. And Siegel, born in 1906 to a poor immigrant Jewish family, was determined to present himself as a civilized, cultured, well-read, sporting man of the world. His charisma, street smarts, and toughness made him a natural leader in the National Crime Syndicate as well as an influential associate of Mafia crime families; yet, he would always be looked on as a hot head, someone for whom violence provided a charge of psychosexual satisfaction. New York City Organized Crime Detective Ralph Salerno told the author that when Siegel's underlings were given a contract to kill someone, Siegel always went with them and often led them into battle. He had a short fuse, or no fuse, and he easily exploded into furious acts of violence; hence, the name Bugsy.

His life of crime began at an early age in the Williamsburg section of Brooklyn, a crowded slum of poor immigrant Jews, all struggling or battling to achieve prosperity. But it was the Lower East Side of Manhattan, where Siegel entered into a life of crime with his lifelong friend Moe Sedway. Together, they threatened peddlers and newsstand operators that if they didn't pay for protection their merchandise would be incinerated. To convince vendors of their seriousness, the two young thugs would overturn a newsstand in the middle of the night and then offer protection the following morning. If the news dealer still proved recalcitrant, the duo would come back that night and set the newsstand on fire. Word of their fiery deeds spread among news dealers, so the dealers paid for protection. When it came to horse-drawn peddlers' wagons, the duo would often kidnap the peddlers' horses and tie them to trees in nearby parks or vacant lots so the peddlers couldn't find their nags. Because peddlers could barely afford to miss a day's work, they, too, paid for protection. By the time they were teenagers, Siegel and Sedway were making more money than their parents.

And then Siegel met Meyer Lansky, another protection racketeer and a protégé of Arnold Rothstein, New York's premier gambling impresario and crime boss. Rothstein was like an octopus, whose arms extended into virtually every illegal activity in the city. Lansky and Rothstein had met at a Bar Mitzvah, and the older man was impressed by the younger man's intelligence and eagerness to earn money, regardless of rules. Lansky was already associated with a young Salvatore Lucania (aka, Charles "Lucky" Luciano); they had met when Luciano's gang attempted to shake down the scrawny protection racketeer, who was short and skinny, hardly posing a potential threat to a gang of strong young Italian toughs. Yet, Lansky not only refused to retreat, but he also told Luciano to go fuck himself. Luciano was so impressed by the kid's moxie that he invited him to join his protection racket. The two future crime bosses cemented an alliance that lasted until Luciano's death in Italy. Lansky, unlike his hot-headed pal Siegel, would always be the cool, brainy, financially sophisticated "Little Man," and Luciano would be the visionary organizational CEO. Their view of crime was as a business to be carried on like any other US business, and that view led them to create the National Crime Syndicate. Once in charge, their word was law, and no other mobster would have the authority to dispute their decisions. But first they had to eliminate two old-world Sicilian Mafioso, Salvatore Maranzano and Joe "the Boss" Masseria. Luciano led Masseria into a trap, setting him up in a Coney Island restaurant, where the two met for lunch. Luciano excused himself to use the men's room, and gunmen burst into the restaurant and pumped Masseria full of holes. For the murder of Maranzano, Luciano retained the services of Siegel, Red Levine, Bo Weinberg, and another member of Murder Inc. They pretended to be agents from the IRS, entered Maranzano's office, and shot and stabbed him to death. The National Crime Syndicate was now in control. (More about these assassinations in chapter 4.)

As National Crime Syndicate executives, Siegel and Lansky complemented each other's skills: Lansky was a superb businessman, a math whiz, and a coolly calculating strategist and opportunist; like his mentor Rothstein, he could quickly figure out gambling odds in his head. Siegel was tops when it came to intimidation. He was tough, fearless, impulsive, and decisive. Prior to the creation of the syndicate, the two had formed one of New York's most successful gangs, the Bugs and Meyer Mob, a name chosen by cops, but hated by Siegel. The two were trailblazers in the history of New York mobsters, and—along with Luciano—would long be remembered as the most iconic gangsters of the Big Apple. Sedway was reduced to a secondary position, never to achieve the prominence that his partnership with Siegel seemed to have portended. Though Lansky always valued Sedway, it was Siegel whom he truly admired.

Of the young Siegel, Lansky said to an Israeli journalist, "Benny never hesitated in a fight. He was faster than the hot-blooded Sicilian boys. He was the first one to hit or shoot."

That appraisal was seconded by another member of their gang, Joseph "Doc" Stacher, who commented, "When it came to fighting, [Benny] was the coolest guy. I never met anyone as decisive as he used to be."[1]

In addition to Stacher, the Bugs and Meyer Mob had attracted other up-and-coming mobsters, such as Abner "Longy" Zwillman and Louis "Lepke" Buchalter. The latter would take what he learned about successful hits to run Murder Inc. with Albert "Mad Hatter" Anastasia. The Bugs and Meyer Mob was an unbeatable force and not even the cops were able to nail them for the many crimes they committed, which included murder, muggings, burglaries, hijacking, fencing of jewels and furs, prostitution, protection, loan sharking, bookmaking, and gambling. The gang's leaders would become well-known characters in Mob history and subjects of numerous legends, particularly Stacher, Zwillman, Buchalter, and Anastasia.

Stacher was the gang's premier diplomat, helping to cement mutually beneficial relations between Italian and Jewish gangsters. He had organized a convention of the two groups of gangsters at the Franconia Hotel and helped to merge them into a national crime syndicate, thus fulfilling the ambitions of Luciano and Lansky. He was an exceedingly clever mobster, who bought his way into a partnership in Columbia Pictures and ran gambling for Lansky at the Sands and the Fremont casinos in Las Vegas.

Zwillman started his career in the rackets as a numbers man, and in just months, he became the leading numbers racketeer in Brooklyn. He was a handsome ladies' man, so well-endowed that he earned the nickname Longy. After making millions of dollars during Prohibition, he became the lover of Jean Harlow. He lent Harry Cohn, head of Columbia Pictures, several million dollars. Part of the interest on the loan consisted of Cohn giving Harlow starring roles in two movies. After Zwillman broke up with Harlow, he married Mary de Groot Mendels Steinbach, whose grandfather was the founder of the American Stock Exchange. Zwillman was a close friend of Joe DiMaggio, and when the IRS was investigating Zwillman, he gave three large trunks full of money to DiMaggio to safeguard. Following Zwillman's death, (which was either a murder or a suicide by hanging), DiMaggio did not return the trunks.

Buchalter rose swiftly in the Mob, heading Murder Inc. with his associate Anastasia. He used the power of Murder Inc. to control labor racketeering in New York's garment center. For the right price, he would keep a nonunion manufacturer free of labor strife and unions. He could also work the other side of the street: for the right price, he could keep a union from striking a unionized manufacturer. With the help of an army of thugs, wielding clubs and lead pipes, he ended union-organizing efforts. As cohead of Murder Inc., he allegedly ordered hundreds of murders and made millions of dollars doing so. As clever and secretive as Buchalter was, he made the mistake of ordering the murder of a recalcitrant garment worker within the hearing range of a stool pigeon. District Attorney Thomas Dewey indicted Buchalter for murder and an arrest warrant was issued. Buchalter, on the FBI's Most Wanted List, hid out at various locations in and around New York City and then gave himself up to gossip columnist Walter Winchell, who turned him over to FBI director J. Edgar Hoover. Buchalter had thought that he would be tried in a federal court for a noncapital crime and, if found guilty, would serve only a few years in a federal prison. But New York wanted him. After a federal trial, he was found guilty as expected, but then his presence was demanded back in New York, where he was tried for murder, found guilty, and executed in the electric chair in Sing Sing prison in 1944. He was the only organized crime boss to be dealt the death penalty.

Of all these, probably the most vicious and notorious gangster was Anastasia, of whom it was said that he killed simply for the pleasure of it. His enjoyment of killing was unlike that of Siegel, who killed out of rage. Anastasia needed to kill on a regular basis because he had a lust for murder, a hunger that could only be satisfied by thousands of executions committed by his own hands. Anastasia (né Umberto Anastasio) was considered the most ruthless homicidal maniac to wear the crown of Mafia boss. He was head of what would become known as the Gambino crime family, one of the two largest and richest of the Five Families. The other is the Genovese crime family. Detective Salerno told the author that he believed Anastasia had killed thousands of people. It is no wonder that he was known as the mob's "Lord High Executioner." As joint chairman of Murder Inc. with Buchalter, Anastasia would have earned that sobriquet even without all the murders that he ordered. Here's an example of his impulsive and gratuitous homicidal impulses: one day, he was watching the local evening news on television. A reporter was interviewing a young man named Arnold Schuster who had noticed famed bank robber Willie "the Actor" Sutton on a New York City bus; he followed Sutton to a garage and then notified the police of the bank robber's whereabouts. Sutton was apprehended and sent off to prison to finish out his term, having previously escaped. Seeing young Schuster explain himself on TV, Anastasia flew into a rage and shouted at one of his henchmen, "I can't stand squealers. Hit that guy!" On March 8, 1952, Schuster was shot once in the groin and once through an eye in front of his home in Borough Park, Brooklyn. The assassin was never caught. Anastasia's lust for death was satisfied but not for long. His murders continued unabated, and he was never charged for all the hits he commissioned. In all of his murders, witnesses either disappeared or suddenly lost all memories of what they had seen. And the murders continued, providing ongoing work for a family-run mortuary. Even his brother, "Tough" Tony Anastasio, head of the Brooklyn docks, commented that the "Mad Hatter" had probably killed thousands of people. Although murders for hire provided a plentiful source of his income, he earned many more thousands of dollars from the International Longshoreman's Association (ILA), which controlled all the docks in New York. Every boat docked at a New York pier was a profit center for the ILA and a source of wealth that flowed into the Anastasia brothers' hidden safes and overseas bank accounts.

Of course, those who live by the ambush often die by the ambush. And so it was for Anastasia. Murder finally found him in a barber's chair at the Park Sheraton Hotel on 56th Street and Seventh Avenue on October 25, 1957. Two men, their faces hidden by bandanas, strode into the barbershop, pushed aside Anastasia's barber and blasted away with a .32 and a .38. Shocked and disoriented, Anastasia leapt from the chair and charged at his assassins' reflection in the large mirror facing his barber chair. He soon tumbled to the ground, blood pooling around his dead head. The killers quickly departed and were never caught. They were thought to be the Gallo brothers, one of whom intimated that he had participated in a close shave, while the gang's leader, Joey Gallo, joked to friends, "You can just call the five of us the barbershop quintet,"[2] even though there were only two killers. Photos of Anastasia's bloody corpse, covered by a sheet, were featured on the front pages of all of New York tabloid newspapers.

Though a partner of such of leading mobsters, Siegel was regarded as sui generis. His reputation as a tough stand-up thug made him a valued member of the syndicate, but he had a quality that none of his compatriots had: he was the only one with movie-star good looks and was often regarded by the crime reporters as a figure cut from a different bolt of cloth than the members of Murder Inc. Siegel was able to pass himself off as a sportsman, a high-level gambler who would never resort to the kinds of tactics employed by the crude members of Murder Inc. It was an image he would cultivate and polish for the rest of his life. Yet, that didn't prevent him from coming to the rescue of some of his notorious pals. For example, when Chicago gang chief Al Capone was on the lam from a murder charge, he was hidden by Siegel in an obliging aunt's apartment in Brooklyn. Siegel never worried about being an accessory to a crime. In fact, he took pride in such activities, feeling that he was untouchable and smart enough to avoid the traps set by law enforcement. And Capone remained grateful for the rest of his life, right through the tertiary stages of syphilis. Capone, unlike the old mustachioed Sicilian Mafioso whom the syndicate had murdered, had no prejudice against other ethnic groups, and his Chicago outfit's top men were Jews, Irish, and Poles. In fact, following his death, the Chicago Outfit was briefly run by Mob financier Jacob "Greasy Thumb" Guzik. And when Guzik died, more Italians were at his funeral in a Chicago synagogue than Jews. The same lack of ethnic narcissism that was characteristic of Capone's outfit was also characteristic of the National Crime Syndicate set up by Luciano and Lansky.

It was at the Atlantic City Conference of mobsters in 1929, attended by Lansky, Luciano, Siegel, Capone, and Costello, among others, that the crime bosses said it would be bad for business for the Jews and the Italians to fight one another. Following the conference, Siegel told one his friends that the "Yids and Dagos will no longer fight each other" as they had on the Lower East Side of Manhattan. It was an alliance that would remain in effect for most of the rest of the 20th century. The reason for its ultimate demise was differing family values: the Italians wanted to create dynasties and so often groomed their sons to take over; the Jews wanted their sons out of the rackets and encouraged them to become doctors, lawyers, accountants. As a character in *The Godfather* says, a lawyer can cheat more people while carrying a briefcase than by carrying a gun. It had always been the ambition of Luciano and Lansky that the syndicate would rival the largest of the *Fortune 500* companies and perhaps even surpass them. In fact, in the 1950s Lansky was recorded on a wiretapped telephone bragging that as a result of the syndicate's governing structure, "We're bigger than U.S. Steel."

The syndicate's dealings were often more like political backstabbing than gangsters shooting and bombing each other out of existence. For example, it was not uncommon for the syndicate to set up rivals, through double dealing and leaks to governmental agencies such as the IRS and FBI, resulting in rivals getting long prison sentences for tax evasion or drug dealing. One of their early victims was their rival bootlegger Waxey Gordon (real name Irving Wexler). He got the name Waxey because, as a teenager, he was so successful at picking wallets out of victims' pockets that the wallets were said to have been waxed. A gang war about disputed bootlegging territory had broken out between the syndicate and Gordon, and men were killed on both sides. Putting an end to it, Lansky arranged for District Attorney Thomas Dewey to receive information that Gordon was a tax cheat. Gordon was tried and sentenced to 10 years in prison. Lansky and Siegel were pleased to be rid of Gordon and that the killing had stopped. Furiously vengeful, Waxey threatened to get even. He paid members of his Mob, the Fabrizzo brothers, to assassinate his two enemies. Siegel learned of the contract and set out to do to the Fabrizzo brothers what they intended to do to Lansky and him. With the instincts of a furtively stalking leopard, Siegel found his prey and dispatched them with several .32-caliber head shots. A third Fabrizzo brother, Tony, decided that the pen was mightier than the sword as weapon for revenge, and he told his indiscreet lawyer that he would write a book about the Bugs and Meyer Mob and the murder of his brothers. On a cold, dark night in 1932, Siegel checked into a New York City hospital. Late at night, with only one nurse on duty, Siegel slipped out of the hospital and joined two of his compatriots. They rang Tony's doorbell, announcing that they were detectives and needed to speak with him about the deaths of his brothers. Tony stepped outside and before he could ask a question of the putative detectives, he was blasted with several bullets from three guns and collapsed in a pool of his own blood. Siegel snuck back into his hospital room, where he had not been missed and awaited his own announcement of an alibi.

There were two more rivals that had to be disposed of: in 1935, two bookmakers and loan sharks, Louis "Pretty" Amberg—who was not only cross-eyed but so ugly that P. T. Barnum offered him a contract to be in circus sideshow, which Amberg turned down—and his brother, Joe Amberg, had attempted to take over the syndicate's territory in Brooklyn; Louis and Joe had been waging war with the syndicate for years. They wanted all of Brooklyn as their domain, and Luciano and Lansky were not about to let the Ambergs take it away from them. The Amberg brothers (there were five of them) left a trail of blood wherever they operated; they were known for their gratuitous viciousness. Louis once drove a fork into the face of Milton Berle after the comedian had insulted him from the stage during a performance. Jabbing a fork into the face of anyone who insulted him was one of Louis's traditional forms of nonverbal retaliation. Louis and Joe knew that bosses of Murder Inc. had decided to eliminate them, and so they hid out in hotels. But in the underworld of hungry rats looking to provide favors in exchange for favors, the Ambergs's hideouts were soon well known. Siegel, deciding not to farm the work out to others as Lansky and Luciano would have, took it upon himself to get rid of the brothers. He had developed a reputation not only as a hard-driving member of Murder Inc., but also as one of its most ardent killers. Siegel killed because he liked the work and he was good at it, rarely being anything more than a suspect.

Nevertheless, by the late 1930s, New York had become too hot for Siegel. Prosecutors wanted to indict him and were hunting for witnesses to his various murders. With the blessing of Lansky, Luciano, and Costello, Siegel left his wife in Scarsdale and boarded the 20th Century Limited to Chicago, where he would change trains and head to Los Angeles. In the years ahead, New York's loss would ultimately be applauded as Las Vegas' gain. Once in Los Angeles, Siegel wasted no time in threatening the local Mafia boss, Frank Dragna, to become his subordinate. He next hired a colorful media hound, former boxer, and all-around thug named Mickey Cohen to be his aide-de-camp and hair-trigger enforcer. Though Siegel succeeded in shaking down Hollywood studios by controlling various unions, he is best remembered today as the man who envisioned the future of Las Vegas. At the time that Siegel entered the dusty desert of dilapidated saloon casinos, the promise of what Vegas could become was only a dream dreamt by one man. Siegel initially had a partner in creating the Flamingo Hotel and Casino: Billy Wilkerson, publisher of *The Hollywood Reporter*. But Siegel had no need for a partner, so he pushed Wilkerson out of the country with the threat of murder. Thereafter, Siegel built the biggest, fanciest, and most luxurious casino in the state of Nevada, bigger and better than anything in Reno, which had previously been the site of Nevada's most popular casinos. His free spending, cost overruns, and costly delays resulted in angry creditors wanting their investments returned. And those angry creditors were members of the National Crime Syndicate. Because Siegel couldn't come up with the money, much of which had been skimmed by Siegel's mistress Virginia Hill, the syndicate decided it was time for Siegel to die. His death warrant was issued by Luciano and seconded by Lansky, Costello, and Joe Adonis.

On June 20, 1947, while reading the *Los Angeles Times* in Hill's home, Siegel was shot multiple times with a .30-caliber carbine. Years later, Ralph Natale, crime boss of Philadelphia, claimed that Siegel's former partner in Murder Inc., Frankie Carbo, had been the assassin. (It is said that in organized crime, one's killer will most likely be one's friend, for he will be the person the victim trusts.)

Though Siegel slept the infinite sleep of the great silent majority, his dreams of Las Vegas as the capital of legal gambling became a reality, whose profits support political candidates throughout the nation.

3

Little Man, Big Gangster

S UDDENLY AND ROUGHLY PUSHED UP against a wall by a gang of young Italian hoods in an alley on the Lower East Side of Manhattan, the teenage Meyer Lansky showed neither shock nor fear. He squinted a hard look of contempt at his attackers. "Hand over your money," demanded the gang's leader, Salvatore Lucania. "Go fuck yourself," said the defiant Lansky. A smile slowly formed on the gang leader's lips as he gazed at the small recalcitrant Jew. Lucania admired the little guy's fearlessness. He was as hard as the cobblestones on the streets of their neighborhoods. During his life, Lucania (later known as "Lucky Luciano") admired guys who stood up to threats, guys who when faced with beatings, drawn knives, cocked revolvers, and the likelihood of death, spit on the face of fate. Lansky was one of those hard-edged teenagers, skinny and short but as ferocious as a wolverine. He would take shit from no one. In Lansky, Luciana saw a partner in crime, a stand-up guy who wouldn't bend to the cops. Words were spoken, and a friendship was born.

As ambitious young gangsters and visionaries of organized crime, Lucania and Lansky were the fathers of a new age of crime in the United States. They would soon create the National Crime Syndicate, which would one day be "bigger than U.S. Steel," as Lansky remarked to an associate while speaking on a wiretapped telephone. They were the underworld's venture capitalists, opportunists looking to make easy money on whatever was illegal. They would create a conglomerate of crime that would underpin US society. Theirs would be a top-down business empire that could have been a case study in a Harvard MBA textbook.

So who was this young genius of crime? How did a tough little Jew, no more than 5'3", become the feared leader of gangland, a man who was respected and feared by celebrity associates such as Frank Sinatra, politicians such as Estes Kefauver, and mobsters of all ranks?

Meyer Lansky (né Meier Suchowlański) was born on July 4, 1902, in Grodno, a part of Poland controlled by Russia. There, Jews were victimized in vicious pogroms that were not only condoned, but also encouraged by the government. Jews, as usual, were the scapegoats as they had been since time immemorial. As a witness to numerous anti-Semitic atrocities in Grodno, Meyer was determined never to bow down to authority, never to bend a knee in obeisance, or to beg a favor. In 1911, he immigrated with his mother and his brother, Jacob, to the Lower East Side of Manhattan. Meyer's father had arrived in New York City 2 years earlier and proceeded to earn enough money working in a tool-and-die shop to pay for his family's steerage boat passage from the port of Odessa to New York harbor. The rough crossing in closed odoriferous and squalid quarters, where passengers breathed stale air that reeked of the stench of vomit from those who had been seasick, was dispiriting and sickening. Yet, the family looked forward to fresh air, sunshine, and financial security, if not exactly prosperity. However, soon after disembarking, the harsh reality of poverty in a slum tenement turned Meyer's dreams into anger. The poverty the family experienced belied whatever fanciful dreams they had entertained of a bright new world of opportunity. The Lower East Side was crowded, dirty, bustling with immigrants hurrying about, and seeking ways to make money, often by being peddlers or small shop owners. The jobs they found required 12-hour days of labor for a few dollars a week. The Lansky family lived in what was known as a "cold-water flat" that was oppressively hot in summer and bitingly cold in winter. At the end of a hallway on each floor of the tenement was a single bathroom lit by a naked light bulb suspended from a skinny, dirt-encrusted chain. The walls were dirty, and the paint was cracked and chipped. There was no window and the tiny room had just one sink and one stained toilet. Summer and winter, the water from the taps was cold and discolored from rusty pipes. The bathroom was shared by other families. An occupant would enter, sniff the stale air that often reeked from a previous occupant and then hold a handkerchief to subdue nostrils. Young Lansky did not want to linger there or any place else that was filthy with poverty. The American dream for him was an illusion, a mirage, a phony reward held in front of the laboring poor just to keep them in line. Yet, to his father, the United States was the land of opportunity, especially compared to Grodno. Meyer's father urged him to earn top grades so that he could obtain a good job following his graduation. Meyer was not so much motivated by his father as he was by his own intellectual curiosity and love of learning: he was a straight-A student and a whiz at math. His hungry mind fed on the nutrition of learning. He enjoyed reading, loved books, and had a memory like a file cabinet. But as the years of poverty continued, young Lansky's attitude about school began to change: good grades were not a sufficient reward for living in oppressive poverty. He wasn't going to be like some young insular Talmudic scholar supported by his family. He saw them in his neighborhood and had no use for the kind of scholarly lives they would lead; for Meyer, the outside world was calling. He wanted money, a lot of money; he wanted out of poverty and out of the miserable tenement in which they lived. Though he quit school after the eighth grade, he never lost his love of books and of learning. His father got him a job in a tool-and-die shop, and Meyer was told that if he applied himself and became expert at his craft, he could earn a dollar a week after 10 years of labor. Meyer wanted no part of that. Legitimate employment meant suffocation and serfdom until death. He wanted to earn big bucks; he didn't want to be anyone's lackey.

He needed a way out. Where could he go? What could he do? He was stumped, but then he learned a lesson that would be the foundation of his career and propel him to the heights of wealth. Following a loss of a nickel in a fixed sidewalk dice game, he understood that betting is for losers: they are suckers taken in by their own greed. They believe that their knowledge and skills will outfox those of the dealers. But the dealers control the game, and they are always the winners; the odds favor them. They are the gamblers, and the suckers are the bettors. Meyer would never forget the distinction. He had to figure out how to become a winner, a gambler, and control the game. He would need the help of a tough partner, someone who could keep competitive gamblers away, by force if necessary.

On his way home one day, he spotted a dice game in an alley. Two boys started fighting. Neighbors called the cops, who swarmed down on the players, clubs flying and heads beaten. One of the fighters dropped a revolver, and his opponent quickly picked it up and aimed it at the cops. The boy with the gun was a raging ferocious Benny Siegel. Before he could squeeze the trigger, Lansky grabbed the weapon and yelled for Siegel to beat it. "You're crazy to shoot a cop!" yelled Lansky. The two boys took off running. Siegel dropped the revolver and was furious that Lansky made him lose such an expensive weapon. "It could have come in handy later on," lamented Siegel. When their emotions cooled, Lansky suggested that they become partners, and so another important friendship was born on the streets of the Lower East Side. With Siegel at his side, Lansky envisioned their criminal future as a pair of gangsters who would get what they wanted by cunning and violence.

Siegel's fearless fighting spirit and his natural ability to control any situation with the threat of violence made the Bugs and Meyer Mob one of the most successful on the Lower East Side. Siegel's violence was complemented by Lansky's cerebral approach to solving problems. Though Lansky never referred to Siegel as "Bugsy" (it was always Benny), he thought the name, which was a translation from Yiddish, was accurate. In the Yiddish-speaking neighborhood in which they lived, Siegel was called "Chaye," which in Yiddish means "untamed" or "animal." Many regarded Siegel's outbursts as a form of craziness, and it was said of him that he was "as crazy as a bedbug"; hence, the name Bugsy. It didn't matter to Lansky. He liked and admired Siegel and appreciated his value to their various criminal enterprises. The two not only formed a lifelong friendship, but also a successful gang that extorted and terrorized news dealers, street peddlers, and store owners. To all their victims, it was apparent that Lansky was the brains and Siegel was the muscle. Or, as New York City detective Ralph Salerno told the author, "One was fire, the other was a calculator." Salerno also stated that the Bugs and Meyer Mob was one of the most vicious in New York.

When a victim didn't immediately acquiesce to Lansky's soft-spoken threats, Siegel closed the deal with an act of violence. They and their other gang members (i.e., Sam "Red" Levine, Joe "Doc" Stacher, Meyer Wassell, and Irving "Tabbo" Sandler) ruled their small domain like all other gangs do: with violence or the threat of violence; the gang's repertoire of beatings with pipes, brass knuckles, wooden clubs, and knives was well known on the Lower East Side, but rarely did they get pinched by the cops. Lansky had learned another lesson: a small bribe to the local beat cop ensured immunity. And desk sergeants were no better: they always had their hands out. They sat behind counters like store owners, but without the presence of cash registers. If one of the gang was hauled into a precinct, the desk sergeant could make the problem vanish for as little as $20. If the gang were known to have enjoyed a big haul, the price of immunity would go up. When the gang's victims had their merchandise ruined, set afire, or stolen in the middle of the night, they might complain at the local precinct, and the cops would write it all down and that's as far as it went. When the gang learned that victims had the temerity to report their crimes to the cops, they were warned that rats got flushed down the sewers. The gang developed such a successful protection and extortion racket that they were earning more money in a week than their fathers earned in 6 months. From protection, they moved on to theft of jewels and furs and arson for hire. The big time lay just ahead.

The Bugs and Meyer Mob had remained exclusively Jewish until Lansky's encounter with young Lucky Luciano. Thereafter, the Italian gang and the Jewish gang operated as a united team of outlaws. Their kind of capitalism thrived on the integration of personnel and resources. Money, neither ethnicity nor religion, was the important factor in all that they undertook.

There was plenty of profit for both of them, and their combined forces meant control over a wider territory than either gang could have obtained on its own. It also meant that their combined forces were more powerful than local Irish gangs. The Jews and Italians would come to dominate organized crime and not just in the Big Apple but also in cities such as Boston, Chicago, New Orleans, Cleveland, Las Vegas, Miami, Newark, and Los Angeles. And it all began on the Lower East Side.

For the ever ambitious and opportunistic Lansky, criminal opportunities increased after he met Arnold Rothstein, the man known as the Big Bankroll, the Brain, the master mind of organized crime in New York and beyond. The two met at a Bar Mitzvah in the Brooklyn. Rothstein was impressed by the young Lansky, his ambition and quick mind; the two sat and talked for 3 hours. The next day Lansky had a mentor as did his cohorts: Siegel, Luciano, and a new recruit, Frank Costello (né Francesco Castiglia). Rothstein directed them to fences for their stolen merchandise and outlets for the gang's drug deals. But their greatest opportunity came in 1920 with the start of Prohibition. Rothstein financed their initial operations for a large piece of the profits. Rothstein would add millions to his already bursting bank account, and the gang would all become multimillionaires. For Lansky, it was light years beyond the Dickensian servitude of a tool-and-die shop. His father, who continued working there, would never forgive his wayward son for abandoning the world of legitimate business and for corrupting his brother, Jacob.

Meyer had no regrets. He and his gang entered into bootlegging with the zest and determination of conquering warriors. They hijacked trucks of liquor and then bought their own trucks; they opened warehouses in Queens and Brooklyn; they had speakeasies throughout Manhattan; and they had boats bringing scotch, whiskey, and bourbon onto the beaches of eastern Long Island. As the illegal liquor poured out of distilleries, the money poured in. It flowed and became a torrent; the profits were enormous. The gang formed alliances with other bootleggers, such as Dutch Shultz and Owney Madden. If someone got in their way, the gang blew holes in him, and if another gang got in their way, they blasted them with sticks of dynamite, leaving shards of bloody human flesh and bones on sidewalks and roads. Lansky, Siegel, Luciano, and Costello had formed the most feared and powerful combination of thugs in New York. They now wore expensively tailored suits and handmade shoes. Their monogrammed shirts, sporting French cuffs, were of the finest softest cotton, their ties of expensive silks, and their shoes of the finest softest leather. These men were no longer rushing, ragged urchins, artful dodgers escaping the clubs of beat cops. They were gangsters who commanded respect and could instill fear in a victim with a single hard stare.

Lansky moved to a swank new apartment on Central Park West with his wife, Anne. Siegel bought a mansion in the upscale Westchester neighborhood of Scarsdale, where Jews had been excluded by what was known as "a gentleman's agreement." He lived there with his wife Esta, but he also kept an apartment in New York's swanky and elegant Waldorf Astoria. Although Costello also kept an apartment in the Waldorf Astoria, he—like Lansky—lived in a large, elegant apartment on Central Park West with his Jewish wife, Lauretta Giegerman. Luciano called the Waldorf his home without having to have another abode. The gang often ate breakfast together in the hotel, but, if dining in public, they were circumspect in their conversation. To onlookers, the men were just conservative-looking, handsomely groomed business executives.

Lansky, Luciano, and Costello had learned how to dress and act from Rothstein. Siegel was his own stylist, preferring loud plaid jackets and colorful ties. Rothstein taught them manners and grammar as well as how to scam and hustle. Among the group, Lansky stood out as the quiet one. He wanted to be inconspicuous and as close to invisibility as possible. To his neighbors and to legitimate businessmen, he was polite, even-tempered, and soft spoken. His suits rarely varied: he usually wore dark, conservative, pin-striped business suits, giving him the image of a member of a distinguished Wall Street banking firm. Though he was short, there was something ineffably imposing about his presence that indicated considerable power and strength of purpose behind his benign smile. Yet when necessary, he could instill fear in someone with a cold, hard stare that seemed to turn his pupils from gray to black. He was developing a reputation among New York mobsters as a financial genius, the chairman of the board of the National Crime Syndicate. That reputation would spread across the country, especially as he did deals with gangsters in Chicago, Cleveland, Los Angeles, Miami, and later in Las Vegas. He was the Bernard Baruch of Gangland, USA.

When not meeting his cohorts in the Waldorf Astoria, Lansky liked to meet his Jewish gang members in Ratner's Delicatessen on Delancey Street on the Lower East Side, where they had a regular table. Waiters who were known for being brusque, if not surly, were always solicitous of Lansky and his table partners. They, in turn, were generous tippers. The waiters dared not slam down a plate of gefilte fish; instead it would be placed before the gangsters as if presenting a delicate jewel.

When Prohibition ended in 1933, the National Crime Syndicate turned to other means of making money illegally. Lansky devoted his attention to gambling but had other businesses as well, including a stake in a company called the Molaska Corporation that made powdered molasses to be used in the making of liquor. Two of his partners in Molaska were Moe Dalitz and Sam Tucker, who would later control much of the gambling in Las Vegas, owning such casino hotels as the Desert Inn, the Stardust, and the Sundance, later named the Fitzgerald and then The D Las Vegas. Lansky would also go into the jukebox business and invest in the careers of several entertainers, hiring them to perform in his casinos.

He first opened what were called carpet joints in Saratoga, New York. Carpets on the floor meant that the casino was not some rip-off joint with sawdust on the floors, where bettors were systematically cheated with shaved loaded dice, marked cards, magnetized roulette wheels, and slot machines whose odds were fixed so that few winnings occurred, usually only when the machine was near empty. No wonder slots were called one-armed bandits. Lansky did not want his carpet joints to be known as clip joints. Lansky never cheated his customers, for he knew, since childhood, that gambling odds always favored the house. And he did not want to run the risk of developing a reputation as a cheat because that would only cause players to stay away from his casinos. From Saratoga, he moved on to opening casinos in Havana, New Orleans, and Florida. Wherever he operated, he made sure that the police were all bribed to let him operate without hindrance. In Havana, he bribed more than mere cops; he bribed the country's dictator, Fulgencio Batista. In fact, he made Batista a junior partner in his two luxurious hotel/casinos: the Hotel Nacional and the Riviera.

By 1946, Lansky was ready to help his pal, Siegel, turn Las Vegas into a gambling kingdom in the desert. He, Luciano, Costello, Joe Adonis, and Abner "Longy" Zwillman, along with others, invested $1 million in the building of the famed Flamingo Hotel and Casino. Unfortunately, the cost overruns plus skimming by Siegel and his mistress, Virginia Hill, resulted in the investors having to replenish the Flamingo's bank balances. The total investment grew to $6 million. Yet, the amount of red ink continued to spill across page after page of the casino's ledgers; after a while, it was no longer a spill here and a spill there: the red ink flowed freely. The investors had had enough. Siegel had to go. Lansky prevailed on the investors for two stays of execution, but the finances of the Flamingo were an open tap of red ink. Enough was more than enough: the investors voted to eliminate Siegel from his position by the power of the gun. Lansky reluctantly agreed to end his boyhood pal's life. Money was the theology of the Mob, and Siegel had proven himself a heretic. He could not be trusted. Frankie Carbo, a former Murder Inc. partner of Siegel's, was given the contract, according to Ralph Natale, former head of the Philadelphia crime family. When the deed was done, two former members of the Bugs and Meyer Mob, Gus Greenbaum and Moe Sedway, took over the operation of the Flamingo and made it a huge success. Lansky was taking in so much money from the venture that he not only sent millions of dollars to a numbered Swiss bank account, but he also opened his own offshore bank.

Prior to Lansky's ventures in Las Vegas, he had become deeply concerned about the rising tide of Nazi-inspired anti-Semitism in the United States. Nazi sympathizers were holding meetings in cities across the country. Lansky had been exposed to the violence of anti-Semitism as a boy in Grodno. In those days, he was just a powerless kid unable to fight against armed men clubbing old Jews and their families. One night in Yorkville, a German immigrant neighborhood on the Upper East Side of Manhattan, there was a German-American Bund meeting and rally in support of the Nazis. Lansky and number of his gangland associates armed with baseball bats, chains, brass knuckles, and razor-sharp box cutters broke into the meeting. They began swinging their bats, knocking the Nazi supporters to the ground. Several had their faces slashed, others suffered broken noses and jaws. One of the gang slashed a picture of Hitler that was mounted on a stage, and another slashed and tore to shreds a Nazi flag. Those who didn't flee fast enough were thrown out of the windows onto the street. Such incidents were like sporting events: the underworld's version of riding to hounds.

With peace in the Western Hemisphere after the war ended, Lansky began to fulfill a dream: to build the largest most luxurious casinos in Cuba. In the late 1940s, Lansky met with Batista at the Waldorf Astoria on Park Avenue, where the dictator kept a suite of rooms. By making Batista his partner, Lansky was not only able to have exclusive rights to run legitimate casinos in Cuba, but he was also put in charge of turning the dishonest ones, the infamous clip joints, into legitimate casinos that would attract tourists from North and South America and Europe. In addition to casinos, Lansky was put in charge of the racetracks. Batista made millions of dollars from his deals with Lansky, and Lansky had a free hand to turn his casinos into machines that had no other function but to take money from bettors. He even gave Frank Sinatra a piece of the marina of the Riviera Hotel, thus ensuring that Sinatra would visit often and entertain the customers. In late 1946, Lansky called for a massive organized crime meeting at his Havana hotel, the Nacional. Gangsters from all over the country attended what became known as the Havana Conference, where Lansky offered each of the attendees the opportunity to invest in casinos and reap substantial rewards. For the conference, Sinatra obligingly entertained the attendees at after-dinner soirees. It was also decided that Luciano should be a boss of bosses. Lansky did not think that some of the Italians would welcome a Jew setting himself up as their leader. Yet, he was in fact the underworld's financial leader, and Luciano told all in attendance that whatever you do, always listen to Meyer and you'll always make money.

By 1958, Cuban rebels fighting in the Sierra Maestra portended an end to Lansky's gambling empire. On January 8, 1959, a victorious Fidel Castro entered Havana after his revolution succeeded. The celebratory populace ransacked the hotels and casinos, and Lansky and his cohorts fled. In October 1960, all the casinos on the island were nationalized. The money, all $18 million, that Lansky had invested in the Riviera was gone as if washed away by a tsunami. Cursing the loss of his casinos, Lansky returned to the United States.

Although Lansky was a preeminent New York gangster, his ambitions and opportunities had drawn him far afield. Cuba and Las Vegas were sources of great sums of money from gambling. His fortune was originally built on the money he earned during Prohibition and that was mainly a New York enterprise. In fact, New York was the easiest city in which to be a bootlegger because the laws were lax and inefficiently enforced. New York State legislators had passed the Mullen-Gage Law to supplement the Volstead Act, which had inaugurated Prohibition in 1920. In 1923, the state legislature repealed the law because it could not be enforced. As a result, in 1925, the World League Against Alcohol complained, "To all intents and purposes, anyone can now engage in liquor traffic in the City of New York."[1]

With his investments in Las Vegas and London casinos, Lansky retired to a modest home in Miami Beach, where he was visited by many of his old cohorts in crime. He died of lung cancer on January 15, 1983, at age 80. Although the FBI believed that he had left behind an estate worth about $300 million, his family let it be known that he was nearly broke, having only $57,000 in a checking account. Of course, a man who stashed millions in Swiss bank accounts and other millions in his own offshore banks could hardly be expected to die a pauper. Then, again, why would he want the IRS to know how much money he had socked away? A man as smart, shrewd, and savvy as Lansky was not about to draw a map to his actual wealth.

Detective Salerno told the author that as much as the government has learned about members of organized crime, it has never been able to figure how they hide all of their money.

4

The Prime Minister of the Underworld

H E ONCE GOT CAUGHT CARRYING A GUN and served 10 months in jail; thereafter, he decided that his wits were more powerful than bullets. It was the beginning of a mobster's life as a politician. And that mobster used his political skills not only to become the prime minister of the Mob, but also to help elect mayors, governors, and even the president of the United States.

It was an unlikely outcome for the young son of poor Italian immigrants. Francesco Castiglia, age 4, had arrived in the United States with his parents Luigi and Maria Saveria Aloise Castiglia in 1895. The family settled into a dank, dark, and dismal tenement in the Italian section of east Harlem. Like many other children of poor laboring immigrant parents, Francesco saw that the only men in his neighborhood who had thick rolls of money, flashy clothes, and drove fancy cars were gangsters. In an environment of crushing poverty, a young boy would rather aspire to be one of the successful hoodlums than a hard-working, badly paid, exhausted laborer.

Francesco met another young man in circumstances similar to his own: Salvatore Lucania. It's interesting to note that they both changed their names: Castiglia to the Irish-sounding Frank Costello, and Lucania to Charles Luciano. While the gangsters of Costello's neighborhood cooperated with other Italian gangsters, Luciano introduced Costello to a broader more ecumenical world where Jewish gangsters were carving out their own territories. Luciano introduced him to Meyer Lansky and Ben "Bugsy" Siegel. The four did not exactly become the four horsemen of the apocalypse of crime, but they certainly became the founding fathers of organized crime in the 20th century. And years later, District Attorney Thomas Dewey would regard them as the infectious bearers of viral criminality and, certainly, as the corruptors of Protestant America, because it was Protestant America that had promoted the ideals of a dry country, and it was primarily Catholics and Jews who profited from Prohibition through their countrywide network of bootleggers.

It's a mystery why Costello was drawn to Jews. Some of his relatives, having funded DNA tests, said that the Castiglias had a small percentage of Jewish genes. In *Top Hoodlum*, Anthony DeStefano writes, "No matter what the anti-immigrant sentiment might have been, Frank Costello always liked Jews. He found a strange kinship in the foreign roots of the Italians and Jews he knew."[1]

It was not surprising then that Costello married a Jewish woman, Lauretta "Bobbie" Geigerman in 1914, just months after meeting her at a dance. Because their parents did not approve of religious intermarriage, the two decided, as a compromise, to be married in St. Michael's Episcopal Church on West 83rd Street. Though the compromise did not please their parents, the Costellos had a long, happy marriage that left Lauretta a widow in 1973, after 59 years of marriage.

So parochial were many of the old-world gangsters that when Costello teamed up with Luciano, the latter was told not to associate with Costello because he was a Calabrian and not a Sicilian. Imagine their anger when the old timers learned that Luciano had, in addition to Costello, partnered with two Jews, Lansky and Siegel. The broad-minded quartet knew that the old-world gangsters, known as Mustache Petes, had to be eliminated, otherwise the goal of a multiethnic National Crime Syndicate could never have been realized.

Into this group came Joe Adonis (né Guiseppe Antonio Doto), Vito Genovese, and Tommy "Three-Finger Brown" Lucchese. Their crimes covered the full menu of illegal activities (i.e., prostitution, drugs, gambling, loan sharking, extortion, murder, theft, arson, etc.). Although Costello never dealt drugs, Genovese and Luciano had no qualms about it. Lansky focused primarily on gambling, and Siegel did a bit of everything, including multiple murders. When Prohibition became the law in 1920 via the Volstead Act, the gangs, ever opportunistic, devoted their efforts to bootlegging. They received their initial financing from Arnold Rothstein, whose money meant that the gang would have access to boats, trucks, cars, warehouses, politicians, distilleries, and all the necessary ingredients for becoming successful entrepreneurs.

Of the gang, only Costello had dealings with the West Side Irish gangsters, William "Big Bill" Dwyer and Owney "the Killer" Madden (whose parents emigrated from England), two of the biggest bootleggers in the city. The association led to the change of surname Castiglia to the Irish-sounding Costello. Surnames could be as fluid as aliases, and if one wanted to fit into one's environment, one could simply tailor one's identity to fit the circumstances. The

Irish combination continued to function until Dwyer was sent to prison for having bribed Coast Guard officers to permit a shipment of booze into New York. Upon Dwyer's incarceration, Costello and Madden took over the operation and excluded Dwyer's furious lieutenant Charles "Vannie" Higgins, who decided to wage war against the two usurpers. The infamous Manhattan Beer Wars erupted, leaving gangsters and civilians bleeding on streets all over the city. Dutch Schultz, the "Beer Baron of the Bronx," allied himself with Costello and Madden. Schultz was also fighting on a secondary front against Higgins's allies, gangsters Jack "Legs" Diamond and Vincent "Mad Dog" Coll; the latter had killed an innocent child during a drive-by shooting, hence the sobriquet "Mad Dog." The tabloids were full of the stories about wild blasts of tommy-gun fire that left corpses leaking blood in the streets and that had caused bystanders to scatter like flocks of startled pigeons. In addition to tommy-gun fusillades, Molotov cocktails and sticks of dynamite were flung into the speakeasies that refused to buy booze from a particular gang. There was no winning for such victims: as soon as they switched vendors, they were bombed by their former suppliers. Hollywood, however, was making a fortune from the mayhem; it turned out one gangster movie after another, each populated by shoot-'em-up gangsters fighting for bootlegging territory.

This was not what Costello and Lansky and Luciano wanted. The less shooting there was, the freer they would be to pursue their own illegal goals.

The young ambitious gangsters wanted less gunfire and more opportunities to pursue their goals without interference. To do so, they needed to rid themselves of their dictatorial, bigoted, parochial, and paranoid dons. In particular, Joe "the Boss" Masseria and Salvatore Maranzano had to go because they were formidable obstacles to the success of Costello, Luciano, Lansky, Siegel, and Adonis.

Masseria, through sheer ignorance and prejudice, was a drag on the fast-moving ambitions of the young bootleggers, who were all men in a hurry. His refusal to put money before prejudice made Masseria an anachronism from the Old Country, a personification of peasant xenophobia. His elimination would clear a path for the bootleggers. Luciano, as devious as any Machiavellian, invited Masseria to lunch at the Nuova Villa Tammaro restaurant in Coney Island. There, on April 15, 1931, Luciano and Masseria were having a pleasant lunch followed by a game of cards during which Luciano excused himself to use the men's room. Four gunmen (Adonis, Siegel, Genovese, and Albert Anastasia) suddenly rushed into the restaurant, their guns drawn and blasting. Masseria was struck by four bullets: three from .32-caliber revolvers and one from a .38-caliber revolver. His four bodyguards, just prior to the shots being fired, had mysteriously vanished: mirages of protection. Masseria lay dead on the floor with a Tally-Ho ace of spades between two of his fingers, a dead man's card. When the cops arrived, they found Luciano standing near the body; he told the cops he had been in the men's room during the shooting and had no idea who killed Masseria but was fortunate to have avoided being hit himself. One of the cops noticed a slight grin on Luciano's face. Though cops subsequently heard rumors of who the killers were, charges were never brought against them.

Masseria received an old-fashioned Mob funeral: a full nursery of floral bouquets decorated the tops of a parade of hearses that trailed his coffin to its final destination, burial in Calvary Cemetery in Queens, New York.

Masseria's death left his chief rival, Maranzano, the top Mafioso in New York. Thereafter, believing himself ever powerful, Maranzano declared himself Boss of all Bosses. This was too much for his underlings and competitors to swallow, because, in addition to thinking of himself as a Caesar of crime, Maranzano was exceedingly greedy and expected excessive tributes from his family. In addition, he was as prejudiced and short-sighted as Masseria had been. But just as his former competitor had nursed a poisoned garden of prejudices, Maranzano cultivated a similar garden to point out that he couldn't abstain from raging against Jewish competitors. To Luciano and Costello, it was the mark of narrow-minded stupidity. Yet, Luciano kept his own counsel so well that Maranzano remained ignorant of the fact that Luciano had partnered with Jews. Nevertheless, he eventually came to distrust Luciano, and not for his partnerships, of which he remained ignorant, but because he thought that Luciano was too clever and ambitious and so could not be trusted. He was right. Maranzano paid "Mad Dog" Coll $25,000 to kill Luciano. When Luciano was tipped off about the contract on his life, he decided that Maranzano would have to be eliminated: better act first and live to become a boss. On September 10, 1931, in the New York Central Building on Park Avenue, Maranzano met his end.

In his book, *Boardwalk Gangster: The Real Lucky Luciano*, Tim Newark writes,

> Word of [the contract on Luciano's life] got to Luciano, and he prepared his response with a degree of irony. If Maranzano so undervalued the importance of Jewish gangsters, then it was they who could deal with him. Luciano recruited a crew of Jewish gunmen from out of town led by Samuel "Red" Levine. An observant Jew from Toledo, Ohio, Levine saw no conflict between his faith and his job; if he had to carry out a hit on the Sabbath he would simply wear a yarmulke under his hat.[2]

Maranzano had been expecting a visit from IRS auditors, so instructed his bodyguards not to bring their guns to the office. When the four ersatz IRS agents arrived, Maranzano invited them into his office. He was stunned when they pulled out switch blades and hunting knives and proceeded to stab him multiple times. Not satisfied with their work, the assassins shot Maranzano a few times and then slit his throat for good measure.

As they were leaving, they ran into "Mad Dog." Levine, a prolific killer and member of Murder Inc., warned Coll to leave because the cops were on their way. Coll left with the killers and got to keep the $25,000 that Maranzano had paid him, but without realizing that he had been warned by men who worked for the man he had been hired to kill. He also didn't realize that those men would soon be scheming to bring about his demise.

Throughout all the battles, Costello kept a low profile, bribing Tammany Hall politicians, including judges and police officials. He was like a man traveling on a toll road, depositing money into the hands of greedy toll takers for each leg of his trip. As he perceived the end of Prohibition with the election of Franklin D. Roosevelt (FDR), he ventured more and more into gambling rackets. With Lansky, he owned carpet joints in Saratoga, New York. In addition, he had hundreds of slot machines placed throughout the boroughs of Manhattan, Brooklyn, the Bronx, and Queens. He had made millions of dollars from Prohibition and was making millions more from his gambling ventures. He continued to see the necessary value of his political connections and served as a delegate to the Democratic convention that chose FDR as its 1932 presidential candidate. Costello even got to meet the great man at the convention.

The election of Fiorello La Guardia as Mayor of New York in January 1934 was another matter that proved an unfortunate event for the mob because a crackdown of gangsters soon ensued. Known as the Little Flower, the colorful and indomitable figure of LaGuardia stood a mere 5'2", but he commanded the respect of a giant. His energy, along with his pursuit of gangsters, was relentless. And one of his biggest targets was Costello's slot machines. He had his police raid one facility after another and slot machines were loaded onto a barge and dumped into New York Harbor. He fought against Tammany Hall and beat it; he instituted a system of hiring city workers based on merit rather than the patronage and pay-to-play schemes that Tammany had employed to fill its coffers.

That, plus the crackdowns against organized crime conducted by Thomas Dewey, led Costello to transfer his slot machine business to Louisiana, where the dominant politician, Huey Long, was happy to accept a $1 million bribe to let Costello and his partner Phillip "Dandy Phil" Kastel operate unimpeded. Kastel, like the founding fathers of the Mob, also got his start with Arnold Rothstein.

Although his slot machines had immigrated south, Costello remained a New Yorker, continuing to bribe political bosses, judges, police commissioners, and anyone who could do a favor for the Mob. He was even able to turn the FBI to other targets for investigation. Because the head of the FBI, J. Edgar Hoover was an inveterate gambler, Costello was quick to advise him on which races had hot horses running. "Hot horses" did not mean those that were especially fast; it meant horses that were sure to win because their races had been fixed. The usual method was to pay jockeys to hold back their horses. Those jockeys then used third parties to bet on the hot horse. There were other methods for ensuring that certain horses won, including drugging the competition or stuffing sponges into the nostrils of horses, thus limiting their breathing capacity. Hoover was not interested in the methods employed to guarantee winners; instead, he was thrilled to bet hundreds of dollars on sure things and then walk away with many more hundreds in his wallet. When asked why he didn't pursue gamblers as he did bank robbers, he responded that robbing banks was a heinous crime that had to be stopped. For the Mob, Hoover was as much a sure thing as any hot horse.

The Mob relied on dependable people—not just like Hoover, but also on those who worked for them in less celebrated positions. When Kastel learned that one of the collectors for the slot machine profits was skimming money, he notified Costello. Furious, Costello, who normally left acts of violence to underlings, flew to New Orleans, where he called a meeting of all his operatives. When they were assembled, Costello called the skimmer up to a lectern as if he expected the thief to make a confession of his misdeeds to the assembled workers. Instead, Costello took out a metal wrench and knocked the man unconscious. As the thief slumped to the floor, his head bleeding, Costello told his employees that if anyone stole from the syndicate his fate would be far worse than what they had just witnessed. His words were few and direct. No one stole from him again. His mission accomplished, Costello boarded a plane and flew back to New York. His behavior was mild compared to that of Siegel who simply shot a skimmer who had been managing one of the syndicate's bookie joints or that of Al Capone who beat John Scalize and Albert Anselmi to death with a baseball bat. The Mob steals and betrays, but no one steals from them, and no one betrays them.

The event in New Orleans was a rarity, for Costello preferred to pay others to enforce his directives with violence. One of his victims was Abe "Kid Twist" Reles, a notorious killer for Murder Inc. He looked like a low-slung ape with powerful arms that could easily break someone's neck. Following his arrest and indictment for multiple murders, Reles cut a deal with prosecutors to avoid frying in the electric chair. He testified against seven members of Murder Inc., all of whom were tried, convicted, and electrocuted in Sing Sing's hot seat, known as "Old Sparky." It was one thing to rat on other low-level thugs; however, it was intolerable to rat on a boss and that's what Reles was doing. Next in his line of fire was Albert "Mad Hatter" Anastasia, the boss, along with Louis "Lepke" Buchalter, of Murder Inc. That was too much for the other bosses to tolerate. It made them all vulnerable. In addition, Reles could provide testimony against Siegel and Frankie Carbo for the death of mobster rat Harry "Big Greenie" Greenberg; Reles had to go. There was no question about it. It was up to the Prime Minister of the Underworld to do his magic and bribe the hands of those who could deliver Reles into the arms of the Grim Reaper. Costello paid the five cops guarding Reles at the Half Moon Hotel in Coney Island to fling him out of a six-story window. The case against Anastasia and Siegel and others went out the window with Reles. The cops claimed that Reles had attempted to escape by tying two sheets together so that he could skitter like a squirrel down five stories and escape. Why he would want to escape into the hands of the Mob made no sense since he had known there was a contract on his life. And if he was so determined to escape why use only two sheets to descend five stories?

Lansky and Luciano reported to associates that Costello had spent $100,000 to bribe the five policemen who had been guarding Reles. All five were subsequently demoted, but they each deposited $20,000 into their individual safe deposit boxes. That was considerably more than their salaries, which were no more than $3,000 annually. For Costello, it was money well spent. Anastasia was delighted that the rat could not finger him. He commented to a crony that "the canary could sing, but he couldn't fly." Of course, his singing career flopped, too.

For Costello, life went on as usual. He continued to dress the part of a successful businessman in his conservative bespoke suits. Indeed, that's how he wanted the world to see him: an honest businessman, who had reformed following his career as a self-confessed bootlegger. When asked his occupation, he would say he was a sportsman and a businessman. So intent was he to alter and polish his self-image that he submitted himself to the care of a psychotherapist for 2 years. The therapist suggested that Costello associate with people other than gangsters. It would make him feel better about himself, and it would not only change his self-image, but it would also offer an attractive image to those in the respectable world. Unfortunately for Costello, reporters learned of his treatment and ambushed his therapist with questions that the therapist had no business answering. Yet, he told reporters that he advised Costello to associate with a better class of people than he normally associated with. When the comments were reported in the press, Costello was furious and subsequently told the press that as a result of his seeing Dr. Richard Hoffman, the therapist now had a better class of patients than he had previously treated. Hoffman was lucky that a certain class of people did not do injury to his body. Costello terminated his treatment.

And because Costello wanted to be accepted by a better class of people than his gangster associates, he moved to a fashionable section of Long Island, known as the Gold Coast, which had been the setting of F. Scott Fitzgerald's *The Great Gatsby*. And like Gatsby, who also wanted the world to think of him as a respectable businessman, Costello hosted parties for captains of industry, politicians, and socialites, none of whom had a rap sheet. Whether they accepted him as a peer is anyone's guess, but they were happy to drink his champagne and eat his caviar and chat with him about his rose garden. For the rest of his life, Costello would relentlessly pursue the often hard-to-believe image he parodied of a conservative businessman. He planted rose bushes and various ornamental flowers, entered horticultural competitions, and lived like a country squire, never commenting for the media about his associates or his neighbors.

However, the image Costello so carefully constructed began to crack and then shatter following his testimony before the Kefauver Committee hearings into organized crime in the early 1950s. Costello had insisted that if he were to give testimony that his face not be televised. Instead, news cameras focused on his hands, which did a nervous dance of the fingers, while his raspy voice added to the impression of a criminal hiding from embarrassing questions. No longer could Costello keep a low profile. It was the turn of politicians who were indebted to him who now kept low profiles: no elected official could afford to be publicly associated with a gangster who was known as the dispenser of bribes or the corruptor of those who supposedly devoted themselves to serving the public good. The Mob also began to feel that Costello had drawn too much attention to himself and his activities; he could no longer operate under the radar of official watchdogs; he reflected badly on the Mob, and he would have to be sidelined.

Costello provided an opportunity that Genovese had been patiently waiting for. Ever since Costello had aligned himself with what Genovese referred to as Costello's Hebe pals, Genovese had harbored a grudge against Costello. And that grudge was a slow-growing cancer that could only be cured by Costello's death. Yet, Genovese still had to suffer and bide his time.

Genovese believed that Luciano should not have appointed Costello as boss of their crime family when Luciano was deported to Italy. He had to go. But Willie Moretti, Costello's cousin, controlled an army of Mob soldiers in New Jersey, and Moretti would have thrown them into a battle to defend Costello's position as boss. Moretti, however, had his own problems: when testifying to the Kefauver Committee, he revealed more information about the Mob than was good for him and for his confederates. He, too, had become too much of a public figure. His talkative outbursts were the result of dementia that was brought on by a case of advanced syphilis. He, too, had to go. On October 4, 1951, Moretti was lunching with four men at Joe's Elbow Room Restaurant in Cliffside Park, New Jersey. They were the only diners in the restaurant. Their waitress had gone into the kitchen to place their luncheon order. At 11:28 a.m., waiters, cooks, and dishwashers, hearing multiple gun shots, rushed out of the kitchen into the dining room. There was Moretti, sprawled on the floor with bullet wounds to the face and head. One leg briefly twitched, and a sheet of blood covered his face. The restaurant staff, as if mesmerized, stood around his dying body, and then one of them called the cops. An embarrassment for the Mob had been silenced. According to Mafia tradition, Moretti's assassination was a mercy killing, and he was shot in the face as a sign of respect. A bullet, of course, shows no respect for its victim, and looking down a gun barrel hardly indicates that one is respected. Alas, those are the conventions.

Because of his many Hollywood connections and his role in getting his godson, Frank Sinatra, out of a contract with band leader Tommy Dorsey and because of his status as a Mob boss, more than 5,000 people attended his funeral. Some in Hasbrouck Heights even flew the US flag at half-mast, such was Moretti's prestige in his hometown.

With Moretti gone, there were two obstacles standing in the way of Genovese gaining control of the Luciano family. They were Costello and Albert "Mad Hatter" Anastasia. Genovese, though seething with anger and envy, had the patience of a turtle on a mission. He waited from 1951 to 1957 to take control.

On the late evening of May 2, 1957, Costello entered the lobby of his apartment building on Central Park West and was followed inside by Vincent "the Chin" Gigante, who pointed a .38 revolver at Costello's head and called out, "This is for you, Frank." The words caused Costello to turn toward his attacker just as Gigante fired. The bullet from Gigante's gun only grazed Costello's skull. Gigante, thinking that he had killed Costello, ran from the building and jumped into a waiting car that sped away into the night. Although the wound was superficial, it persuaded Costello to relinquish power to Genovese and retire. Genovese then controlled what is now called the Genovese crime family. Joe Bonanno, boss of an eponymously named crime family, would later credit himself with arranging a sit-down, where he kept Anastasia from immediately taking lethal action against Genovese.

Yet, Genovese knew that Anastasia would have to be eliminated. He decided to remove the possibility of a war between families by offering Carlo Gambino, Anastasia's underboss, the position of boss of the dead Anastasia's family. Gambino apparently agreed not to act against Genovese, if he had Anastasia hit. In addition, Genovese sought and got the approval from Lansky, who was angered that Anastasia had demanded more than his fair share of the profits from Lansky's casinos in Cuba. Lansky nodded his approval of the hit.

Ever watchful and cautious, Genovese moved stealthily: he knew that if Anastasia suspected a hit, he would go after Genovese. On the morning of October 25, 1957, an unsuspecting Anastasia entered the barber shop of the Park Sheraton Hotel at 56th Street and Seventh Avenue in Midtown Manhattan. After dropping off Anastasia, his driver-cum-bodyguard parked the car in an underground garage and then took a walk outside, leaving his boss unprotected. As Anastasia relaxed in the barber's chair, a hot wet towel covering his face, two men, wearing bandanas over their faces like old-time bank robbers, rushed into the barber shop, shoved the barber out of the way, and fired multiple shots at Anastasia. After the first volley of bullets, Anastasia leapt from his chair and attempted to lunge at his killers. The attack had disoriented him, and he lunged at the reflections of his killers in the wall mirror opposite his chair. The gunmen continued firing until Anastasia finally fell dead on the floor. The gunmen then ran from the shop and disappeared into the crowds on the sidewalk. They were never caught, though gangland informers identified them as the Gallo brothers.

Genovese was not home free. Though he proudly set himself up as boss, he had not factored in how his enemies might react to his duplicity and murderous deeds. They had no intention of letting him sit undisturbed on his new throne. Luciano, Costello, Gambino, and Lansky conspired to entrap Genovese with a narcotics conviction; they bribed a drug dealer to testify that he had personally worked with Genovese to buy and distribute drugs. On July 7, 1958, Genovese was indicted for narcotics trafficking. He was found guilty, and on April 17, 1959, he was sentenced to 15 years in state prison. The betrayer had been betrayed, and he impotently cursed the men who had engineered his imprisonment.

Costello, though pleased to have removed Genovese, had other problems. He had to withstand several indictments during his last years and wound up briefly serving time in the same prison as Genovese. Old and resigned, the two tired bosses made peace. There was no point in carrying on a fight that would have ended in both of their deaths.

Death came with neither guns nor knives to kill Genovese; he died of a heart attack at the US Medical Center for Federal Prisoners in Springfield, Missouri, on February 14, 1969. He is buried in Saint John's Cemetery in Middle Village, Queens.

Costello lived on for a few more years. Following his release, he divided his time between Manhattan and Sands Point, Long Island, where he attended to his roses and ornamental flowers. In Manhattan, he continued to meet with cronies for lunch or breakfast at the Waldorf Astoria Hotel, where he also received his haircuts and manicures. He would return to his apartment on Central Park West from where he and his wife would venture out to have dinner with friends. Wise guys would seek out his advice, and he would often chat about old times with his boyhood pal, Lansky. In early February 1973, he keeled over from a heart attack and was rushed to a nearby hospital. He died on February 18 and is buried in the Costello Mausoleum in St. Michael's Cemetery in East Elmhurst, Queens County, New York. His wife insisted that no mobsters attend his funeral. She had abided by her husband's wishes that he be seen as a businessman and not a mobster. However, he achieved lasting mobster fame when the character of Vito Corleone, in *The Godfather*, was based on him. Marlon Brando even studied recordings of Costello's raspy voice for his portrayal of the Prime Minister of the Underworld and gave the old gangster everlasting cinematic life.

In the real world, however, Costello was not permitted to rest in peace. On the morning of January 26, 1974 (Costello's birthday), the doors of his mausoleum were bombed. The metal doors were blown off the hinges. Carmine Galante, boss of the Bonanno crime family, had ordered the bombing. What was his motive? The Mafia rumor mill said that Galante was furious that Costello had banned the sale of drugs during his reign, and Galante was going full steam into the drug trade. In addition, Costello acted as if he had retired from the Mafia, and no one is allowed to do that. Membership lasts a lifetime.

Unfortunately for Galante, he was not long for this world, and on July 12, 1979, Galante was killed just as he finished eating lunch on the patio of Joe and Mary's Italian-American Restaurant at 205 Knickerbocker Avenue in Bushwick, Brooklyn. Galante had been dining with Leonard Coppola, a Bonanno capo, and restaurant owner/cousin Giuseppe Turano, a Bonanno soldier. Also sitting at the table were Galante's Sicilian bodyguards, Baldassare Amato and Cesare Bonventre. At 2:45 p.m., three masked men strode into the restaurant, entered the patio, and opened fire with shotguns and handguns. Galante, Turano, and Coppola were killed instantly. A news photo of Galante showed the dead man sprawled on the ground with a cigar clenched between his teeth. Amato and Bonventre, who hadn't reached for their guns to protect Galante, were left unharmed. The killers ran out of the restaurant; it was reminiscent of the murder of Masseria.

Fate seems to have protected Costello from his enemies who either died in prison or were felled by bullets. Though a gangster, Costello did not share the fate of so many mob bosses, who endured long prison sentences, deportations, or assassinations by young Turks. Costello, the gangster who refused to carry a gun and aligned himself with politicians, came the closest to being a legitimate businessman. His path was apparent as far back as 1932 when he was a delegate to the National Democratic Convention; there, with Big Apple pols and Tammany Hall bosses, he helped to secure the presidential nomination for FDR. And why not? As Ralph Salerno told the author, "Frank Costello was a great statesman. Who, as far as I know, never killed anyone.

In addition, he and Lansky changed the face of gambling in the US following World War II."[3]

And as a businessman he owned Wall Street office buildings and Texas oil leases.

5

Mr. Lucky

WHEN HE WAS A SCRUFFY KID roaming the streets of the Lower East Side with his gang, mugging people and running a protection racket, no one thought of him as lucky. He was named Salvatore Lucania, the poor, angry son of Italian immigrants. His future looked bleak; if he continued as a delinquent and graduated to being a career criminal, he would need more than luck to survive. Over a 20-year period, 1916 to 1936, he was arrested 25 times for a full menu of crimes, including robbery, pimping, drug dealing, gambling, and blackmail. (His clients could choose from a wide variety of skills.) Yet, Lucania spent no time in prison. He was indeed lucky at beating raps, at least until 1936, when special prosecutor Thomas Dewey set his gun sights on Lucania. But the ambitious gangster really developed the sobriquet "Lucky" after being kidnapped, taken to Staten Island, severely beaten, knifed, and left as a bloody and bruised mess. The surname on his rap sheet also underwent a slight bit of tailoring: he was now Lucky Luciano. The tough young thug was not going down. He was up and ready for anything that came his way. Anyone else would have died from the beating he took, but Luciano knew he was lucky to have escaped with his future still intact. From that near-death experience, he wore a scar on his face, and one droopy eyelid because some nerves had been cut.

Many years later, those who saw the film *Mr. Lucky*, starring Cary Grant, thought it might be fancifully based on an idealized version of the career of Luciano. In fact, Luciano believed that if a film of his career were ever made, it should star Grant. Luciano saw himself not only as lucky but also as a sharp, elegantly tailored ladies' man who loved the good life.

He was born in 1897 in Lecara Friddi, Sicily; there, he and his two brothers and two sisters grew up tasting the dirt of poverty. By April 1906, the Lucanias had finally saved enough money for steerage passage on a boat sailing from Palermo to New York City. The family, like many poor Italian immigrants, settled on the Lower East Side of Manhattan, a neighborhood also teeming with poor Jewish and Irish immigrants, none of whom got along well. They had brought with them their Old World prejudices, including fears and distrust of those who were different. It was a time and place that bred crime. Lucania was no exception. He was a tough, ruthless, and resourceful teenager. He and his gang often beat up other kids and then demanded 10 cents weekly for protection. One day, the gang confronted a skinny young Jewish kid on his way home from school. Lucania, the leader of the gang, demanded protection money. The kid told Lucania to "go fuck yourself." Lucania was impressed by the kid's guts and moxie: that a kid so small and ostensibly vulnerable would stand up to a gang and its leader was impressive indeed. And so began the lifelong friendship of Luciano and Meyer Lansky, two criminal masterminds, who would create the National Crime Syndicate, an illegal corporate enterprise that controlled most of the crime in the United States. Even Mafia families, many of whose bosses were members of the syndicate, had to obey the syndicate's dictates.

Luciano and his pals, Lansky, Frank Costello, and Ben "Bugsy" Siegel, were all being mentored by Arnold Rothstein, who had a jeweler's eye for discerning criminal brilliance in his young protégés. In addition to teaching them the skills of professional criminals, Rothstein taught them how to dress and even how to treat society ladies; he corrected their grammar and improved their diction. He was a Fagin in a three-piece suit. He wrapped his pupils in the veneer of gentlemen, while providing a road map leading to incredible bounties from illegal enterprises.

When the Volstead Act was ratified in 1919 and took effect in January 1920, Rothstein and his protégés, ever opportunistic, became what is known as bootleggers. (The term supposedly originated as a reference to high boots in which one could conceal a weapon or illegal whiskey.) Rothstein lent them money that they invested in boats, trucks, warehouses, distilleries and was used to grease the itchy outstretched palms of police, prosecutors, and judges. The bootleggers all became millionaires. Unfortunately for Rothstein, he was shot and killed by a fellow gambler, George "Hump" McManus, during a card game at the Park Central Hotel in 1928. Rothstein supposedly owed $320,000 to McManus but refused to pay because he said the card game was fixed. Rothstein's bloody exit opened doors for his protégés to take over many of their mentor's operations.

Luciano was now on a fast track to becoming a millionaire. And by the late 1920s, he had reportedly earned more than $12 million from bootlegging. He and five other gangsters (Lansky, Siegel, Owney "the Killer" Madden, Abner "Longy" Zwillman, and Waxey Gordon) had become the predominant bootleggers in the East. Costello also had his hand in bootlegging and often partnered with Lansky and Luciano. In Boston, Joseph Kennedy controlled much of the bootlegging and kept his association with Costello sub rosa.

With the elimination of bosses Joe "the Boss" Masseria and Salvatore Maranzano in 1931, Luciano set himself up as the boss of the National Crime Syndicate and operated it with his longtime colleagues, Meyer Lansky, Costello, Siegel, and Vito Genovese. They all respected Luciano and admired his business acumen. Together, they grew rich. Lansky played a particular role that none of the others were able to perform: he invested the syndicate's money in licit and illicit businesses, ensuring that each of the investors received regular dividends. Though smarter than his partners, Lansky was happy to remain in the shadows. Better to pull strings than be the marionette on the stage for everyone to see: a successful gangster is one who maintains a low profile, which is a maxim that neither Luciano nor Siegel chose to follow.

Independent of the syndicate, Luciano established his own crime family, making Genovese his underboss and Costello his consigliere. He also appointed five caporegimes: Joe Adonis, Willie Moretti, Anthony Carfano, Michael "Trigger Mike" Coppola, and Anthony Strollo.

Next, Luciano set up the Mafia Commission, which was created to settle all disputes that arose among the different families. As head of the commission and the syndicate, he was able to negotiate territorial disputes, approve or disapprove of murder contracts, and impose cease-fires, thus preventing the onset of gang warfare. His power was like that of a fascist generalissimo.

In addition to the five New York Mafia families, the commission comprised the Mafia families of Chicago, Buffalo, Detroit, Cleveland, Philadelphia, Los Angeles, and Kansas City. Though the Mafia members were all Italian, the commission had seats for Irish and Jewish gangsters, a fact never mentioned in movies or popular fiction. The commission was like the United Nations of the underworld. And for its creation and governance, Luciano was regarded by his contemporaries as the Mob's most innovative leader in its history. In later years, reporters often opined that if Luciano had gone straight, he could have been the CEO of a *Fortune 500* company. Such opinions were complemented by Lansky's remark that the syndicate was bigger than US Steel.

Keeping the peace while earning millions of dollars was the guiding theme in the business plan of the Luciano and Lansky partnership. But Dutch Schultz, a less reasonable man, was prepared to shred that business plan out of sheer homicidal fury. The hot-headed, sadistic gangster wanted to assassinate special prosecutor Thomas Dewey before he would be indicted; and Dewey, out of an almost religious sense of righteousness, along with calculated political ambition, was determined to prosecute not only Schultz but also Luciano, Louis "Lepke" Buchalter, Jacob "Gurrah" Shapiro, and members of Murder Inc. He wanted to rid New York of its gangsters, while elevating himself into the governor's mansion. Rather than plow fields of promise in new territories, as did Siegel in Los Angeles and Lansky in Florida, Shultz removed himself to the commuter jurisdiction of Newark, New Jersey, where he could still orchestrate a hit on Dewey. Luciano and Lansky conferred with Lepke, Shapiro, Albert "Mad Hatter" Anastasia, and other syndicate powers about Schultz's wild plan, and although Anastasia and Shapiro approved of it, the majority of the governing body, including out-of-state members Moe Dalitz and Zwillman, were adamantly against it; they finally agreed it was crazy. To kill Dewey would aim every weapon at the command of law enforcement at the Mob's operations. Schultz, always a hot head, shouted that he would kill Dewey on his own and strode out of the meeting. He had signed his own death warrant, which would be assigned to Murder Inc.

As hard as the syndicate continued to try and convince Schultz that his plan was madness, they could not reason with him; he was consumed by the idea of killing Dewey. Schultz enjoyed killing people and took pleasure in killing not only opponents but also members of his own gang whom he suspected of betrayal. To accuse him of being a psychotic, paranoid man would not be an understatement. The syndicate believed that killing judges, cops, prosecutors, and reporters would result in the issuance of a blizzard of indictments and inordinately long prison sentences. Better to operate in the shadows. And if indicted, it was smarter to fight the prosecutors with the aid of smart lawyers in court than with guns. Besides, one could always bribe judges and jurors, and if necessary, witnesses could be killed. Without corroborating testimony, convictions were unlikely. Yet, an obsessed Schultz refused to listen to subsequent arguments; he told the syndicate he was determined to go at it alone. Charles "the Bug" Workman and Emanuel "Mendy" Weiss, Murder Inc. gunmen, were given the contract to kill the Dutchman before the law could swing a wrecking ball at the syndicate's operations.

On October 23, 1935, Shultz and his henchmen, Otto "Abbadabba" Berman, Lulu Rosencrantz, and Abe Landau, were having dinner at the Palace Chop House on 12 East Park Street in Newark, New Jersey. After reviewing the accounts for their numbers operation, Schultz had left the group to go to the men's room. Shortly thereafter, Workman and Weiss rushed into the restaurant and fired their guns at the three diners. The diners fired back but failed to hit their assailants. Workman then burst into the men's room and fired a couple of shots at the urinating Schultz. One bullet entered Schultz's upper abdomen and exited his back. The Dutchman and his henchmen all died in hospital. (For more about the assassination of Schultz, see chapter 6.)

There is an irony to the syndicate's decision to spare Dewey and kill Schultz: if the syndicate had approved Schultz's plan, who would have followed through on Dewey's many successful prosecutions? Although Luciano was strongly against Schultz's plan to kill Dewey, Luciano was the fox who Dewey would hunt and drive to ground with the single-minded intensity of one delivering the wrath of God. In the underworld, ironies abound like ricocheting bullets.

Luciano and his cohorts divvied up Schultz's rackets. Luciano was particularly eager to get his hands on Schultz's policy racket, which was raking in millions of dollars a year. Luciano was growing richer and more powerful day by day, and his thirst for further riches seemed unquenchable. Dewey, free from threats of gangsters, was determined to end their reign of lawless entrepreneurial exploitation. On February 2, 1936, just months after Schultz's assassination, Dewey ordered his assistant Eunice Carter to raid more than 200 houses of prostitution in Brooklyn and Manhattan. To avoid tipping off the brothels of the upcoming raid, Carter did not use vice cops, who were known to be on the take for letting the brothels operate. Instead, she used local beat cops and kept them at the ready until just minutes before the raids took place. The 160 cops assigned to the raids arrested 100 prostitutes and madams as well as 10 pimps and managers. Bail was set for each of them at $10,000, a figure too high for any of them to pay, which meant that they could all be interrogated. If they cooperated, they would not have to go to prison. Three of the prostitutes claimed that Luciano was the kingpin operating the brothels, personally taking profits, and forcing prostitutes to submit to his friends at parties. The garrulous testimony of intimidated prostitutes led to Luciano's indictment. But as soon as he learned of it, he fled to Hot Springs, Arkansas, a city run by former New York bootlegger Madden. Hot Springs had not only become a safe resort and retirement center for gangsters, but it was also place where many of them hid out from law enforcement. Luciano was welcomed there in March 1936, but his vacation was cut short when he was arrested on an extradition warrant on April 3. He was sent back to New York under heavy guard. On May 13, he went on trial for pandering, which comprised 60 counts of compulsory prostitution. On June 1, he was convicted on all counts, and on July 18, he was sentenced to 30 to 50 years in prison, a virtual life sentence. He was astounded not so much at being found guilty as he was at the length of his sentence. A rap for murder two would have resulted in less time, and no one accused him of murder. He was shipped off first to Sing Sing Prison in Ossining, New York, and then to the Clifton

Correctional Facility in Dannemora in northern New York; inmates referred to Clifton as Siberia because in winter the small damp cells were freezing and in summer, the cells were as stifling as sweat boxes. While in prison, Luciano appointed Genovese as the boss of his family; however, that appointment was short-lived because Genovese was indicted for murder. Not wishing to be a neighbor of Luciano in prison, he fled to Italy, where he aligned himself with Benito Mussolini. Though the dictator had suppressed the Mafia, Genovese found ways to ingratiate himself and run his own criminal enterprises, ones that helped fill the dictator's coffers. Genovese even arranged to have the Mafia kill the antifascist editor of an Italian newspaper in New York's Little Italy; Mussolini was grateful.

With Genovese's self-deportation, the role of boss had to be filled, so Luciano appointed his boyhood chum Costello to run the family in his absence. Costello was smarter than Genovese, slow to anger, and rarely resorted to violence.

Though Costello profited handsomely from being a boss, he was willing to give up the position if he and Lansky could extricate Luciano from prison. After numerous failed legal appeals, a new tactic was tried. With the outbreak of World War II, a fortuitous opportunity arose: there had been acts of sabotage on the docks of New York City, and there was tremendous fear that Nazi saboteurs would do whatever they could to destroy US shipping. The Mob needed a shocking event that would cause government officials in Washington and New York to lose sleep. And there was the vulnerable SS *Normandie*, just sitting there as potentially sacrificial as a tethered goat. And what made her even more desirable was her acclaimed beauty, a glamorous ocean liner on full display at dockside, bathing in the sunlight. She had been extolled as the fastest and largest ship on the oceans. It was the most powerful steam turbo-electric-propelled passenger ship to sail the seven seas—what a perfect target for sabotage.

One day, fire broke out on the ship; it spread throughout, consuming all that was flammable. Flames lit up the sky above the Hudson River where the ship had been docked. The fire was rapacious, destroying all that it engulfed. It did not take long for the wounded, burned-out hulk to roll over on its side, stricken like a dying animal. The ship, which had been designated as a troop carrier to transport thousands of US soldiers to England, was mourned by thousands who had traveled on the luxurious ocean liner. Many assumed the fire was set by arsonists working for enemies of the United States. Government officials in New York were stunned that such devastation had occurred on their watch.

For the ever-opportunistic Mob, the death of the *Normandie* gave birth to a strategy to win Luciano's release from prison. To wit: it was well known that the Mob controlled the waterfront. The longshoremen's union was controlled by Anastasia's brother "Tough" Tony Anastasio (Albert had altered the spelling of his last name, replacing an o with an a), while mobster Socks Lanza was the commandant of the fishing fleets that did business at Fulton Fish Market. Lanza claimed that he could get all the fishing boats to be on watch for enemy submarines; Tough Tony, while ostensibly controlling just the Brooklyn docks, had influence over all dock workers and would let it be known that they should be the eyes and ears for ascertaining the presence of Axis spies. Lansky, ever loyal to his boyhood pal and partner in crime, presented a deal to naval intelligence: Luciano's supervision of Mob members would mean that there would be no sabotage on the docks and piers and no sabotage of ships in port. To facilitate the program, the Navy arranged for Luciano to be transferred to Great Meadow Correctional Facility in Comstock, New York. The location was much closer to New York than Clifton and so was easier for Lansky and Costello to visit. And while Luciano had endured bitter cold winters and hot-house summers in Dannemora, the climate in Great Meadow was less severe. Whenever Lansky, Costello, and others visited Luciano, they were given the use of the warden's office. The warden would discreetly absent himself during those meetings, thus ensuring that the mobsters could talk about more than just the docks, piers, and boats. Luciano was treated like an honored guest rather than a convict. Whatever he wanted in the way of food, reading material, and clothing was made available to him. Luciano had become the key for preserving New York's waterfront. And as soon as the US military leadership planned to land troops in Europe, Luciano was called on again to provide assistance.

Just prior to the US invasion of Sicily, the Navy asked Luciano for the names and contact information for Mafioso on the island who could be of help. Luciano readily provided the government with an address book full of names. The program was secretly known among naval intelligence officials as Operation Underworld, and gratitude for Luciano's help was growing in important spheres of influence.

Following the end of the war, Luciano's emissaries appealed to Governor Dewey for a commutation of Luciano's sentence. They were confident that a positive decision would be forthcoming. On January 3, 1946, Governor Dewey commuted Luciano's sentence but only on condition that Luciano accept deportation to Italy. (Dewey's dual roles as prosecutor and then as agent for Luciano's release did not go unnoticed by the media, politicians, and gangsters.) On February 2, Luciano was escorted from his prison cell by immigration agents and taken to Ellis Island. Seven days later, he was put aboard a freighter to be taken to Italy. The night before his departure, Luciano was enlivened by six guests, including Lansky, Costello, and Anastasia; they gave him an extravagant bon voyage party. It was extravagant not so much in the quality and abundance of the food and drink but in the merriment of Luciano and his associates celebrating the success of their strategy in terminating a long prison sentence. To this day, there is only uncertainty about how the fire on the *Normandie* was started and why it was permitted to burn so rapaciously. But years after the event, Anastasia claimed that he and his brother, Tony, set the fire.

In Italy, Luciano missed New York and looked for ways to return, but the closest that he would come to the Big Apple was when he attended the Havana Mob conference at Lansky's Hotel Nacional de Cuba on October 29, 1946. The conference had been organized by Lansky, who also retained Frank Sinatra to entertain the gangsters. Sinatra also acted as a bag man, carrying a million dollars in an attaché case for Luciano. The main topics of the conference were gambling, drug distribution, and the fate of Siegel. In a side conversation, Genovese told Luciano that he wanted to become the boss of the Luciano family and its eponymous head could become the boss of bosses. Luciano barked a strong negative response at Genovese, refusing the offer and instructing Genovese to never bring it up again. Genovese, as patient and scheming as a fox, would wait 11 years to enact his short-lived dream of power.

For the remainder of his life, Luciano operated from various domains in Italy, accepting regular payments from Lansky from their joint gambling interests. Though living with a beautiful ballerina named Igea Lissoni who was 20 years his junior, Luciano—ever a suave ladies' man—carried on numerous affairs. Luciano and Lissoni argued about his relationships with other women, and he would often terminate their arguments with a slap to her face; yet, she never left him.

With Luciano no longer a presence, Genovese had been eliminating those who stood in his way to achieving ultimate power as a boss. He ordered a series of assassinations—his version of the legendary Night of the Italian Vespers. His actions brought down on the Mob a shower of negative publicity. Who would be next? No one who was an obstacle on Genovese's road to power was safe. The Mob believed he had eliminated Anastasia, who had been aligned with Costello. It was time to get rid of the ambitious Genovese. In 1959, Luciano invited Costello and Carlo Gambino to visit him in Palermo. There the trio, along with Lansky's consent, decided to frame Genovese as a drug dealer and send him off to a life in prison. Upon conviction, Genovese was sentenced to 15 years in prison and died in 1969, 5 years short of his release date. It was one of Luciano's last clever manipulations of the law. He, Gambino, and Costello had always preferred the double cross, acts of betrayal, and the planting of evidence to the use of guns and knives. They had disposed of numerous opponents, such as Gordon, with such tactics. They thought a long prison term was often worse than death. And for Genovese, the 15-year sentence was a death sentence.

The sands in the hour glass of Luciano's career were quickly running down. While waiting at Naples International Airport to meet a US film producer who wanted to make a movie of his life, Luciano dropped dead of a heart attack on January 26, 1962. Three days later, his body was enclosed in a coffin that was placed in a horse-drawn black hearse and conveyed to a Naples cemetery. However, his relatives claimed his body, and he was finally laid to rest at St. John's Cemetery in Middle Village, Queens, New York. As 2,000 mourners looked on, Gambino gave the eulogy of the man who had been a Mafia visionary. So admired was Luciano for his business acumen that *Time* magazine wrote in 1998 that Luciano, a criminal mastermind, was among the top 20 most influential business titans of the 20th century. The magazine failed to include his partner and advisor, Lansky, of whom Luciano stated, "Always listen to Meyer, and you'll always make money."

6

The Dutchman

I FIRST LEARNED OF DUTCH SCHULTZ when my father informed me that a great uncle and bootlegger named Irving K. had been indicted but never tried for the murder of the Dutchman. That dubious honor, plus a conviction, went to Charlie "the Bug" Workman, a member of Murder Inc., who served a 23-year prison term for killing the Dutchman. Following his release, Workman was employed as a salesman in the garment center of New York City. Much of the garment center was controlled by the Tommy "Three-Finger Brown" Lucchese and Carlo Gambino crime families.

There were many people who wanted to kill Schultz and not only because he was a sadistic son of a bitch but also because his irrational anger was a threat to the rational criminality of the National Crime Syndicate. In addition, his ability to charm others was zero, and he often went out of his way to humiliate other gangsters whose support could have been beneficial. For example, Carl Sifakis writes in *The Mafia Encyclopedia*,

> Schultz, one of the flakiest of big gang leaders, couldn't resist sticking it to Joe Adonis, a gangster always vain and proud of his good looks and star quality. Schultz, at the time, had the flu and had been ordered by his doctor to stay in bed, but he showed up at the meet. When Adonis dropped a cute remark in the discussion, Schultz, looking to top him, suddenly pounced on him with a hammerlock and breathed right in his face, saying, "Now, you fucking star, you have my germs," . . . If organized crime connotes anything it is that the rackets have to operate by some universally accepted rules. For Schultz there were no rules—other than those he liked or made. For those who broke his rules ended up dead;

not only was he the flakiest of the bosses, he was also the most cold-blooded. In the end, he had to be blown away.[1]

So from where did this obnoxious sadist of the underworld emerge? Schultz's real name was Arthur Simon Flegenheimer. He was born in 1901 in the Bronx; his parents were German Jewish immigrants. Schultz's father deserted the family when the boy was 8 years old. To help support his mother and siblings, Schultz dropped out of school in the eighth grade and went to work for several companies before winding up at a trucking company, where he worked off and on from 1916 to 1919. His work was menial, and his compensation was penurious. Desperate for money, Schultz committed several burglaries during that time but was caught by police. Indicted and convicted, Schultz served time in prison, where he proved to be rebellious and defiant of authority. He escaped once and, after being caught, had additional time tacked onto his sentence.

Out of prison in 1920, he found a job that comported with his angry temperament. He was hired as a bouncer for a Bronx nightclub, the Hub Social Club, which was owned by a small-time mobster named Joe Noe, a man with whom Schultz would develop a nearly fraternal relationship. Noe was impressed by the truculent Schultz, who proved to be a violent and resourceful bouncer. Noe decided to make Schultz a partner. With the outset of Prohibition, the two formed a gang known to the cops as the Noe-Schultz Gang. They opened several more nightclubs and went into the bootlegging business, buying several trucks to deliver booze not only to their own nightclubs but also to numerous others throughout the Bronx. Owners who resisted the opportunities to become customers of Noe and Schultz were met with violence, which invariably resulted in their ultimate capitulation. The gang, unfortunately, met resistance from the Rock brothers, a pair of minor bootleggers and club owners. Following a series of threats and acts of sabotage engineered by Noe and Schultz, the older Rock brother capitulated and agreed to become a customer. However, the younger brother, Joe, was made of tougher (and perhaps stupider stuff) than his brother: he refused to cooperate with Noe and Shultz. There was only one way to melt Joe's icy resistance. They did not use a blow torch. Instead, Schultz kidnapped and beat Joe senseless, repeatedly knocking him into unconsciousness, reviving him and then beating him again. Joe's face left Schultz's fists sticky with blood. Schultz complained about having to repeatedly wash his hands. Joe, who had been tied to a chair, was next suspended from a meat hook and beaten some more. The warehouse in which the beatings took place was empty and echoed with Joe's screams, moans, and whimpering. Finally, unable to control his sadistic rage, Schultz took a gauze bandage that had been permeated with the evidence of gonorrhea and tightly wrapped it as a blindfold across Joe's swollen, bloody eyes. Schultz then notified the Rock family that if they wanted to welcome Joe home, they would have to pay a ransom.

The delivery of Joe's still breathing body cost the Rock family $35,000. Several days after his return home, Joe went blind from the infection in his eyes. When word of Joe's torture spread among bootleggers, club owners, and mobsters, there was no further resistance to the Noe-Schultz Gang.

Noe and Schultz had become the bootleg kings of the Bronx. However, that was not enough for them. They wanted to expand their kingdom, to conquer and control new lands. Fueled by greed and ambition, Noe and Schultz planned their attack and, without firing a shot, took control of bootlegging in northern Manhattan. However there was resistance farther south. There, the competition was less compliant than in the Bronx and north of 96th Street. In much of Manhattan, they would have had to deal with Lucky Luciano, Meyer Lansky, Arnold Rothstein, and the men whom they bankrolled and who operated their subsidiary companies. In addition, there was Owney "the Killer" Madden, whose illegal brewery took up an entire block on the Lower West Side. He was one of the most successful bootleggers in New York during Prohibition, and only he could supply the nightclubs he owned, such as the famous Cotton Club. Though the Cotton Club operated in the midst of Schultz territory, Madden made sure that it was as inviolable as police headquarters. Schultz dared not threaten it or Madden. Schultz knew that Madden owned politicians who could put him out of business with one phone call. There were others, however, against whom Schultz was prepared to wage war. His first bullet-flying Manhattan battles were waged against the notorious Jack "Legs" Diamond, a rival bootlegger, who had been a bodyguard for Arnold Rothstein. He was as violent as Schultz but not as clever. In addition to being a bootlegger, he also owned a Broadway nightclub, the Hotsy Totsy Club, located at 1721 Broadway, between 54th and 55th Streets. One night he had shot a man there and then went into hiding in upstate New York. However, his war with Noe and Schultz, known as the Manhattan Bootleg Wars, waged on with few interruptions. In one of the battles, Noe was an early casualty: on the night of October 16, 1928, Noe was gunned down in front of the Chateau Madrid on West 54th Street. Who killed him? Schultz believed that Diamond's gang, following orders from Rothstein, had murdered his partner. For a cold-blooded killer, Schultz was deeply bereaved. Noe was one of the few people and, perhaps, the only person, that Schultz had loved as a brother. Schultz was enraged and determined to get even. He subsequently arranged for George "Hump" McManus to kill Rothstein in the Park Central Hotel following a 3-day card game during which Rothstein ran up a debt of $320,000. The press reported that Rothstein was murdered for not paying the debt, for he was widely known up and down Broadway, as a welcher. He regularly made excuses to those to whom he owed money, saying he would pay them next week or next month, as soon as he received payment of a big gambling debt. Although the press bought the story that Rothstein was killed because he hadn't paid McManus his winnings, the Mob knew better. They believed that Schultz had ordered the killing because shortly after the shooting of Rothstein, Bo Weinberg, a member of the Schultz gang, arrived by car, picked up McManus, and drove him to a safe haven. Eventually McManus was arrested and tried for Rothstein's murder, but he was ultimately acquitted, and neither Weinberg nor Schultz was indicted for it.

As the Manhattan Wars raged, bullet-ridden bodies, scattered like debris, were photographed for the tabloid newspapers. Those papers were having a field day keeping track of all the killings and publishing photos of bodies lying in bloody puddles on sidewalks, streets, and alleys. Some bodies were thrown from rooftops; others were found floating in one of the city's rivers, where they were fished out by police boats. Often the names of the victims were either omitted or misidentified. The public was fascinated by all the murder and mayhem but also cautious enough not to visit particular clubs where gangsters had killed one another. A tommy gun, wildly spraying bullets, can just as easily mow down the innocent as well as the guilty.

Diamond, unlike many of his cohorts, proved hard to kill. He had been ambushed and shot full of holes during two attempts on his life, but each time he managed to survive. He thought of himself as being indestructible. Yet, before his survival rate could reach the limit of the mythical nine lives of cats, Diamond was tracked down to a rooming house in Albany, where two men pinned him to his bed, while one of them fired a pair of bullets into the back of his cranium. Among Mob insiders, it was believed that Schultz was behind Diamond's assassination. According to Sifakis, Schultz commented about Diamond's death, that he was "just another punk caught with his hands in my pockets."[2]

Another gangster as ambitious but more vilified than Diamond was Vincent "Mad Dog" Coll. He earned his sobriquet as a result of a failed assault against Shultz when Coll sprayed a sidewalk on East 107th Street in Spanish Harlem with more than 60 tommy-gun bullets, killing 5-year-old Michael Vengalli and wounding four other children in front of Joey Rao's Helmar Social Club. Coll became the most hated gangster in New York; other gangsters ostracized him and figured he would die in a gun battle with the cops who might miss and kill them. Better to stay away and pursue one's own interests. It was one thing for gangsters to kill each other, but it was quite another thing to be so careless and heartless as to shoot down innocent children. If Schultz, acting as an outraged vigilante, had immediately killed Coll after the Vengalli murder, he would have been celebrated as a folk hero.

Instead, Schultz—fearful of being killed by Coll in an ambush—stayed out of the limelight. He knew that Coll was crazy, careless, and unpredictable. The longer Coll was on the lam, the more nervous Schultz became. In fact,

Coll drove Arthur to such distraction that the Dutchman went around to the 42nd Police Precinct in the Bronx one day in 1931 and offered to put a bounty on his head, the way they used to do it in the Old West. Of course, it strains the imagination, but it happened. Schultz simply walked into the detective's squad room and said, "Look, I want the Mick killed. He's driving me out of my mind. I'll give a house in Westchester to any of you guys who knocks him off." There were three detectives on hand and the one who knew the beer merchant best, Fred Schaedel, from the old neighborhood, answered him.

"Arthur," the big cop said, "do you know what the hell you're saying? You know you're in the Morrisania station?"

"I know where I am," Schultz snapped. "I've been here before. I just came in to tell ya I'll pay good any cop that kills the Mick."

"Then get your ass out of here before we pinch you. You hafta be out of your head."[3]

When asked years later why Schultz wasn't pinched, the detective said that the cops couldn't make it stick. Schultz would have said he was only kidding, and his lawyer would have gotten him released as quickly as the cops could have arrested him.

The war between Schultz and Coll had been a long time gestating: Coll had originally worked for Schultz, from whom he received a modest salary. But tired of being a salaried employee, Coll wanted a piece of the action, a partnership. Schultz, for whom money was everything, refused. Coll furiously quit the gang, formed his own gang, and decided to take over his former boss's action. He would kill all who stood in his way. To say he was reckless would be an understatement.

It would have been typical of Schultz to have killed Coll moments after his employee quit. Yet, Schultz did not act with his customary impulsive violence. When others told Schultz they were quitting, they usually disappeared, never to be heard of again. Schultz regarded enlistment in his organization as a lifetime commitment.

During the war between Schultz and his treasonous henchman, Schultz had to endure the allegations of law enforcement. He went on trial and everyone, mobsters and prosecutors alike, thought the final of a series of trials would end with Schultz's conviction. Not wanting to be left high and dry with neither an income nor a pension, Schultz's top lieutenant, Weinberg, approached Luciano and Lansky about taking over his boss's business. All Weinberg wanted in return was an ongoing portion of the profits, a kind of lifetime royalty. In a world of betrayals, double crosses, and set ups, Schultz learned of his conniving lieutenant's treason and determined to have him executed. Schultz stoked the flames of his anger through the trial and beyond. When he was acquitted, he met with Luciano and vented his fury. Luciano, a snake charmer with mongoose instincts, assured the furious Schultz that he had only been "looking after the shop" in Schultz's absence. What a good fellow he had been—selfless to a fault. Schultz departed the meeting, but his anger was still at a boil. Luciano knew that Schultz would kill Weinberg, and eventually Schultz would have to be whacked, too. He and Lansky would patiently wait for the right time and then take over Schultz's business. Schultz, meanwhile, invited Weinberg to an evening on his boat. Waiting for Weinberg was a pair of buckets, each filled with wet cement. Soon after boarding the boat, Weinberg was knocked unconscious, and each of his feet was placed in a bucket of cement. When the cement hardened, Schultz aroused Weinberg into wakefulness and wished him good riddance. Weinberg was thrown overboard and descended into the depths of the East River, from which a few bubbles of air rose to the surface and popped.

Coll did not think he would die at Schultz's hands; he thought he was such a tough guy that no one would succeed at killing him. In his arrogance, he never suspected that his time might be up. He may not have heard that there was a $50,000 contract out on his life. Had he known, he would have left town. Instead, he was staying at the Cornish Arms Hotel on 23rd Street. Coll left his room at 12:30 a.m. and strode across the street to the London Chemists drug store. He was unarmed, which was unusual for Coll. Once inside the drug store, he cocooned himself into a phone booth. He was there for about 10 minutes, animatedly talking on the phone, when a limo pulled up outside the drug store. The limo contained three men, all with fedoras pulled low on their foreheads. One man emerged, entered the store, told the proprietor and customers to remain quiet, and then raised a tommy gun out from under his overcoat, pointed it at the phone booth in which Coll continued talking, and then blasted away. Fifteen bullets blew Coll against the back wall of the phone booth. As soon as the machine gun went silent, Coll fell out of the phone booth onto the floor of the drug store. The killer, reported to be Ben "Bugsy" Siegel, strode out of the store and got into the limo that sped off. A uniformed cop, walking his beat, heard the shots, saw the killer run from the store and get into the limo; the cop quickly commandeered a taxi, leaping onto one of its running boards and shouting that the taxi driver should follow the speeding limo up Eighth Avenue. The taxi's engine was not as powerful as the one in the limo and the driver could not overtake the speeding getaway car. The taxi fell farther and farther behind, and the cop finally gave up the chase. The limo was later found abandoned in the Bronx with the deadly tommy gun peacefully lying on the back seat. No one was ever prosecuted for the hit.

Two of Schultz's primary enemies were now dead. Schultz was a happy man. As far as he could tell, there were no further competitors to his business enterprises. He figured he could work something out with Luciano and Lansky and recover what they had taken. Schultz wanted to run his businesses as monopolies, and with Diamond and Coll dead, he believed that he had succeeded. Price-fixing was a fait accompli.

From bootlegging, Schultz moved into the policy racket. Throughout Harlem, poor residents played the numbers in which they would bet on three numbers to win. The numbers were derived from the amount that was bet at the Belmont Park racetrack. Using the threat of murder, Schultz was able to take over the banks of numerous Harlem policy operations. The owners were forced to become salaried employees and were promised a percentage of the profits, which were rarely paid to them. If they complained, their legs were broken. If they continued to complain, they were permanently silenced.

Policy was as profitable as bootlegging. And to maximize profitability, Schultz retained the services of a brainy accountant named Otto "Abbadabba" Berman, who in just minutes could calculate the minimum amount that had to be bet to change the final numbers at Belmont. Because Berman could create the final three numbers, he minimized the number of winners and the amount of the payouts. A small number of winners meant that Schultz's profits would amount to millions of dollars per month—all of it tax free. Because Berman was necessary to the operation and could not be easily replaced (unlike Coll), he was paid $10,000 a week by his otherwise stingy employer. Not satisfied with the millions of dollars that poured in from his numbers racket, Schultz also formed a corrupt union, The Restaurant and Cafeteria Owners Association, whose business agents, led by Jules Modgilewsky, a fearsome thug, threatened owners into making regular payments to ensure labor peace. Modgilewsky, also known as Jules Martin, was so inspired by his own entrepreneurial ambition that he embezzled thousands of dollars from the Association's treasury. Not one to take such thievery lightly, Schultz confronted the embezzler. At first, Modgilewsky denied having taken any money, then—after being relentlessly berated—confessed that he took only what he was entitled to. Schultz showed him exactly what he was entitled to by suddenly pulling a revolver out of his waistband, sticking it in Modgilewsky's mouth and blowing away half of his head. According to Schultz's lawyer, Dixie Davis, it was all done in one quick motion. As Modgilewsky crumpled to the floor, pieces of his brain and skull splattered on the floor and a wall, Schultz went right on talking with his lawyer and another man as if nothing had happened. Not long afterward, Modgilewsky's body was found by police in a snow bank. The police discovered that, in addition to its bloody head wounds, it had multiple stab wounds. When asked about the condition of the corpse by his lawyer, Schultz claimed that he had cut Modgilewsky's heart out of his chest.

While most mobsters committed murder as part of their way of doing business, Schultz impressed them as a man who enjoyed killing and looked for excuses to do it. While a Frank Costello could hit a thief with a metal wrench in front of an audience to discourage him from ever embezzling again, Schultz provided no second chances. Steal from him and he would kill you. It was as simple as that.

In the eyes of New York's other crime bosses, Schultz was too volatile, too violently unpredictable. They knew that if Schultz didn't get what he wanted from Lansky and Luciano, he would start another war to recover what had been taken from him while he was on trial. Schultz was not only planning on going after Luciano and Lansky for their thievery, but he also wanted to assassinate special prosecutor Thomas Dewey, who had set his prosecutorial gun sights on Schultz. Dewey was as determined and persistent as a beaver and would not rest until he could get Schultz sentenced to a long prison term. That was the lesser of the punishments that Dewey had on his agenda. At the top of his agenda was his intention of convicting Schultz for murder and dispatching him to fry in the electric chair at Sing Sing.

Schultz was acting like an enraged and wounded lion, ready to lash out at all of his tormentors. He demanded a meeting with the National Crime Syndicate. At the meeting, he said he needed their permission to assassinate Dewey. A few members, including Albert "Mad Hatter" Anastasia and Jacob "Gurrah" Shapiro, thought it was a good idea; however, the majority voted against it, believing that such a murder would bring the entire weight of law enforcement down on them, causing many of their businesses to cease operating. The boss of the Bonanno crime family, Joe Bonanno, said that Schultz was crazy to even consider such action. Schultz angrily rose from his seat, yelled that they were all cowards, and that the syndicate was just out to take over his operations. Schultz told them he would take care of Dewey himself. That, in effect, sealed his doom. After he left the meeting, the syndicate issued a death sentence on Schultz.

At 10:15 on the night of October 23, 1935, Schultz was having dinner and reviewing his account books with Berman, his new lieutenant Abe Landau, and bodyguard Bernard "Lulu" Rosenkrantz at the Palace Chop House in Newark, New Jersey. Emanuel "Mendy" Weiss and Charlie "the Bug" Workman, hit men for Murder Inc., entered the restaurant, guns drawn. Schultz had gone to the men's room to urinate; Workman found him there and fired two bullets, one hitting Schultz in the abdomen. Workman then joined Weiss and the two repeatedly shot Landau and Rosenkrantz. Though Landau's carotid artery was pierced and blood flowed from his neck, he not only managed to return fire, but he also chased the two hit men from the restaurant. Out on the street, Landau continued firing until he collapsed onto a garbage can, then tumbled onto the sidewalk. The garbage can clattered to the sidewalk and rolled several feet. Weiss panicked, leapt into a waiting car, and told the driver to take off, leaving Workman behind. Workman, not hit by any of Landau's bullets, ran to safety and found transportation back to New York City. Schultz had managed to stumble out of the bathroom; he sat at his table for a moment, then fell face forward onto the table. Rosenkrantz, who was badly wounded and dripping blood from several bullet holes, painfully trudged to the bar, where he demanded five nickels as change for a quarter, so that he could use the pay phone to call for an ambulance. (He didn't want to waste an entire quarter on a 5-cent call.) He dialed the number of the local police and demanded that an ambulance be sent to the chop house. Before he could wait for an answer, he collapsed onto the floor, and four nickels rolled out of his outstretched hand.

In an ambulance, on the way to the hospital, Schultz handed $3,000 to a medical intern, stating that he wouldn't need the money where he was going. Fearing that Schultz might live and demand the return of his money, the intern handed the money back to Schultz, who took it as a sign that he would survive.

Berman and Landau, each shot multiple times, were pronounced dead in the hospital. Schultz lingered on, amazing the doctors. Workman had loaded his pistols with rusty bullets, hoping that if the wounds didn't result in Schultz's death, then he would die of blood poisoning. During the last 22 hours of his life, Schultz uttered what some consider to have been a poetic stream of consciousness. William S. Burroughs published a novel with the title *The Last Words of Dutch Schultz*, and Schultz biographer, Paul Sann, devoted an entire chapter in *Kill The Dutchman!* to those final words.

Here are some of the last strange words uttered by Schultz and recorded by the police:

"Talk to the Sword. Shut up. You got a big mouth."

"Please Mother, Mother, please the reaction is so strong. Oh mama, mama, please don't tear; don't rip, that is something that shouldn't be spoken about; that is right."

"No, No! There are only ten of us and there are ten million fighting somewhere in front of you, so get your onions up and we will throw up the truce flag."

"The sidewalk was in trouble and the bears were in trouble and I broke it up."

"Oh, Oh, dog biscuit, and he is happy, he doesn't get snappy."

"I had nothing with him; he was a cowboy in one of the . . . Seven days a week fight. No business, no hangout; no friends, nothing; just what you pick up and what you need."

"A boy has wept . . . nor dashed a thousand kin."

"Oh Duckie, see we skipped again."

"If that ain't the payoff. Please crack down on the Chinaman's friends and Hitler's commander. All right, I am sore and I am going up and I am going to give you honey if I can. Look out. We broke that up. Mother is the best bet and don't let Satan draw you too fast."

"I know what I am doing here with my collection of papers, for crying out loud. It isn't worth a nickel to two guys like you or me, but to a collector it is worth a fortune; it is priceless. I am going to turn it over to . . . Turn your back to me, please, Henry."[4]

Though born a Jew, Schultz had converted to Catholicism and so was entitled to last rites according to Catholic doctrine. He was buried in the Gate of Heaven Cemetery in Hawthorne, New York. His mother, an Orthodox Jew, requested that her son be buried with his tallit (i.e., a Jewish prayer shawl). Prior to his death, Schultz allegedly put millions of dollars into a safe. He and Rosenkrantz then drove to upstate New York and buried the safe. To this day, fortune hunters with metal detectors have combed through the Catskill Mountains looking for the safe. It has never been found. Such is the legacy of Schultz, who—had he killed Dewey—would have saved Luciano from prison and Louis "Lepke" Buchalter and members of Murder Inc. from the electric chair. Sometimes the craziest of the crazies is correct.

7

The Gorilla Boys

CHARLIE, "THE BUG" WORKMAN, who had killed the Dutchman, did so on the orders of Louis "Lepke" Buchalter, the man who was the boss and—in effect—the biggest client of Murder Inc. Buchalter, along with Albert "Mad Hatter" Anastasia, issued murder contracts with the nonchalance of guys ordering cups of coffee. They ordered more than 1,000 hits in cities and towns across the country.

Had the National Crime Syndicate permitted Schultz to assassinate District Attorney Thomas Dewey, he would have saved Buchalter from frying in the electric chair; Buchalter was the only Mob boss to be sentenced to death.

Once Schultz was out of the way, Dewey turned his prosecutorial sites on Buchalter and his partner Jacob "Gurrah" Shapiro. They had become the biggest labor racketeers in the United States. It was Schultz's death that permitted Buchalter and Shapiro to take over his restaurant union. From there, they took control of the entire garment industry. Paul R. Kavieff in *The Life and Times of Lepke Buchalter*, writes,

By threat and sometimes violence, the Lepke mob took control of one union local after another. Big labor leaders who were used to having East Side gangsters withdraw from the field after they put down strikes found themselves sharing their leadership with Lepke [and] Shapiro. . . .

Lepke completely changed the face of labor racketeering in the New York City needle-trade unions. He was methodical in this approach, and as a result, organized crime gained a permanent foothold not only in the needle-trade unions, but in the entire New York City garment industry. Early in their association, Buchalter and Shapiro won the label of the "Gorilla Boys" for their efficiency in strong-arm work. Later when they raked in millions of dollars a year from the captive garment industry, they became known in the underworld as the "gold dust twins."[1]

The garment and restaurant industries were not the only ones that Buchalter and Shapiro controlled: they also took over trucking, bakery, and poultry workers unions. Very few had the nerve to stand in the way of the duo's ambitions. Recalcitrant union bosses viewed the gorillas as a pair of blood-thirsty goons who would likely kill them if they resisted.

In the world of unions and union organizing, Buchalter and Shapiro were certainly pioneers who knitted together related industries into a single fabric that they either owned or controlled. In fact, they not only owned unions, but they also forced their way into taking control of manufacturing companies, some of which were unionized and some of which were union free. There were two ways in which they took control: (i) they provided strikebreakers to management and, instead of a payment, demanded a portion of their clients' businesses. If management resisted, their merchandise was destroyed by acid, their employees beaten up, and the trucks that carried their garments were fire bombed. (ii) Many garment manufacturers were unable to keep up with changing styles without borrowing money to finance the purchase of new material. If they were in arrears with a bank or a factoring company, they would have no choice but to turn to gangsters. And those gangsters were Buchalter and Shapiro who lent money at exorbitant rates of interest. If borrowers couldn't afford the interest rates, they would be forced to take on the duo as new partners, and Buchalter and Shapiro had no intention of being minority partners. They might later demand a larger share of a company, and if their partner resisted, the Gorilla Boys would call a strike and drive the company deep into debt. Unable to pay off the additional debt, the original owner would have to sign over his company to his new partners.

For manufacturers who didn't acquiesce to the Gorilla Boys' demands for sweetheart deals, payoffs, or portions of their businesses, they were met with threats, threats of strikes, threats of death, and if threats didn't produce the desired results, there was always death by gunfire, knife, or in one case, being thrown out of a window.

The Gorilla Boys' methods for taking control of unions consisted of getting their gang members to join a union and then voting for the gangsters as new directors. Once in control of various union locals, Buchalter and Shapiro siphoned off millions of dollars by invading the treasuries of those unions. They were, in effect, taking money earned by their working-class members.

No one competed with Buchalter and Shapiro in the domination of labor unions, and unlike Lucky Luciano, Buchalter and Shapiro were not involved in gambling, prostitution, and bootlegging (though Buchalter later invested in the drug trade). Their focus remained the two primary needs of the middle class and working poor: food and clothing. And to achieve their goals, they used gunmen from Murder Inc. to remove obstacles that stood in their paths to power and riches.

Luciano seemed to criticize the Gorilla Boys and exculpate himself by claiming that his crimes of bootlegging, gambling, and prostitution were essentially victimless crimes, whereas the Gorilla Boys stole money from poor working-class stiffs who could ill afford to part with even a few dollars, especially during the hard times of the Great Depression. The Gorilla Boys didn't care about the men they robbed, though they were generous to their own families. Or as Robert Rockaway titled his book about Jewish gangsters: *But He Was Good to His Mother.*

Because trucking was the lifeblood of the garment and food industries, the Gorilla Boys knew that control of the truckers was absolutely essential. If trucking was withheld from garment manufacturers, restaurants, supermarkets, and bakeries, their businesses would cease operating. The Gorilla Boys offered deals to truckers that they better not resist. For those truckers who refused to accept their offers, assaults, bombings, or the denial of business followed. The truckers, with a few exceptions, capitulated.

So who were these labor gangsters and where did they come from?

Buchalter was born on the Lower East Side of Manhattan in 1897. He was the youngest of five children. He was the only one to become a gangster; his sister became a school teacher; one brother became a college professor and rabbi; another brother became a dentist; and a third brother became a pharmacist. Louis was his mother's baby, and she called him "Lepkeleh," which means "little Louis" in Yiddish. His schoolmates shortened it to "Lepke." When, years later, Buchalter was introduced to Luciano by Meyer Lansky, Luciano wanted to know what kind of name Lepke was. Buchalter replied that it was what his mother called him when he was a child. Luciano was touched and quipped that any man who thought so highly of his mother that he kept her nickname for him couldn't be all bad. Luciano shook hands with Buchalter and thereafter always called him Lepke. (The name would later be featured on FBI posters as belonging to America's Most Wanted criminal, a name synonymous with cold-blooded murder).

In 1909, Buchalter's father died, and the family had to deal with increased poverty. His mother tried to make a living by selling kosher food door to door. Young Buchalter was appalled that his mother slaved day and night to earn a few dollars a week. He took a few menial jobs, but the remuneration added little to the household income. His mother was quickly descending into debt. It was too much for Buchalter, and he quickly found his métier in small-time criminal activity; he was unlucky in his endeavors and caught and sent to a reformatory. Following his release, he upped the ante and attempted to pull off more high-stakes crimes. Again, he was caught, but this time he was sent to Sing Sing prison. He didn't return to civilian life until 1922, stating—upon his release—that he would never spend another day in prison. From that time on, he would operate behind the scenes, directing others to commit crimes, which is how he met his future partner, Shapiro.

One day, Buchalter decided to steal the content of a peddler's wagon, but he suddenly encountered Shapiro, who also had the same plan. Buchalter approached Shapiro. Soft spoken and diplomatic, he suggested to Shapiro that they operate together: Buchalter would be the lookout and—because Shapiro was big and strong—he should do the actual robbing. The husky, muscular Shapiro agreed, and the slender 5'6" Buchalter held back and scanned the street looking for the possible approach of a cop. No cops passed by, and the heist came off without a hitch. For Buchalter and Shapiro, it was the beginning of one of organized crime's most important partnerships.

Shapiro treated Buchalter as if he were his brother, and Buchalter reciprocated. The two poor Jewish boys with an aptitude for crime realized that the brains of one and the brawn of the other would be the means for achieving vast criminal wealth.

Shapiro had been born in Russia in 1899 and brought to the United States as a small boy. Not much is known of his parents, other than that they were poor and illiterate. Shapiro lived on the streets of Brooklyn, where he found comfort with other young criminals, who valued him for his fearlessness and quick-tempered violence. He believed the most convincing argument was a punch to the jaw—one that resulted in a few teeth being knocked out. Not only were his fists a feared weapon, but his angry, gravelly voice by itself could instill fear. He would growl, lion-like at someone he had intimidated, "get outta here!" But it was heard as "Gurrah!" Gangsters often tacked nicknames onto their compatriots, and Shapiro was not one of the exceptions. For the remainder of his life, he was invariably referred to as "Gurrah." The frightening growl fit with the appearance and reputation of the stocky threatening gangster who cops and reporters said was an angry gorilla in an expensive businessman's suit.

Shapiro and Buchalter learned the ways of gangsters in the gang of Jacob "Little Augie" Orgen, a small-time labor racketeer, who hired out an army of thugs to unions and to management. It didn't matter which side hired him as long as they paid his price. If management wanted to end a strike, they called up Orgen, who would send a platoon of thugs who were armed with bats, clubs, blackjacks, and chains. The thugs would beat the workers into a bloody retreat and defeat. If a union boss called Orgen because management had hired scabs to break through picket lines, Orgen would send a platoon of thugs to beat up the scabs. Orgen's army of thugs became known as professional sluggers, who could beat all opponents into bloody submission. In addition, Orgen had a price list for those who wanted to hire individual thugs who could inflict pain and suffering on others: there was a price for a broken arm, a broken leg, a murder, murder by drowning, murder by gun, murder by knife, and murder by garroting. Buchalter and Shapiro, who had been tutored by Arnold Rothstein, the great brain of organized crime, realized that more money could be made by controlling unions than by being hired out by union bosses. They decided that their fortunes lay with taking over unions. The days of the freelance labor sluggers were numbered. If Buchalter and Shapiro didn't act soon, some other criminals would realize the potential wealth that could come from controlling unions. Their plan was simple: hire thugs to be employed by garment manufacturers and then join a union and run for positions as board members. Once in power, the thugs could either front for Buchalter and Shapiro or let one of them become a union president. Regardless of the choice, they could siphon money from their treasuries and force manufacturers to pay to avoid strikes. It was a plan that Orgen was too myopic to appreciate. He couldn't be persuaded to see the big picture of large-scale labor racketeering. Buchalter and Shapiro decided to leave Orgen in their past, but they knew that he would resent their departure and attempt to put an end to their lives. Orgen, not trusting Buchalter and Shapiro, replaced them with the Diamond brothers: Jack "Legs" Diamond and Eddie Diamond as his bodyguards. The Gorilla Boys worried that the Diamond brothers might be employed to end their budding partnership. It would be smart to take action sooner rather than later. One night on the Lower East Side as Orgen was strolling on Norfolk Street, Buchalter pulled his car alongside his boss. Shapiro leapt from the car, guns blazing as Buchalter shot at Orgen from inside the car. "Legs" Diamond was wounded, but Orgen lay dead on the sidewalk, a bullet in his head. Their mission completed, the assassins departed as quickly as they had arrived. No one identified them. They were now on their own, and they would not only take over the unions that had been clients of Orgen but also many of the garment manufacturers that had hired Orgen's sluggers to beat up striking workers.

One union after another, all that handled every aspect of commerce in the garment center, fell under control of the Gorilla Boys. They had risen so high and so fast that they were invited into the National Crime Syndicate where they were the equals of Luciano, Lansky, Ben "Bugsy" Siegel, Frank Costello, Joe Adonis, Abner "Longy" Zwillman, and others. The FBI believed that the Gorilla Boys were taking in more than $20 million annually from their labor rackets.

In short order, Buchalter and Shapiro formed a mutually beneficial alliance with Tommy "Three-Finger Brown" Luchesse, head of the Luchesse crime family, who had an interest in much of the trucking industry in the garment center. Lucchese also realized that if you controlled the garment truckers, you could control the entire industry. He told manufacturers that if they wanted their suits, dresses, blouses, shirts, coats, and gowns shipped to stores, they had to pay the prices that the trucking companies demanded. Those manufacturers who refused to cooperate with the trucking companies were driven out of business.

Here is a firsthand example: in the 1970s, I went to visit my mother's cousin, a famous dress designer who had designed dresses for Jackie Kennedy. I entered a showroom in an office building at 37th Street and Seventh Avenue. Not seeing anyone in the empty showroom, I called out my cousin's name. In less than a minute, a large man wearing a shoulder holster erupted out of a nearby room, like an angry bear out of cave. "Who the fuck are you?" he demanded. "I'm (blank's) cousin. We're going to have lunch today." He turned and strode back into the room from which he had emerged. A few minutes later, my cousin entered the showroom. When I asked who the thug was, he replied, "I'll tell you at lunch." "The thug," he explained over a bowl of chicken noodle soup, "is my partner. I was forced to take him into the business if I wanted my dresses shipped to department stores. He belongs to a crime family that controls garment industry trucking."

The trucking and garment industries, as lucrative sources of business for the Gorilla Boys, were not sufficient to satisfy their greed. Using their standard strong-arm techniques, they ventured into and took over the bakers' union, poultry workers' union, and a cleaning and dyeing workers' union. In the bakery business, they not only controlled the union, but they were also paid a tribute of 1 penny for each loaf of bread sold in New York.

The National Crime Syndicate was so impressed with the success of the brainy Buchalter that they asked him to take control of what the Mob called "The Combination," which became better known as Murder Inc. Murder Inc. would act as the enforcement group on behalf of the syndicate. Kavieff writes, "This group would maintain discipline within the ranks of the organized crime cartel to ensure that all moneymaking ventures operated smoothly. Thus was born what journalists would later refer to as Murder Inc. Lepke became the overseer of this group."[2]

The Combination comprised squads of executioners, cadres of Jewish and Italian gangsters. Among the more notorious hit men in the organization were Abe "Kid Twist" Reles, Frank "the Dasher" Abbandando, Emanuel "Mendy" Weiss, "Blue Jaw" Magoon, "Buggsy" Goldstein, "Pittsburgh" Phil Strauss, Vito "Chicken Head" Gurino, "Happy" Maione, Workman, and Louis Capone (no relation to Chicago's Al Capone). Several of those hit men met their ends in the tight grip of Old Sparky, the electric chair, in Sing Sing

Prison. Among those fried were Strauss, Capone, Weiss, Goldstein, Maione, and Abbandando, and most infamous of all—their boss, Lepke.

Murder Inc. was structured so that the syndicate's bosses could order hits without their names being involved. A chain of command was instituted: Buchalter would give Anastasia the name of someone to be hit. He, in turn, would pass the information onto one of his lieutenants, usually Reles, Capone, or Weiss. One of them would then give the contract to another hit man. Only syndicate bosses could order hits; lesser members needed their permission. No outsiders could use the lethal talents of the Murder Inc. hit men, each of whom received a regular retainer plus payment for each hit.

Victims were invariably gangsters who were not members of the syndicate, former members who had become rats, labor and management personnel who did not submit to the syndicate's demands, or those who attempted to steal from the syndicate. Other than those involved in labor unions and management, Murder Inc. rarely killed civilians; hence Siegel's comment to Del Webb, "We only kill each other." And the number of those killed ranged from as few as 400 to more than 1,000.

The hit men met at a small, all-night candy store in the shadow of the elevated subway in the Brownsville section of Brooklyn. The store was located at the corner of Livonia and Saratoga Avenues. Because it was owned by Rose Gold and she kept it open 24 hours a day, it became known as Midnight Rose's. As the Mafia discussed business in Italian social clubs, so the Italian and Jewish hit men of Murder Inc. turned Midnight Rose's not only into a social club where egg creams, ice cream sodas, and hot fudge sundaes were enjoyed, but also into a war room for the syndicate's soldiers. It was there that they received their contracts, each one usually by way of a phone call. Many of their hits were out of town, and there was nothing to connect the victims to the hit men. Neither motives nor relationships were apparent clues for cops who investigated the hits.

Buchalter not only relayed contracts from other bosses, but he also ordered a number of the hits himself; that would ultimately prove to be his undoing.

One of the men who would bring down Murder Inc. and send Buchalter on a path that would end in the electric chair began his mission in 1935. He had been appointed by Governor Herbert Lehman as special prosecutor to rid New York of organized crime. The syndicate, through bribes and favors, controlled the Democratic Party of New York City through its instrument Tammany Hall. Because judges and district attorneys owed their jobs to Tammany Hall, they rarely indicted or even convicted members of the syndicate. Governor Lehman, though a Democrat, felt pressure to appoint a man without political debts to be special prosecutor. Four prominent Republicans turned down the appointment, but they all recommended Dewey. Lehman accepted their recommendation, and Dewey wasted no time in putting together New York's most effective anticrime group of prosecutors. In quick order, he had hired 60 assistants.

Following his pursuit of Schultz and Luciano, Dewey went after Buchalter with the determination of an avenging warrior. He was known for his unbending probity: neither the syndicate nor politicians could bribe him with money or the promise of political office. He would become the most celebrated gangbuster in the United States. The only man more celebrated in the 1930s than Dewey was aviator Charles Lindbergh.

As Dewey lined up a series of potential witnesses who could testify to Buchalter's murderous deeds, Buchalter decided that his best protection would come from Murder Inc., which could destroy whomever Dewey had lined up. Dewey arranged for New York City to post a $25,000 reward for Buchalter, dead or alive. Buchalter decided to go underground. From hideouts in Brooklyn, he ordered one hit after another. Murder Inc. hit man Reles visited him daily and received orders about who should be killed. If Anastasia thought the cops had been tipped off about Buchalter's hideouts, he arranged for Buchalter to move to a different location.

Kavieff writes,

> Over a more than two-year period that Lepke was a fugitive, an estimated sixty to one hundred underworld characters in the New York area disappeared completely. Some became brutally murdered corpses left in conspicuous places as a warning to potential Dewey witnesses. Others ended up in shallow graves covered with quick lime to help the body decompose. . . . It was Lepke's paranoia and the chaos that this caused in the underworld that in the end would destroy him.[3]

As if there weren't enough reasons for Buchalter to feel extremely anxious, Shapiro, who had been sentenced to prison in 1936, was also on the lam. Every time Shapiro's name was mentioned, it was linked to Buchalter's. Shapiro angrily told Buchalter that this never would have happened if he had agreed with him, Anastasia, and Schultz that Dewey should have been killed. Killing Schultz was a mistake that only opened the door for Dewey to go after the Gorilla Boys. It was Dewey that should have been killed; Schultz was no real threat to the syndicate.

Buchalter's ongoing fugitive status, resulting in Dewey's crackdown on Mob activities was making the top Big Apple gangsters furious. The loss of revenue was getting worse day by day. Cops were harassing them by arresting low-level members of the syndicate who kept the gears greased. It had to stop.

Luciano and Lucchese finally decided that Buchalter should give himself up for the benefit of the syndicate. They conspired to find a reason for Buchalter to agree that surrender was his best option, but they knew he would need some convincing. Buchalter had to believe that if he gave himself up to the FBI, he would be tried on federal charges and serve only a few years in a federal prison. By the time his sentence would be completed, Dewey would be out of office and state charges would have vanished for a lack of witnesses. Buchalter would be a free man.

To convince Buchalter that a deal had been made with J. Edgar Hoover, head of the FBI, Luciano dispatched one of Buchalter's trusted friends, Morris "Moey Dimples" Wolensky, to make the offer. Luciano told Wolensky that the deal was genuine, the fix was in, and he only had to relay it to Buchalter. In August 1939, when Buchalter had been on the lam for 2 years, Wolensky approached him; Buchalter carefully considered the offer and agreed to take the deal. He insisted that Anastasia drive him to a location where he would turn himself over to Hoover, and no one else. Anastasia attempted to convince Buchalter not to go through with the surrender because he didn't believe the deal was genuine and thought Buchalter could continue to operate from hideouts for many years.

New York Daily Mirror columnist Walter Winchell was a friend of Hoover and an acquaintance of Costello. He received a call from Costello asking him to set up the meeting where Buchalter would turn himself over to Hoover. Winchell did as he was asked, for it would be an exclusive journalistic scoop not only for his column but also for his radio program.

Shortly after 10 p.m. on August 24, 1939, Anastasia drove his colleague to 28th Street and Fifth Avenue. He parked directly behind Hoover's car, from which Winchell emerged and escorted Buchalter to Hoover's car. Winchell opened a back door, and Buchalter got in beside the head of the FBI. Winchell said, "Mr. Hoover, this is Lepke." "How do you do," said Hoover. "Glad to meet you," replied Lepke."[4]

On January 2, 1940, Buchalter was found guilty on a federal charge of drug trafficking and was sentenced to 14 years in a federal prison. He thought that would be the end of his troubles with the law; however, he was soon turned over to the State of New York to be tried for labor racketeering and extortion. He realized that he had been betrayed by his colleagues in the syndicate, that his pal Wolensky had lied to him, and that there never was a deal. He was somewhat gratified when he later learned that Wolensky had been gunned down.

On March 2, 1940, Buchalter was found guilty on all 15 counts of the indictment for extortion in the bakery and trucking industries. As a "four-time loser," he received a life sentence. Buchalter accepted the fact that he would be spending the rest of his life in prison, first doing 14 years in Leavenworth and then the remainder in a New York State prison, probably Sing Sing, where he had served time in his youth.

To his shock, the scenario he had imagined was not going to play out. In September 1940, New York District Attorney William O'Dwyer discussed with Harold Kennedy, US Attorney for the Southern District of New York, how to have Buchalter delivered to authorities in Kings County for the murder of Joseph Rosen.

Rosen had been a disaffected truck driver, put out of business by Buchalter. He opened a small candy store in Brooklyn and threatened to reveal Buchalter's criminality to the district attorney. That threat led to his killing by Murder Inc. Unfortunately for Buchalter, his order to kill Rosen was made in the presence of Albert "Allie" Tannenbaum, a killer for Murder Inc.

O'Dwyer flew to Leavenworth and offered Buchalter a deal: Testify to all that you know about Murder Inc., and you won't be tried for Rosen's murder. Buchalter foolishly turned down the offer and, meanwhile, had arranged for one witness after another to be killed before anyone could testify against him.

On May 9, 1941, Buchalter was brought into court in Brooklyn and arraigned for Rosen's murder. While in court, Buchalter received a note from Shapiro that read, "I told you so," referring to Shapiro's belief that Dewey should have been killed. It was too late for that. It was Buchalter's life that was targeted, and Tannenbaum's testimony was a bullet aimed at that target. On November 2, 1941, at 2 a.m., the jury found Buchalter guilty of first-degree murder. On December 2, 1941, he and his henchmen, Weiss and Louis Capone, were sentenced to death in the electric chair. Buchalter's lawyers immediately filed an appeal, but the New York State Court of Appeals upheld the conviction by a vote of four to three. Next, his lawyers appealed to the US Supreme Court, which agreed to hear the appeal. It, too, affirmed the conviction. On January 21, 1944, after much wrangling, Buchalter was taken from Leavenworth prison to Sing Sing Correctional Facility (in reality a maximum-security prison) in Ossining, New York. After several delays, Buchalter was executed in the electric chair on March 4, 1944; he was 47 years old. His execution was preceded by those of Weiss and Capone. Buchalter is buried in Mount Hebron Cemetery on Flushing, New York.

Shapiro died of a heart attack in prison on June 9, 1947. He was 48 years old and is buried in Montefiore Cemetery in Springfield Gardens, New York. The Gorilla Boys, who had become the Gold Dust Twins of labor racketeering, ended their lives in ignominy with a deep sense of anger at the world, at the syndicate which they believed had betrayed them, and most of all, against Dewey. To his dying day, Shapiro believed that if he, Anastasia, and Schultz had been permitted to kill Dewey that neither he nor Buchalter would have wound up as they did.

8

The Mad Hatter

GOING BACK TO 1931, Mob bosses knew that Albert "Mad Hatter" Anastasia was kill-crazy. He drew unwelcome attention to his psychopathic personality after he ordered a hit on civilian Arnold Schuster. Anastasia was not just the Mad Hatter; he was also the Lord High Executioner. It was said of him that he enjoyed killing as much as Ben "Bugsy" Siegel did, but he lacked Bugsy's charm and good looks.

Schuster thought he was simply being a good citizen. It was a clear cold day in February 1952 when Schuster, an amateur detective riding in a New York City bus, was surprised to see escaped convict and infamous bank robber, Willie "the Actor" Sutton, on the streets of Brooklyn. The 24-year-old Shuster quickly disembarked from the bus and surreptitiously followed the bank robber to a garage. There, he saw Sutton working on his car. Schuster found a nearby public phone and called the police. When they arrived, they found Sutton removing a dead battery from his car; he was quickly identified and then immediately arrested.

Schuster was acclaimed as a hero, a good kid who had done the right thing. He looked forward to collecting the $500 reward for Sutton's capture. Schuster was profiled in local newspapers and interviewed on local TV news programs. When asked if he was afraid of being targeted by Sutton's underworld friends, he replied that he wasn't initially afraid but became worried after he got home.

Anastasia, while living in his New Jersey mansion under the threat of deportation to Italy, saw a brief TV news interview with Schuster and flew into a rage; one could say a homicidal rage. Allan R. May, in *Gangland Gotham*, writes,

> According to Joseph Valachi, Anastasia became enraged, and even though he did not know Sutton, he exploded, "I can't stand squealers. Hit the guy!"
>
> On the night of March 8 [1952], Schuster was walking home from work and was ten houses away from his home on 45th Street in Brooklyn. A man walking toward him suddenly pulled out a gun and began firing. It was a brutal killing. Schuster was shot once in each eye and twice in the groin and left dying on the sidewalk. According to Valachi, Frederick J. Tenuto was the killer. With all the publicity of the brazen killing, to cover himself, Anastasia ordered Tenuto killed and his body was never found.[1]

Schuster's family was devastated by the brutal death. They were not members of organized crime and did not know who was responsible for the murder of their son. With nowhere else to turn, Schuster's family, acting on behalf of his estate, sued New York City for failure to provide protection. Their lawyer claimed that because Schuster had acted on behalf of a request from law enforcement to report the whereabouts of Sutton, the state had an obligation to protect anyone who acted on the state's request. The court disagreed because the law did not permit actions against the state. In an appeal that became a landmark decision, New York's highest court reversed the decision of the lower court, stating that in a case in which a member of the public has furnished information that the police have publicly requested, there is an obligation on the part of the police to protect a person who comes forward to assist them.[2] The Schuster estate again filed its suit against the City of New York, which agreed to settle the case for $41,000, which at the time was considered a large amount of money, although it hardly represents the amount of money that Schuster could have earned had he lived into old age.

Anastasia's order to murder Schuster was seen by Lucky Luciano and Meyer Lansky as the manifestation of the kind of crazy and impulsive violence that could bring down the forces of law and order on the Mob's numerous enterprises. Such behavior was reminiscent of Dutch Schultz and his plan to assassinate District Attorney Thomas Dewey. In addition, Anastasia had broken a syndicate rule not to kill civilians; murders needed to be approved by the syndicate commission. It was one thing to kill gang members who betrayed the organization, but it was something else to kill a civilian who was no threat to the Mob, for Sutton was an independent operator. Unlike Luciano, Lansky and Frank Costello, Vito Genovese was gratified by Anastasia's hotheaded action because it demonstrated that Anastasia couldn't be trusted and would one day have to be killed. Genovese looked forward to that day when an obstacle to his ambitions would be permanently removed.

The FBI had also considered Anastasia a violent loose cannon. And after the agency heard rumors that Anastasia had ordered the hit on Schuster, it too felt that Anastasia's days as one of the Mob's most deadly criminals were numbered. If the government failed in its efforts to deport Anastasia to Italy, then surely he would be hit. He was just too unpredictably violent to be ignored.

Former New York Police Department Detective Ralph Salerno told the author that he believed Anastasia had murdered thousands of people during his reign as a top mobster. And that figure was considered correct by former FBI Assistant Director James Kallstrom. Even Anastasia's brother, Mob member and boss of the Brooklyn docks, Anthony "Tough Tony" Anastasio (he kept the original spelling of his family's surname) stated that his brother killed many people.

Like many of his contemporary gangsters, Anastasia was born into a world of poverty and meanness. His birth took place in Calabria, Italy, in 1902 and his parents, Raffaele and Luisa Nomina de Filippi Anastasio named their son Umberto. He kept the spelling of the family name until he became a professional thug in the United States. At age 17, disgusted with the poverty of his native village and eager for a change of scenery, young Anastasio decided to go to the United States where the streets were supposedly paved with gold. He and his three brothers got jobs as deckhands on a boat headed for New York. When it docked in Brooklyn, the brothers jumped ship and soon thereafter got work as longshoremen on the docks in Red Hook. Anastasia proved to be more than a hard worker: he was a hard man, who was quick to settle an argument with a longshoreman's hook, a blackjack, or brass knuckles. One day, he got into an argument with another longshoreman named George Turino; words were rapidly replaced by fists and hooks. Anastasia killed Turino and went on trial for murder. On March 17, 1921, he was convicted of that murder and sentenced to death in the electric chair at Sing Sing prison. His lawyer, however, was able to win his client a new trial. At the outset of the trial, prosecutors soon discovered that the original witnesses had all disappeared, never to be heard of again. Such vanishing acts of potential witnesses would become standard practice for Anastasia, especially when he and Louis "Lepke" Buchalter were the coheads of Murder Inc. Knowing that a gun was far more effective than a hook or a blackjack, Anastasia took to carrying a gun wherever he went. It was another one of his early mistakes because he was arrested and convicted of illegally possessing a firearm in 1923. This time no witnesses vanished, and he was sentenced to 2 years in prison. Following his release, he returned to the docks of Brooklyn and bullied his way into the International Longshoreman's Association (ILA). Using threats and violence, he rapidly rose to a leadership position in the ILA. No one dared challenge him. In short order, he took control of six local chapters of the union. In that position, he was able to determine who worked and who didn't; he extracted payment as tribute from those who were chosen to work at the morning "shape-up." In addition, he controlled loan-sharking, gambling, and cargo thefts on the docks. He put his brother Tony in a position to look after his interests and make sure that money flowed into his hands. If a dock worker was foolish enough to question Tony's authority, Tony only needed to mention his brother's name and the challenge to his authority quickly vanished, as if by magic. As a top official of the ILA, Anastasia was able to invade the treasury of the union and use it as his private bank. The poor boy from Calabria was raking in thousands of dollars a month.

His reputation as the czar of the docks and his ready resort to violence to achieve his goals brought him to the attention of Luciano, who invited Anastasia to a meeting. When Luciano explained his plans to take over the crime families of Joe "the Boss" Masseria and Salvatore Maranzano, Anastasia was hooked. Carl Sifakis writes,

> [Luciano] knew the Mad Hatter, as Anastasia had become known, would enthusiastically kill for him. Anastasia responded by seizing Luciano in a bear hug and kissing him on both cheeks. "Charlie," he said, "I been waiting for this day for at least eight years. You're gonna be on top if I have to kill everybody for you. With you there, that's the only way we can have any peace and make the real money.[3]

Luciano arranged for Anastasia to be appointed as underboss to the crime family of Vincent Mangano. It was a natural fit for Anastasia because the syndicate had put the Mangano family in control of the Brooklyn waterfront. In addition to Anastasia's position as underboss of the Mangano family, Tony was also inducted into the family. Anastasia made sure that the family received payment from every ship that docked in Brooklyn and, subsequently, in Manhattan. His method of operation was quite simple: shipping companies had to pay tribute to the family or their cargoes would not be unloaded. When the shipping companies complained to local politicians, nothing happened because the politicians and local police were all paid to look away from what happened on the docks.

While the extortion of shipping companies ran smoothly, Anastasia's relationship with his boss, Mangano, did not. The two men disliked one another, and if Luciano hadn't insisted that Anastasia be made underboss, Mangano would have had nothing to do with him. Mangano was old-world Mafia but not quite as narrow-minded as Masseria and Maranzano. He resented Anastasia's relationships with Luciano, Costello, and the Jewish gangsters. He particularly disliked Anastasia for doing business on his own with Luciano and Costello. From such dealings, Mangano received nothing. He would berate Anastasia, and a vociferous argument would ensue, occasionally bordering on violence. More than a few times, the men had to be separated by underlings. If not, the younger and stronger Anastasia would have imposed a bloody beating on his boss. Anastasia, as cohead of Murder Inc., would become known as the Lord High Executioner, but Mangano was known merely as the Executioner.

While underboss of the Mangano family, Anastasia was smart enough never to be indicted for murder. Law enforcement suspected him of various hits, but there was never sufficient evidence to arrest him. As cohead of Murder Inc., he continued to avoid indictment by insulating himself from the hit men: his orders went down a chain of command. He was luckier than his partner Buchalter, who was overheard ordering a hit on Joseph Rosen. Anastasia and Buchalter, until the testimony of Albert "Allie" Tannenbaum and Abe "Kid Twist" Reles, operated like a dual-headed monster, ordering thousands of murders. Anastasia and Buchalter not only operated as partners, but they were highly protective of one another. And when Buchalter was named America's Most Wanted criminal, Anastasia did all in his power to keep his partner in hiding and tried to convince him not to surrender to the FBI. The two pieces of advice that Anastasia offered to Buchalter, to let Schultz kill Dewey and don't surrender, would have saved Buchalter from the electric chair.

As careful as Anastasia was, he came close to making a mistake. He had ordered a hit on an ILA union activist named Peter Panto, who had been urging fellow ILA members to oust the corrupt leadership of the union. Anastasia's minions first offered bribes to co-opt Panto, and when that failed, they threatened him. That, too, had no effect. Panto had a mission to reform the union, and he would not let anything dissuade him. He was able to organize 1,250 ILA members to demand the end of kickbacks, extortions, and other illegal union activities. He decided to sue the union leadership and expose their wrongdoing in court. He hired a lawyer named Marcy Potter, who agreed to represent the rank-and-file members of the union. Potter also told Panto that his life was in danger, and he should never go about alone; there would be safety in numbers. May in *Gangland Gotham* quotes Potter's testimony to an investigative committee:

> [Panto] had been shaving when someone came in to tell him there was a telephone call for him down at the corner—either the candy store or drug store—and there was with him at the time a brother of the girl to whom he was then engaged to be married. He went to answer the telephone call and when he came back he spoke to the young lad, and said there was something funny about the telephone call. He said "I don't think it is entirely on the square." He had to meet two men, and he didn't know what was going to happen, but he told his

intended brother-in-law, this young boy, that if he didn't show up by 10 o'clock the next morning he should notify the police.

According to May, the men who killed Panto were:

James Feracco, Joseph Florino, Anthony Romeo, and Mendy Weiss. Burton Turkus [the district attorney who prosecuted Murder Inc.] relates the story by Reles, who claims he was told by Weiss that he strangled Panto. During the murder, the younger and lighter Panto put up a terrific fight and at one point managed to get one of Weiss's fingers in his mouth and nearly chewed it off, forcing Weiss to later see a doctor. Reles claimed "Mendy strangled him as a favor for Albert." Relating the conversation with Weiss later, Reles recalled the killer saying, "Gee, I hated to take that kid. But I had to do it for Albert, because Albert has been good to me."[4]

Panto's bloody body was discovered on a farm in New Jersey on July 14, 1939. To make sure that Anthony Romeo, who had been arrested for Panto's killing, couldn't testify against him, Anastasia had him killed. His body was discovered in Guyencourt, Delaware, in 1942; he had been brutally beaten and shot several times.

Anastasia thought he should temporarily remove himself from Mob activities because the Panto murder had gotten too many headlines, and politicians were feeling pressure to do something about the ILA and the thugs it employed. In an effort to present himself as a patriot and not a killer, Anastasia enlisted in the army. Rather than be a troublemaker, he appeared to be a dedicated soldier, and through hard work, he rose in rank to be a technical sergeant. World War II had been raging for a year, and Anastasia hoped that his participation in the war effort would be seen as more important than the possibility of linking him to a murder for which there were no witnesses. Meanwhile, Anastasia's erstwhile partner, Buchalter, was sitting on death row in Sing Sing, and though Anastasia had been devoted to him, he did not want to meet the same fate. The US Army was certainly a more attractive alternative than prison. He had made a good bet; he was honorably discharged, and as a reward for his service, he was given US citizenship. While wanting to profit from the ILA, but not wanting to be seen as involved in its activities, Anastasia made his brother Tony the head of union. As its boss, Tony became known as Anthony "Tough Tony" Anastasio, or just "Tough Tony." Anastasia, draping himself further with the aura of legitimacy, purchased a dress-manufacturing company in Hazleton, Pennsylvania.

Anastasia's disguise as a legitimate businessman did not convince senators investigating organized crime in the United States. He was called to testify before the US Senate Special Committee to Investigate Crime in Interstate Commerce. From 1950 to 1951, the committee investigated members of organized crime whose criminal enterprises crossed state borders. The committee became popularly known as the Kefauver Committee because of its chairman, Senator Estes Kefauver. The committee's investigation generated dozens of newspaper headlines and enraptured TV audiences throughout the country.

In 1951, Anastasia was one of several Big Apple gangsters called before the committee in a closed-door session. Anastasia refused to answer questions, invoking his Fifth Amendment right not to incriminate himself. Later, in a public hearing, Senator Kefauver threatened him with contempt if he didn't answer questions. At that hearing, Anastasia stated that he owned an interest in a dress company and had worked for 6 months for his brother in the ILA. When asked about his finances, he still refused to answer questions as he did when asked who built his mansion in New Jersey. Kefauver said that his ongoing refusals would result in a contempt-of-the-Senate citation. Anastasia again blew off the committee's authority and was neither fined nor jailed.

Another mobster called to testify was Mangano. Not only did he not show up, but he also was never heard from again; he simply vanished. However, his brother Phillip's body was found in a swamp in Sheepshead Bay, Brooklyn. Police figured that because one Mangano had been killed, so had the other. At a meeting of the Mafia Commission, Anastasia was elevated to boss of the Mangano family. His elevation was backed by Costello, who wanted Anastasia's guns and soldiers as a bulwark against Genovese's ambitions to take over the Luciano family. Although not admitting that he had killed Mangano, Anastasia claimed that Mangano had been planning to kill him. The inference was that Anastasia had acted in self-defense. The commission agreed to rename the Mangano family as the Anastasia family. The new underboss would be Carlo Gambino, a man of devious plans and an opportunist as sly as a fox. Genovese looked on Gambino as a possible ally for his future plans.

As the head of his own family, Anastasia was of even more intense interest to law enforcement than he had previously been. Following the lead of the Kefauver hearings, the New York State Crime Commission was established and began looking into Mob activities. On December 19, 1952, Anastasia was called to testify. He refused to answer 97 questions, again citing his right not to incriminate himself provided by the Fifth Amendment. Nevertheless, his cooperation was not needed for the hearings to result in the establishment of a Waterfront Commission Act and Compact, which required that all supervisory personnel be licensed and that anyone with a criminal record be denied the opportunity to work on the docks. It also eliminated the "shape-up," which often required longshoremen to pay for the privilege of working. Each man would indicate his agreement to pay for work by placing a toothpick between his ear and the side of his head or simply having one poking out of the side of his mouth.

Frustrated by Anastasia's evasiveness at the hearings, the government decided the best way to nail him was to deport him. He wasn't the only one. More than 100 gangsters were on a list of those to be deported, and most prominent among those was Costello, to whom Anastasia was devoted. On December 9, 1952, US Marshals went to Anastasia's mansion in New Jersey to serve him with a summons and complaint. His son told them that his father was sick in bed. After numerous delays, the case went to trial, and on April 14, 1954, Anastasia's citizenship was cancelled. However, in 1955, the US Court of Appeals for the Third Circuit overturned the decision of the lower court. Still looking for ways to get Anastasia, the government resorted to what it usually did to nail many gangland bosses: it filed a case against Anastasia for income tax evasion. The government's case was based on the difference between the huge cost of building Anastasia's mansion and the comparatively modest income he said he had earned. There was no way that Anastasia's reported income could have paid for the building and the upkeep of the mansion, even though Anastasia said that his wife had money of her own that she contributed to the building and upkeep. The government didn't buy that explanation and called Charles Ferri to testify. Ferri had supplied all the plumbing and heating for Anastasia's home, and the cost of that alone exceeded Anastasia's declared annual income. At trial, the jury deadlocked, and a retrial was scheduled. However, in the interim, Ferri, who had been subpoenaed, disappeared. When police searched Ferri's Miami home, all they found were blood stains. The bodies of Ferri and his wife were never found. Without a witness, the case died. But the government was preparing to retry Anastasia. He and his lawyer realized that the government would not give up in its attempt to convict him of tax evasion. They simply had to assemble all the financial data necessary for a conviction. Anastasia preemptively decided to plead guilty. On May 23, 1955, he pled guilty to tax evasion for underreporting his income during the late 1940s. On June 3, 1955, he was sentenced to 1 year in federal prison and ordered to pay a fine of $20,000, which had to be paid before he could be released. Anastasia served 10 months of the 1-year sentence. He was released on March 26, 1956, but the government was not finished with its tax case against him. In 1957, the government filed suit to recover $250,000 for unpaid back taxes and penalties for the years 1946 to 1952. That case would never go to trial.

Genovese had paid close attention to Anastasia's trials and tribulations and realized that his opportunity to take over the Luciano family was fast approaching. He assigned Vincent "the Chin" Gigante to assassinate Costello, the head of the family. On May 2, 1957, Gigante confronted Costello in the Central Park West lobby of Costello's apartment building. With revolver in hand, Gigante shouted, "This is for you, Frank." Costello quickly turned as

Gigante fired a single bullet that grazed the side of Costello's head. Thinking he had killed Costello, Gigante turned and fled into a waiting limo. Costello got the message and decided to retire as boss. Yet, Genovese was concerned that Anastasia might start a war over the attempted murder of his friend and protector. Genovese convinced Joe Bonanno that a war would be detrimental to all the families, so Bonanno had a talk with Anastasia, convincing him not to take action until the commission could come to an agreement about what should be done.

Genovese's next target was Anastasia, but before he could order the hit, he needed permission from Lansky. During the 1950s, prior to Fidel Castro's takeover of Cuba, Lansky owned or controlled all of the casinos in Cuba. He distributed a percentage of profits from those casinos to various Mob bosses but kept the lion's share for himself. Anastasia had not been happy with the arrangement and demanded a larger share of the profits. When Lansky refused, Anastasia decided to open his own casinos on the island and take away some of Lansky's income. The Anastasia invasion had to be stopped before it could be launched. Shortly after Genovese approached Lansky for permission to kill Anastasia, permission was given with a nod of the head.

On October 25, 1957, around 10 a.m., Anastasia entered the barbershop of the Park Central Hotel on Seventh Avenue between 55th and 56th Streets. His bodyguard parked his car and went for a walk. Anastasia took his usual seat in chair number 4. The barber placed a hot towel over Anastasia's face as two men, bandanas covering the lower half of each of their faces, entered the shop. Each pulled out a pistol, walked to the back of chair number 4 and blasted away at Anastasia. He leapt from his chair and ran at the image of the gunmen in the mirror opposite the chair. A few more bullets felled him, and he lay on the floor. The gunmen ran from the barbershop and disappeared into the crowds of pedestrians on the street. They were never caught; only their discarded pistols were recovered. Anastasia was denied a Catholic burial by the Archdiocese; he was laid to rest in nondenominational Green-Wood Cemetery in Brooklyn. The cemetery is considered one of the most beautiful cemeteries in the country and is a designated a National Historic Landmark. It is also the final resting place of "Crazy" Joey Gallo, one of the men who claimed to have killed Anastasia.

Following Anastasia's death, Gambino (who had secretly agreed with Genovese to Anastasia's killing) ascended to the position of boss of the family, which soon became known as the Gambino family. As boss, Gambino reduced the power of "Tough Tony," who could no longer use his brother's name to instill fear on the docks or any place else where the name Albert "Mad Hatter" Anastasia was as good as pointing a gun at someone. According to Sifakis, Anastasio once confronted a reporter and demanded to know:

"How come you keep writing all those bad things about my brother Albert? He ain't killed nobody in your family . . . yet."[5]

Angered and humiliated by his loss of power, Anastasio became an FBI informant. He died of a heart attack in 1963. His son-in-law Anthony Scotto took over the Local 1814 of the ILA, which—at the time—had 15,000 members. There is now a scholarship in the name of Anthony Anastasio for the sons and daughters of members of Local 1814.

9

Don Vitone

V ITO GENOVESE WAS NOT A MAN who let obstacles stand in his way. When he wanted something or someone, he gratified himself regardless of the cost. In 1931, Genovese fell in love with a beautiful blonde named Anna Vernotico; she was 22 years old, and he was a 34-year-old widower. Genovese was determined to marry Vernotico, but there was a singular problem: she was already married. Her husband, Gerard Vernotico, had a rap sheet for numerous crimes. If killed, he would not be regarded as an innocent civilian. On March 16, 1932, his bloody, beaten, and strangled body was found on the roof of a building at 124 Thompson Street in Manhattan. Twelve days after the discovery of the body, Mrs. Vernotico became Mrs. Genovese in a civil ceremony. Years later, Mafia turncoat Joe Valachi testified that Genovese had ordered two of his thugs to get rid of Mr. Vernotico. Nothing was going to stand in Genovese's way.

Was it any wonder that he was one of the most feared gangsters in the National Crime Syndicate? Though a short man, either 5'6" or 5'7", he was as intimidating as a pair of cocked .38-caliber revolvers. Though he was useful to Mob bosses, he was distrusted by Lucky Luciano, Meyer Lansky, and Frank Costello. They believed that the pleasure he derived from violence would be his undoing. In the 1950s, looking back on his career, Luciano confessed that he had been initially impressed by Genovese's eagerness to fight ferociously for what he wanted; however, Luciano confessed that he had made a mistake, much to his regret, in thinking that Genovese would be a loyal soldier and then underboss. Genovese's only loyalty was to himself.

From the time he was a boy growing up in the small village of Risigliano near Naples, Italy, where he was born on November 27, 1897, Genovese had fought for everything he wanted. Life in the small village, which today has a population of only 1,116 people, was predictable and dull. There were no avenues to wealth. Like many poor immigrants dreaming of financial opportunities, the Genovese family thought that the United States would be the land of opportunity. Young Genovese did not know that it would also be a land for great criminal opportunities. At age 15, he arrived in Little Italy with his family; he and his two brothers found numerous opportunities to make easy money from protection, extortion, and muggings. The United States was like an orchard filled with ripe fruit, except the Genovese family didn't own the orchard. If Genovese wanted easy pickings, he would have to use violence to get what he wanted. The opportunities were so plentiful that he dropped out of elementary school, and rather than books and pencils, he would make do with an assortment of weapons: brass knuckles, a blackjack, a knife. All those push carts and peddlers on the Lower East Side of Manhattan were targets for theft and protection rackets. Young Genovese attracted the attention of older hoodlums, who were impressed by his fearless acts of violence. They engaged him to run errands and directed him to fences who would buy his stolen merchandise. Life was certainly more exiting and profitable in Little Italy than it had been in the town from which the Genoveses had departed. Genovese was a young man in a hurry, and he was quickly moving up in the underworld.

By the 1920s, he was employed by Joe "the Boss" Masseria, who appreciated the young man's aptitude for using violent solutions to solve disturbing problems. One such problem was posed by Gaetano Reina, a Bronx-based gangster and gang leader. Though Reina had worked for Masseria, the Boss didn't trust the Bronx gangster because he thought he was too ambitious and might have aligned himself with Masseria's enemy, Salvatore Maranzano. Not willing to tolerate such a possible threat, Masseria ordered Genovese to kill Reina. No mere revolver would do: Genovese decided to use a shotgun. On February 26, 1930, Genovese waited for Reina to leave his mistress's home. He came up behind the unsuspecting Reina, raised the shotgun, and blasts from both barrels crashed into and cratered the back of Reina's cranium. He collapsed onto the sidewalk, blood pooling around his head. When Genovese reported the success of his deed to his boss, Masseria gratefully took over the Reina gang. Genovese was impressed how quickly murder could advance one's career and expand one's business. He would never fail to use murder to advance his own career and to silence witnesses who might testify against him.

Masseria's and Maranzano's murders certainly proved to be the solution for ending the Castellammarese War and the means by which Luciano became boss of the National Crime Syndicate. In addition, it resulted in the formation of the five Mafia families that developed a stranglehold on many industries in New York.

Once the war was over, Luciano, now top dog, appointed Genovese as the underboss of his family. Though pleased by his new position, Genovese, like Masseria, was annoyed that Luciano partnered with Jewish gangsters, such as Ben "Bugsy" Siegel and Lansky. According to Martin Gosch and Richard Hammer in their book, *The Last Testament of Lucky Luciano*, Genovese flew into a rage when Costello suggested that they form a partnership with Dutch Schultz: "Vito screamed, 'What the hell is this! What are you tryin' to do, load us up with a bunch of Hebes?' Before Benny or Meyer could even open their mouths, Frank almost swung on him and he said, very quiet, 'Take it easy, Don Vitone, you're nothin' but a fuckin' foreigner yourself."[1]

Genovese would never forget nor forgive the insult, and he resented being referred to as Don Vitone, though the sobriquet stuck.

In addition to carrying grudges, Genovese was also greedy to the point of failing to deliver on promised payoffs. In 1936, Genovese engineered the murder of Ferdinand Boccia (aka Fred Bocci), who had pestered Genovese for his share of the money they had scammed during a crooked card game. The take from the scam was $150,000, and Bocci wanted his cut, an agreed upon $35,000. Genovese let it be known that Bocci was a rat and had to be killed; it was cheaper to have him killed than to pay him.

Genovese was always on the lookout for the main chance and for opportunities to increase his wealth and power. And on July 18, 1936 he thought that a singular opportunity had finally arrived, one which would let him ascend to the head of the Luciano family. It was on that date that Luciano was sentenced to 30 to 50 years in prison after having been found guilty on June 7 of 62 counts of compulsory prostitution; in effect, pimping.

Shortly after ascending to Luciano's vacated throne, Genovese became worried that he would soon be prosecuted for Boccia's murder. He filled a suitcase with $750,000, booked passage on an ocean liner, and sailed for Italy, which was under the control of Benito Mussolini and his National Fascist Party.

For Genovese, Mussolini was another Mob boss with whom he could do business. While Mussolini had prosecuted the Mafia in Sicily (forcing Carlo Gambino and Joseph Bonanno to flee to New York), he gave Genovese a free hand to operate as he liked. In addition to giving money to the Fascists, Genovese gave money and cocaine to Mussolini's son-in-law Galeazzo Ciano.

As Allan R. May writes in *Gangland Gotham*,

> By spreading his money around, Genovese was able to gain favor with some of the leaders of Mussolini's Fascist government. At one point, he contributed $250,000 toward the construction of a new government building in Nola, a town

a few miles from his birthplace Risigliano. Risigliano was rumored to have a strong presence by the Camorra, a secret crime society with its roots in Naples.[2]

In addition to spending lavishly on the behalf of the Fascists, Genovese was making money from various illicit activities. He had simply brought his experience as a successful New York gangster to the country of his birth. The money he spent on the Fascists was no different than paying off cops, judges, and politicians back home. What worked in the United States also worked in Italy.

In a show of gratitude, Mussolini awarded Genovese the Order of Saints Maurice and Lazarus and made him a *commendatore* in the Fascist Party.

In addition to providing financial support for the Fascists, Genovese did them a symbolically important favor, one for which Mussolini was personally grateful. It involved Carlo Tresca, a dashing elegant socialist with a neatly trimmed goatee, who was an indefatigable critic of the Fascist regime and the Mafia. Tresca was a courageous idealist, who not only put his ideals into words but also into actions. He demonstrated against corrupt government officials and union leaders, led strikes for decent wages, picketed factories with unsafe conditions for employees, and spoke forcefully against the evils of dictatorship. He edited a fiercely anti-Fascist newspaper, *Il Martello*, in which he published scathing denunciations of Fascism, Stalinism, and the Mob's infiltration of organized labor. In addition to editorials, he wrote mordant exposés of the Mob's corrupt union practices on the waterfront. Though an ardent idealist, he found time to have a pair of long-running affairs with Sabina Flynn and her sister Elizabeth Gurley Flynn, a socialist labor organizer and author. (Tresca's son, Peter Martin, a friend of the author made a name for himself in the world of books after he founded the City Lights Publishing Company and the City Lights Bookshop in San Francisco with the poet Lawrence Ferlinghetti; Martin later founded the New Yorker Bookshop on the Upper West Side of Manhattan.)

Tresca's articles did more than annoy the Mob; they could be used to incite prosecutorial investigations into the Mob's control of various industries. His articles were also more than an annoyance to Mussolini because the dictator wanted Italian Americans to rally in support of the Fascists, and Tresca instead offered a rallying cry for liberals and communists who were against Fascism. The Mob and the Fascists wanted to get rid of Tresca, and Genovese, eager to oblige, thought that a dramatic hit on Tresca would further ingratiate him with his Fascist protectors.

Shortly after Tresca left his office on January 11, 1943, a short stocky man quickly exited a black Ford and ran up behind Tresca. He pointed a revolver at the back of Tresca's head and fired a single bullet that lodged in Tresca's brain. Tresca died immediately. The shooter was Mafioso Carmine Galante, who went on to become boss of the Bonanno crime family. He, too, died by the gun: on July 12, 1979, following his attempt to take over a massive drug-trafficking business in New York and his refusal to share profits with other Mob families, he was shot to death while having lunch on the outdoor patio of Joe and Mary's Italian restaurant in Bushwick, Brooklyn. His trademark cigar was stuck in his mouth as he lay on the patio bleeding amid scattered napkins and an overturned chair; his bodyguards were nowhere to be found.

Mussolini was grateful for Tresca's death, but his gratitude would be short-lived. As for Genovese, his benefits would also be short-lived, for the landing of the US soldiers and the revolt of Italian partisans would alter the focus of Genovese's loyalty.

Following the Allied victory in southern Italy, Genovese changed sides as easily as a chameleon adapts to new surroundings. He ingratiated himself with his new hosts by offering his services as a translator and guide to the Allied Military Government for Occupied Territories (AMGOT). He also presented Colonel Charles Poletti, former governor of New York and the army officer in charge of the occupation, with a 1938 Packard that became the colonel's official staff car. Ironically, Poletti had confiscated cars that had been used by the Fascists. Genovese stole many of those cars and then sold them on the black market. To accuse him of opportunism would be an understatement.

Genovese, however, was not as slick as he thought, for the army had gotten information about Genovese's various illegal activities and had begun an investigation. Orange Dickey, an investigator, began compiling evidence of Genovese's various black market activities. When he compiled enough irrefutable evidence of Genovese's criminal activities for a likely indictment, he had Genovese confined to a jail cell in Nola. Yet, AMGOT was not happy with the outcome. They did not want Dickey to pursue Genovese because they did not want him jailed. So Dickey was made to understand that Genovese should be released; but a short time later, using additional evidence of Genovese's criminal activities, Dickey arrested and jailed him again. Genovese offered Dickey $250,000 to release him, but Dickey turned him down, whereupon Genovese threatened to kill Dickey. Such was the back and forth, which finally ended when Genovese's indictment for the murder of Boccia became known. Genovese was extradited back to Brooklyn to stand trial for the murder. On June 2, 1945, he was arraigned in the Kings County Court. He was represented by Hyman Barshay, Louis "Lepke" Buchalter's former lawyer. Considering Buchalter's murder conviction and execution in the electric chair, the choice of attorney may not have been a good sign. Buchalter and Genovese had something else in common: Buchalter had eliminated many possible witnesses in his murder trial, and Genovese resorted to the same tactic. Unlike Buchalter, Genovese only had to arrange for the murder of two witnesses: Peter LaTempa and Jerry Esposito.

Genovese's trial judge was Samuel Leibowitz, noted as a hanging judge who regarded the death penalty as a deterrent and often referred to criminals as "rats." Before becoming a judge, Leibowitz had been a famous criminal defense attorney who defended Al Capone, but he refused to defend Luciano and members of Murder Inc. His most famous case was in defense of the Scottsboro Boys, nine young African American men who had been accused of raping two white women. Leibowitz was tireless in his defense of the Scottsboro Boys, refused a fee, and took the case all the way to the Supreme Court. In 1976, Clarence Norris, the last surviving defendant in the Scottsboro case, said on the occasion of Leibowitz's death that "Mr. Leibowitz was a beautiful man. He really did a job for me and the rest of the fellows. The world is a little different now and he helped change it."[3]

As passionate as Leibowitz had been in defense of the Scottsboro Boys, he was just as passionate in ridding the world of gangsters. (His values had obviously changed since he defended Capone.) Leibowitz was furious that the case against Genovese fell apart as the result of the murders of LaTempa and Esposito. Before Genovese could walk out of court a free man, Leibowitz sternly told him that if the two dead men had been able to give testimony against him the result would have been that Genovese would have been condemned to sit in the electric chair at Sing Sing. With that, he banged his gavel and the case ended.

Genovese had said nothing in response. He was now free to pursue his ambitions to become a Mob boss. After the murder of Willie Moretti, Costello offered Genovese the position of underboss of the Luciano crime family.

The road ahead was not as smooth as Genovese thought it would be because his drive to become a Mob boss briefly stalled when he was publicly embarrassed by his wife. Genovese and Anna had separated; she claimed that her husband had beaten her and used their Atlantic Highlands, New Jersey, home for sex orgies and various decadent acts. She sued her husband for financial support, and the newspapers ran stories that made Genovese look weak, for made men were not supposed to be sued by their obedient wives, who were supposed to live in the shadows. For a Mob boss, even an underboss, to be sued for support by his wife was a public humiliation. One can only imagine other mobsters snickering behind Genovese's back.

To make his situation even worse, the government decided that the time had come to bring a denaturalization case against Genovose in which it claimed he had lied about his criminal activities. If the denaturalization case proved successful, then Genovese would be deported.

Genovese's anger boiled over. He found a target for his anger in the person of Stephen Franse, whom Genovese had charged with looking after Anna while he was in Italy. Franse never reported any misgivings about Anna, with whom he owned a restaurant. Genovese, never a trusting soul, decided that Franse had likely seduced Anna in Genovese's absence. On June 18, 1953, Franse was lured to a meeting with Pat Pagano and Fiore Siano in an empty restaurant. Before anyone sat down, Pagano and Siano viciously beat Franse into bloody unconsciousness, then they strangled him. Franse's body was found in his car on West 37th Street. Police initially thought that Franse had been the victim of a brutal mugging.

Genovese was now ready to make his move to the top. Following the wounding and retirement of Costello and the murders of Moretti and Albert "Mad Hatter" Anastasia, Genovese was ready to appoint himself boss of bosses. In November 1957, he organized what became known as the Apalachin Conference to be held in the stone mansion of Joseph Barbara in Apalachin, New York. More than 60 bosses from all the La Cosa Nostra families in the United States were in attendance; as they were drinking and gossiping and joking, there was an unexpected knock on the front door of Barbara's mansion. It was the state police who came to make arrests, and with that knowledge, mobsters bolted like a startled herd of cattle. They climbed out of windows and dashed out of back doors. They took off running in all directions. Immaculately tailored men in their 50s, 60s, and 70s were seen by the cops as they huffed and puffed, trotting, stumbling, and running through the surrounding woods. Most were not as fleet of foot as they had been in their youth when outrunning cops on city streets. Of the more than 60 attendees, 58 were netted by the state troopers. According to Carl Sifakis in the *Mafia Encyclopedia*, "The arrest roster bore the names of men whom law enforcement had tried for years to net: Trafficante, Profaci, Genovese, Maglioco, Bonanno, DeSimone, Scalish, Riela, Gambino, Magaddino, Catena, Miranda, Zito, Civello, Ida, Ormento, Coletti, Galante."[4]

No one in attendance believed that the state police simply showed up because they had seen lots of cars arriving at Barbara's mansion, though that was the official police explanation. The mobsters figured the cops had been tipped off. Those who chose not to show up and who wanted Genovese removed from power included Costello, Lansky, and Joseph "Doc" Stacher, and their absence did not go unnoticed. Luciano, who was deported and living in Italy, didn't want Genovese to become boss of his family. And although Gambino attended the meeting, he, too, was against Genovese becoming boss of bosses. He was playing a double game as the inside man for the outside men.

Sifakis writes,

> Genovese had been set up beautifully by Costello/Luciano/Lansky, none of whom were present, and by Carlo Gambino who was. . . . they tipped off the authorities about the meeting. Instead of emerging the foremost Mafioso in the

nation, Genovese succeeded in angering the nation's bosses, who blamed him for the Apalachin disaster.[5]

Genovese's reputation was in rapid decline, and there was little he could do to change course. Luciano, Lansky, and Costello needed one final plan to dispose of Genovese and make sure that his removal was permanent. They decided that Genovese should be convicted for drug dealing. Lansky and Costello arranged for a Puerto Rican drug courier named Nelson Cantellops to be paid $100,000 plus a lifetime pension for implicating Genovese in drug trafficking.

In the book, *Meyer Lansky: Mogul of the Mob*, the authors write,

The bait was set by one of Meyer's couriers, Nelson Cantellops. Meyer had been angry with Nelson after he got himself mixed up running drugs at the same time he was working for Meyer. When Nelson was caught, Meyer refused to help him and he went to Sing Sing on a narcotics charge. Then, using his brother, Jake, Meyer passed the message to Nelson that he would forgive him if he would take on a little job. Cantellops was promised a pension for life. So our friend Nelson Cantellops, despite the danger he would be in, asked for an interview with the Narcotics Bureau in New York and told an agent, George Gaffney, that he would provide information about how Genovese and his partners were smuggling narcotics from Europe to the United States.[6]

Although the feds may have been doubtful that a low-level drug dealer would have dealings with a major crime boss, they were willing to overlook their doubts and go after Genovese. The government won a conviction against Genovese for drug trafficking on July 7, 1958. Following failed appeals, Genovese was sentenced to 15 years in prison on April 17, 1959. More appeals followed and failed. On February 11, 1960, Genovese went off to the Atlanta Federal Penitentiary in Georgia. Once in prison, Genovese railed against those whom he suspected of setting him up. Unlike most paranoids, Genovese had good reason to feel people had been out to get him. He lashed out at several mobsters and arranged for each of their murders. Those who were killed included his assistant, Tony Bender, Anthony Strollo, and Anthony Carfano. He also suspected his cellmate and Mob soldier Joseph Valachi of betrayal. In 1959, Valachi had been found guilty in a drug case and sentenced to 15 years in prison. Then in 1961, Valachi was taken from his Atlanta prison cell for another trial in New York City. This, too, was a drug case, and he was found guilty again and sentenced to 20 years in prison. Valachi was returned to the cell he shared with Genovese and complained bitterly about his sentence. Shortly thereafter, Genovese was told that Valachi had testified against him, and that's all it took for the paranoid Genovese to act. In their cell, Genovese gave Valachi the kiss of death, an old Mafia custom.

Fearful of being murdered, Valachi misidentified Joe Saupp, a fellow prisoner, as the man who had been hired to kill him. Saupp was the wrong man; Joe DiPalermo was the one given the contract to kill Valachi. Valachi snuck up on Saupp in the prison yard and beat him over the head with a steel pipe. Saupp died from a fractured skull and severe brain bleeding. Valachi was now worried that he would be convicted of capital murder and sentenced to death, so he decided to make a deal with the feds and agreed to testify before the McClellan Committee.

Valachi was the first member of the Italian American Mafia to break the code of omerta. During his testimony, he described the structure of the Mafia, its rituals, and its rules. He also named members of the Five Families and provided information about unsolved murders. In 3 days of testimony, Valachi lifted the veil that kept the Mafia hidden in shadows, where even J. Edgar Hoover had not looked; Hoover was the man who had claimed that the Mafia did not exist. The embarrassment that Mob bosses experienced as the result of Valachi's testimony was blamed on Genovese. In addition to blaming Genovese for that, the Mob blamed him for the failed and embarrassing Apalachin Conference; both events completely destroyed Genovese's reputation among the Mob.

So that he could not issue orders and threaten any other inmates, Genovese was moved from the Atlanta prison to Leavenworth in Kansas. In an attempt to isolate Genovese, there were new restrictions placed on visitors. While in Leavenworth, Genovese developed heart problems, so he was transferred to a medical facility in Springfield, Missouri. There, on February 14, 1969, Genovese died. It was the anniversary of the notorious St. Valentine's Day Massacre. He is buried in St. John's Cemetery in Middle Village, New York, a stone's throw from Luciano's grave. The contrast between the two gangsters is striking: Luciano, along with Lansky, was the visionary creator of an organized crime syndicate and then served as its brilliant CEO; Genovese, conversely, embarrassed the Mob with the failure of the Apalachin Conference, followed by becoming a patsy who was set up by his Mob enemies, and then provoked Valachi to reveal Mob secrets to the world.

Standing in the wings was Gambino, who would rename the Anastasia family and take it to new heights.

10

Carlo Gambino: Fox of Bosses

H E WAS SLY, CUNNING, SUBTLE, AND WILY. When a drunken gangster loudly made insulting remarks to Carlo Gambino in a restaurant, Gambino showed no emotion. The corners of his lips, as always, turned up slightly in an inscrutable smile. His emotions were always cloaked by that Mona Lisa smile. He never seemed rattled, panicked, furious, or intimidated. He operated in the shadows. The next day the loudmouthed gangster who had insulted Gambino was killed, which sent the message: don't attack the boss of the crime family that bears his name—which also happened to be the richest and most powerful of the five Mafia families. And that family's interests extended, octopus-like, across the country and even into Italy.

Gambino did not believe that publicity was good for his profession. He was not in the mold of Ben "Bugsy" Siegel, John Gotti, or Al Capone. Even in the few photos of him that are publicly available, he does not attempt to be the center of attention; he was not a showboat. There is an infamous photo of Gambino, members of his *borgata*, and Frank Sinatra that was taken backstage at the Westchester Premier Theater in 1976. Two gangsters flank Sinatra, one of whom stands between the singer and Gambino. While Gambino looks as if he would like to disappear from the photo with his closed eyes and perfunctory smile, the others (with one exception) are broadly grinning. Sinatra, the celebrity actor and singer, is the focal point of the photo, grinning along with his gangster pals. (Sinatra once told an interviewer that given the choice of being president of the United States or of being a Mafia boss, he would choose to be a Mafia boss.)

For Gambino, who came to the United States looking for criminal opportunities, keeping a low profile and looking after business was his modus
operandi. It was the source of his enormous success.

Gambino was born in Palermo, Sicily, in 1902. His father was a member
of a loosely organized crime family on the island; but there were greater opportunities for Gambino with his cousins and uncles in the United States.
So at age 19, he boarded a freight boat named the SS *Vincenzo Floria* and
sailed to Norfolk Harbor, Virginia. Jumping ship, he arrived on US soil as
an illegal immigrant 2 days before Christmas 1921. He made his way to New
York City, where he was welcomed by his Castellano relatives; he and his
uncle, Giuseppe Castellano, soon became members of the Salvatore "Toto"
D'Aquila crime family. As an up-and-coming young criminal, Gambino associated with Lucky Luciano, Meyer Lansky, Tommy "Three-Finger Brown"
Lucchese, Vito Genovese, Albert "Mad Hatter" Anastasia, Frank Costello,
and Siegel, all of whom became his friends. Seeing the enormous sums of
money that could be earned from bootlegging, they all turned to Arnold
Rothstein to finance their operations. By the end of Prohibition, they had
all become millionaires. It was Gambino's first fortune. And when Rothstein was murdered in 1928, Gambino and some of the others took over
his various illegal operations. While the others turned from bootlegging to
gambling, prostitution, labor racketeering, and murder for hire, Gambino
stuck with the alcohol business. He bought alcohol stills in four states and
distributed untaxed alcohol to restaurants, nightclubs, and bars in cities
throughout the northeast and mid-Atlantic regions of the country. It was the
basis for his second fortune.

From that, he ventured into a wide array of legal and illegal businesses:
trucking, labor racketeering, construction, and food distribution. He conducted all transactions in his head and everything was done in cash. He would
always feel safe if there were no records that could be used as evidence against
him. Whenever possible, he spoke with his compatriots in his Sicilian dialect,
which was incomprehensible not only to mainland Italians, but also, and
more importantly, to law enforcement.

As sensitive to new opportunities as Geiger counters are to the presence of
radiation, Gambino took advantage of a government opportunity to add to
his fortune during World War II. He did so first by stealing and then buying
and selling ration stamps. The stamps were issued by the government to limit
wartime shortages of gasoline, meat, and groceries. Consumers used the limited number of stamps they were issued to purchase those commodities. For
many, the limits imposed by ration stamps represented a hardship. So they
began to pay premium prices for extra stamps on the black market.

When Gambino and others saw the profits that could be made from being the supplier of these stamps, several break-ins occurred at the OPA [Office of Price Administration] administrative offices; safes were broken into and stamps stolen. . . . Before he could contemplate his next move, OPA officials handed him the solution on a silver platter. These government jobs [were] mostly low-pay positions, many staffed by volunteers. . . . Unscrupulous officials found out how they could make money, too. The ration stamps were soon being sold to the mob.[1]

Gambino, while raking in millions of dollars, patiently waited to move up in the ranks of the Mob. It had naturally occurred in 1931, following the murders of Joe "the Boss" Masseria and Salvatore Maranzano. Vincent Mangano, an ambitious gangster, was approved by Luciano to take over the remnants of the Mineo crime family following the murder of its boss, Manfredi Mineo. Gambino was an unobtrusive member of the family, making money and paying tribute to his boss as he watched and waited for his opportunities. He played it safe, never riling his colleagues or bosses. He was secretive and cunning. While Mangano trusted Gambino to be a loyal member of their *borgata*, he disliked his underboss, Anastasia, who was quick to discount his boss's orders and do what he liked. As Anastasia worked private deals with Costello, Luciano, and Louis "Lepke" Buchalter, Mangano grew increasingly angry. On occasion his anger would heat to an uncontrollable fury, and Mangano would physically strike out at Anastasia, whose hair-trigger temper pushed their encounters to the very edge of gladiatorial combat. The two were fortunate, however, that several capos would rush in to separate them because surely Anastasia, the bigger, younger, and stronger of the two would have killed his boss. Although the murder of bosses by underbosses was not uncommon, it often triggered further warfare that was injurious to each of the Five Families.

Anastasia reached a point where he could no longer contain his anger. He knew that Mangano's murder would result in a trial by the Mafia commission, but he believed he would be acquitted in such a trial and then be permitted to become the boss of his own family. He decided to go forward with a plan to eliminate his boss. On April 19, 1951, after 20 years as head of his own crime family, Mangano disappeared. Each of the bosses figured that Anastasia had murdered Mangano. That same day, the bloodied body of Vincent's brother, Philip, was found in a marsh near Sheepshead Bay, Brooklyn. He had been shot in the head three times. The body of Vincent Mangano has never been found.

Having told the bosses that Mangano had planned to kill him, Anastasia said he acted in self-defense. He was backed up by Costello, who needed Anastasia's army of soldiers to protect his own family, the one he inherited after

Luciano was deported to Italy. Anastasia quickly took the reins of the Mangano family, renaming it the Anastasia family and appointing Gambino as his underboss. He treated Gambino as if he were nothing more than a gofer, a mistake that would ultimately be ruinous to Anastasia. The "Mad Hatter" would regularly yell at Gambino, treating him as if he were a slow-minded employee, a vassal to be ordered about.

Gambino continued to live his life out of the spotlight. Other than the famous photo of himself with Sinatra, he was never seen with celebrities, politicians, or professional athletes.

Ralph Salerno told the author that neither Gambino nor Lucchese would ever meet with fellow gangsters in public places such as Italian social clubs or nightclubs. They had business offices, and that's where they would meet. In his home office, Gambino had a large living room that contained a conference table. There, he would meet with his capos and make business decisions. It was all low key. Gambino, playing his cards close to his chest, felt comfortable maintaining relationships with other Sicilians, especially his Castellano relatives. It is why he chose his cousin, Catherine Castellano, as his wife. He was 24, and she was 19. They had four children: Thomas, Joseph, Phyllis, and Carl, Jr. The family resided in a 13-room, two-story home located at 2230 Ocean Parkway in Brooklyn. It was a middle-class neighborhood of Jews and Italians. When asked about Gambino, his neighbors said that he was a quiet unassuming man, pleasant and kind. He and his wife were often seen strolling in the neighborhood.

A myth has been perpetuated by movies and several mobsters that drug trafficking was not permitted because it would result in a crackdown by law enforcement. In fact, one of the reasons that Gambino maintained such a low profile was that he was an importer of massive amounts of heroin, resulting from a deal he made with the deported Luciano. Yes, there would be a crackdown but only if the government discovered the drug deals. If undiscovered, many millions of dollars could be made from the drug trade. Drug trafficking was condoned if done by bosses but forbidden if carried out by soldiers and Mob associates. If a low-level drug dealer were arrested, there might be a good chance he could be flipped and give evidence against his higher-ups. It was better to outlaw all drug dealing.

John H. Davis, in *Mafia Dynasty*, writes,

> It has long been a myth about the Mafia that the big bosses did not deal in hard drugs; Mario Puzo's 1969 novel *The Godfather* and its film adaptation helped publicize the myth, as did Joe Bonanno's 1980 autobiography, *A Man of Honor*. But the truth is that La Cosa Nostra families have been active in the drug trade since the late forties and Carlo Gambino was in the thick of it. The bosses may

have banned their family underlings from dealing in drugs, under penalty of "death without trial," but the ban did not apply to the bosses themselves.[2]

Gambino's drug dealing was so inconspicuous that it did not attract attention. Slowly but surely he earned the trust of all the Mob families; when Vito Genovese decided to eliminate Anastasia, whose army of soldiers had been a bulwark of protection for Costello, Genovese offered Gambino the opportunity to take over the Anastasia family. Gambino nodded his agreement, and Anastasia was murdered. An expert in the double and triple cross, Gambino now formed an alliance with Lansky, Costello, and Luciano to get rid of Genovese. They set him up to be prosecuted for drug trafficking. He was sentenced to 15 years in prison, and it turned out to be a life sentence. Gambino even arranged for his friend, Genovese capo Alphonse "Funzi" Tieri, to become head of the Genovese family. By doing so, Gambino had quietly asserted his undeniable power and became the de facto boss of bosses, yet he never declared that title for himself. He was not going to alienate the other bosses as had Maranzano when he arrogantly declared himself boss of bosses, rather like Napoleon crowning himself as emperor. Gambino was not only modest compared to Maranzano, but he was also beneficent to those in need, a quality lacking in Maranzano's greedy persona. As boss, Gambino acted much like the godfather depicted in the movie of the same name. He would stroll down Mulberry Street in Little Italy, nodding and smiling at those who greeted him. He would take a seat at the Café Biondo, where he would listen to tales of woe and deal out favors and arrange for doctors' bills to be paid, for rents to be paid, and even for parochial school tuitions to be paid. He also instructed his capos to meet with people in their neighborhoods and offer help as needed. All that goodwill generated immense gratitude in thousands of people who would be eager to sit on juries and acquit Gambino and his men of any crimes they might be accused of having committed. Gambino created the kinds of bonds that had shaped the relationships between peasants and Mafia bosses in Sicily.

Gambino was just a smart practitioner of public relations. As head of the newly named Gambino crime family, he set about making it the largest and richest of the families. The FBI estimated that it had between 800 and 1,000 made members plus thousands of associates.

As Gambino solidified his power, eliminating those who were loyal to Anastasia, he surrounded himself with trustworthy caporegimes, such as his cousin Paul Castellano, (representing the white-collar business elements in the family) and Aniello Dellacroce who represented the blue-collar guys (one of whom, John Gotti, would kill Castellano years later to become the family's boss and assert the prominence of his blue-collar *borgata* over the white-collar elites). Under Gambino, the family's control extended over the garment industry, trucking, private carting, and the International Longshore-men's Union. Gambino also ventured into seemingly legitimate businesses, such as S.G. S. Associates, a public-relations and labor-relations company that guaranteed labor peace through bribery and extortions.

Gambino was not free of government scrutiny. Following his appointment as US Attorney General, Robert Kennedy waged an unrelenting, even zeal-ous, war against organized crime; two of his most visible targets were Jimmy Hoffa, head of the Teamsters Union, and Carlos Marcello, crime boss of New Orleans. But Gambino was also a specimen under Kennedy's prosecutorial microscope: the government was bugging his phones and eavesdropping on his capos and soldiers. With the government indicting one organized crime figure after another, Gambino wisely kept a low profile; he became even more secretive than he had been. By the end of his term as Attorney General, Ken-nedy had won more than 400 convictions against organized crime figures. He had done more to cripple the activities of organized crime than any other prosecutor—and the Mob hated him for it. They wanted him dead. The Mob was eager to be rid of the Kennedy brothers, and FBI tapes of bugged conver-sations proved the Mob's intentions.

"Kennedy's not going to make it to the (1964) election—he's going to be hit," Santo Trafficante, the top Florida mobster, said to an FBI informer in August 1962.

"You know what they say in Sicily: if you want to kill a dog, you don't cut off the tail, you cut off the head," said Carlos Marcello, Mafia boss in New Orleans, to an acquaintance that same month, explaining why President John Kennedy, not Robert Kennedy, would be killed.[3]

And once JFK had been assassinated, Robert Kennedy's war against or-ganized crime began to cool. In anguish, the Attorney General questioned whether his pursuit of the Mob was the cause of his brother's murder. Of all the murders that benefited the Mob, certainly none was more beneficial than that of JFK.

By 1964, following a reduction of Mob indictments, Gambino felt less threatened and aggressively went after new business opportunities. He ex-panded his activities into unions, focusing not only on the waterfront but also on the cargo and freight handlers' unions at Kennedy International Airport, Wall Street securities fraud, major construction projects in New York City, pornography distribution, topless bars, and expanded drug trafficking.

In *Mafia Dynasty*, John H. Davis writes,

> In the less profitable realm of legitimate business, Gambino gained a lucrative foothold in the Castro Convertible furniture (exclusive control of mattresses used in Castro beds, and the trucking of Castro furniture from factory to showroom to retail outlets), Pride Meat Supermarkets (run by his cousin and

brother-in-law Paul Castellano), fuel oil trucking, pizza parlor equipment, meat packing companies.[4]

To maintain the profitability of his various business endeavors, Gambino relied on the loyalty not only of his own capos and soldiers but also on the capos of other families. To generate that loyalty and diminish the power of rival bosses, Gambino would secretly side with one faction against another. In the war that raged between the Profaci family and the Gallo brothers, which was led by Joey Gallo, Gambino secretly supported the Gallos. The war came to an unexpected conclusion following the death of Profaci as a result of liver cancer and the imprisonment of Joey Gallo for murder and racketeering. Gallo's relatively small *borgata* no longer had the fire power to battle the Profaci gang, so it retreated. During the war, Joseph Bonanno, head of the Bonanno crime family, had supported the Profacis. With the war's end, Bonanno then decided it was time to eliminate Gambino and his allies. Bonanno wanted to become boss of bosses. He gave the murder contract to Joseph Colombo, a capo in the Profaci family, now run by Joseph Magliocco. Colombo thought the murder of Gambino would just prolong a needless war and hurt everyone's business interests. He told Gambino of the plot, and Gambino called a meeting of the Mafia Commission. Magliocco, though a boss of one of the Five Families, was not a member of the commission. He was summoned by the full commission to appear. At his trial, Magliocco informed the commission members that Bonanno had issued the murder contract on Gambino's life and it was not his idea. The commission decreed that Magliocco would have to give up his position as head of the Profaci family and pay a $50,000 fine. Magliocco quickly accepted the verdict, grateful that he wouldn't be killed. Bonanno had refused to appear before the commission, fearing that he would be sentenced to death. To preserve his life, he went into hiding. The commission concluded that Bonanno had wanted to kill Gambino and his allies so that he could become boss of bosses. Instead, Bonanno lost his allies in the Profaci family and faced Gambino's undying enmity. As a reward, Colombo was elevated to the position of boss of the Profaci family, and Magliocco retreated into illness. His retirement did not last long; a month later he died of a heart attack.

Although Colombo could have quietly operated as the boss of his newly named eponymous family, he chose to add a public role to his life. He was the first boss of a Mafia family born in the United States and took pride in his US citizenship. As such, it was not surprising that as a media-conscious man of 41, and not afraid of publicity, that he would tap into the churning zeitgeist that was capturing the attention of newspapers, television, and movies. He was not one of the old-school dons who operated in the shadows, sub rosa and sotto voce.

In spring 1970, Colombo created the Italian-American Civil Rights League suggestively imitative of the Urban League, the NAACP, and the Anti-Defamation League, all organizations created to fight bigotry and oppression of particular racial and religious minorities as well as to advance the interests of those it represents. Colombo was a master of publicity: he got Sinatra to agree to be the chairman of the League and then perform at Madison Square Garden in a huge fundraising concert for it. Sinatra brought Dean Martin, Sammy Davis Jr., Jerry Vale, Connie Francis, Vic Damone, and others with him. Colombo appeared on the *Dick Cavett Show*, got Cavett to be a member of the League, and was interviewed on numerous news programs. He was profiled in countless newspaper and magazine articles. He even arranged for the producer of *The Godfather* not to use the words "Mafia" and "Cosa Nostra" in the movie. He led demonstrations against the FBI and even convinced Attorney General John Mitchell not to use the word "Mafia" in official Justice Department documents and press releases. His publicity efforts resulted in his signing up 45,000 dues-paying members within the first 2 months of founding the League. He aligned his group with the militant Jewish Defense League (JDL) and its leader, Rabbi Meir Kahane. When 11 members of the JDL were arrested, Colombo posted their bail.

All of that publicity made Gambino and other Mob bosses unhappy. Bosses were supposed to keep low profiles, to eschew publicity, and focus on making money, which was the ultimate goal of organized crime.

Meanwhile, an enemy of the Profaci family, Joey Gallo was released from prison in 1971. As a peace offering, Colombo invited Gallo to a meeting and offered him $1,000 as a token of his good intentions. Gallo spurned the offer and said there would be no peace without the payment of at least $100,000. An underboss of the Colombo family thereupon allegedly issued a murder contract on Gallo.

Gallo was not the only one who now had sufficient motive to kill Colombo. Off in the shadows was Gambino who was finding Colombo's antics as a publicity hound worrisome; he could jeopardize the quiet workings of the Mob. On June 28, 1971, during the second Italian Unity Day Rally in Columbus Circle, a black street hustler named Jerome Johnson, sporting press credentials and posing as a photo journalist, approached the podium from where Colombo was about to address the crowd. He pulled out a revolver and fired three shots, hitting Colombo in the head and neck but did not kill him. Johnson was wrestled to the ground, shot, then killed by a Colombo bodyguard. While Johnson's body lay on the ground, an ambulance rushed Colombo to a nearby hospital. Though his life was saved, he would spend the next 7 years in a vegetative state.

There have been two divergent theories about who ordered the hit on Colombo. Was it Gallo or Gambino? The Colombo family and the police believed it was Gallo. Organized crime figures thought it was Gambino. But it would be Gallo who would pay the price.

Nearly a year later, on April 7, 1972, at 4:30 a.m., while eating dinner with his family and friends at Umberto's Clam House (a restaurant partly owned by Genovese crime family capo, Matthew "Matty the Horse" Ianniello) in Little Italy, Gallo was gunned down by members of the Colombo family, thus ending a potential and disruptive war.

The Colombo family, the Gambino family, and the commission were now rid of an unpredictable and volatile character who could inflict injury on the mob. Gambino went about his business as usual; his fingerprints were on neither the Colombo nor the Gallo murder. He had operated as usual, craftily behind the scenes. Business returned to normal for the Mob, and the Gambino family continued to thrive and expand.

Seven years later, Colombo died. *The New York Times* reported,

Joseph A. Colombo Sr., the reputed Mafia leader who was a founder of the Italian American Civil Rights League—and who was gunned down and left almost totally paralyzed at a 1971 league rally in Columbus Circle—died Monday night at St. Luke's Hospital in Newburgh, N.Y. He would have been 55 years old on June 16. Mr. Colombo had been taken in a coma to the hospital on May 6 from his nearby five-acre estate in Blooming Grove. Dr. John C. Bivono Jr., a member of the hospital's staff who had been attending Mr. Colombo, said that while the immediate cause of death was cardiac arrest, Mr. Colombo's condition stemmed from the seven-year-old gunshot wounds.

In a 1975 court ordered evaluation of his condition, Mr. Colombo was described as being able to move only the forefinger and thumb of his right hand. A year later, he was reported able to utter a few words and recognize people.[5]

Throughout the 1970s, the government attempted to deport Gambino; he was considered an illegal alien because he had entered the country illegally by jumping ship in 1921. The fact that Italy refused to accept Gambino did not deter the government from proceeding with its case. Appeals and stays by Gambino's lawyers delayed the government's actions to have him deported. Then on the morning of October 15, 1976, Gambino died of a heart attack at his home. A funeral cortege of some 30 cars followed the hearse bearing the Mafia boss to his final resting place in the family mausoleum at St. John's Cemetery, where numerous other Mafioso also rest in peace.

The cemetery is not the only place where Gambino is remembered. There was a military school in Oakdale, New York, which Mr. and Mrs. Gambino supported and where one of their sons was a student and where Gambino and Lucchese headed the Fathers' Club. A plaque at the school honors the Gambinos for their generous fundraising.

And what of the Gambino crime family? As Carl Sifakis writes in *The Mafia Encyclopedia*, "In his reign from 1957 to 1976 Carlo Gambino took a second-string crime family and built it into the Mafia's jewel in the crown, far more wealthy than even the family originally ruled by Lucky Luciano, far more powerful than the Capone-descended Chicago Outfit."[6]

11

Paul Castellano: White-Collar Gangster

FORMER NEW YORK DETECTIVE and mob authority, Ralph Salerno, told the author that "Paul Castellano was not a typical mob thug; he didn't carry a gun and personally never killed anyone."[1] Though Castellano hadn't personally killed anyone, he had ordered the murders of various others. It was done sotto voce, with a nod of the head or a hand gesture. He ordered that his son-in-law should be killed because the man had beaten Castellano's daughter. Roy DeMeo, a homicidal member of the Gambino family, carried out the hit.

Castellano wanted to be perceived as a legitimate businessman, just as Frank Costello and Meyer Lansky wanted to be respected as legitimate businessmen. The three men usually went about unarmed, but each could order a hit that was carried out with alacrity. No one argued against their orders, no matter how softly uttered. Of the three, Castellano was the most powerful; with a phone call, he could call a strike of garment industry truckers, could shut down the ports of New York, and could bring major construction sites to a halt. Told that he looked like a legitimate businessman, he would smile because it was one of the highest compliments anyone could pay him.

This man of vast power and wealth was born into modest circumstances on June 26, 1915, in Brooklyn, New York. His father, Giuseppe, was a butcher and member of the Mangano crime family. His mother, Concetta, was an old-fashioned, stay-at-home wife and mother. The one relative who would play a major role in his life, helping to elevate him to being a Mafia boss, was his cousin Carlo Gambino.

Young Paul was a bright boy, but he aborted his education when he dropped out of school during the eighth grade. Although most boys who drop out of school do so because they have a learning disability or have a strong need to rebel against the confines and rules of schools, young Castellano dropped out to learn the butchering profession from his father as well as to run numbers for him. Giuseppe set his son on the path to becoming a gangster.

Though a gangster in the making, Castellano was cautious and did what he could to avoid being noticed by cops; however, in 1934, he made a mistake that would not only bring him to the attention of law enforcement but also garner the respect of the Mafia. Castellano and two friends robbed a men's clothing store in Hartford, Connecticut. The trio drove away with the modest loot of $51, each of them netting $17. As if that were not sufficiently disappointing, their getaway car's license plate was noted by a witness and handed over to local cops. The car was registered to Castellano, and he was tagged with the crime. Understanding Mob culture, Castellano knew better than to squeal on his two compatriots. He served 3 months of a 1-year sentence and never let on who his accomplices were. The Mob took note of his silence and agreed that Castellano was a stand-up guy and that he could be counted on. His sponsor would now be his clever cousin, Carlo Gambino. In addition, it hadn't hurt that Castellano's sister, Catherine, had married Gambino in 1926.

Castellano was proving to be good earner and was moving up in the Mangano family. When Albert "Mad Hatter" Anastasia took over as boss, following Mangano's disappearance, he promoted Castellano from soldier to capo. Castellano formed the Dial Poultry Company, which supplied chickens to supermarkets throughout New York City. From that point of entry, he developed interests in several chains of supermarkets. He was so powerful in the supermarket and poultry distribution businesses that famous chicken entrepreneur Frank Perdue sought his help.

As Selwyn Raab writes in *Five Families*,

[Perdue] acknowledged to the FBI in 1981 that he had directly solicited Castellano's aid at least twice. The first occasion was to ask if Castellano could derail attempts by the mob-tainted United Food and Commercial Workers Union to organize his main processing plant in Accomac, Virginia. A second difficulty Perdue thought Castellano could resolve was his inability to get his chickens into many of the chain supermarkets in the huge New York area.

Perdue never clarified to the FBI what help Castellano offered or provided. At first he said he contacted Castellano because of his expertise as an investor in beef, poultry, and wholesale food companies. Pressed by Gambino Squad agent Joseph F. O'Brien as to why he had singled out Castellano rather than supermarket and meat business officials, Perdue, with a high-pitched cackle replied "Why? Because he's the godfather."

[Perdue later amplified to investigators from a presidential fact-finding commission that he sought Castellano's intervention because he was known to have "long tentacles as an organized crime figure. Yeah, the Mafia and the Mob."[2]

In addition to the food business, Castellano was deeply involved in the concrete business and supervised what was known as the "Concrete Club." It was a club in which all of New York's Five Families had an interest. If a New York real-estate developer was going to use more than $2 million worth of concrete, he had to pay a fee that was divided among the Five Families. To ensure that their wishes were carried out, the Gambino family put Castellano in charge of dealing with Teamsters Local 282 whose members poured concrete in all major developments in New York City and Long Island. To add to his wealth and responsibility, Castellano owned several concrete companies. He had become a multimillionaire and enjoyed all the comforts and luxuries that money could buy, and the money from his multiple operations poured in faster than concrete was being poured throughout the city.

On October 15, 1976, Gambino died in his bed, one of the few bosses who was neither executed nor sentenced to a long prison term. He had outwitted his pursuers and created the largest and most powerful Mafia family in the United States. He had decreed that his successor should be his cousin and brother-in-law Castellano. A large number of Gambino soldiers and capos, especially those who dealt in such street crimes as hijacking, loan-sharking, burglary, fencing of stolen goods, and extortion, thought that Aniello Dellacroce should have been named boss. He was truly a tough gangster, not one who attempted to pass himself off as a legitimate businessman. Though Dellacroce was in prison, he would soon be released and could have taken charge of the family. But Gambino had figured that Castellano could grow the family's wealth and power through his development of white-collar criminal enterprises as well as through legitimate businesses. Dellacroce, meanwhile, could continue to oversee blue-collar street crimes of his *borgata*, which was being controlled in his absence by the ambitious John Gotti. Gambino's choice of successor did not take into consideration that it might cause a schism in the family, one that ultimately led to Castellano's murder and the decline of the Gambino family.

> Paul Castellano was a very different species of Mafia don than the three men who had bossed the family before he took over. He was much more of a diplomat than they had been, was more polished and soft-spoken, and cultivated a more elegant appearance. . . . When someone told him he looked more like a businessman than a mobster, it pleased him no end.[3]

The 6'3" Castellano cut an imposing figure in his conservative bespoke suits and cashmere overcoats. His black horn-rimmed glasses gave him a somewhat owlish look that camouflaged the savagery that was the source of his power and essential to his modus operandi. As a man of prominence, he enjoyed patronizing the finest restaurants in Manhattan and Brooklyn, where the waiters and maître d's paid obeisance by catering to every criteria that he had for fine food and drink. One of his favorite restaurants in Manhattan was Sparks Steak House, located at 210 East 46th Street, between Second and Third Avenues. Though the staff could not have been more accommodating to him, Castellano resented that they never offered him a free bottle of wine, though he spent many thousands of dollars there.

To go along with his status as boss of the wealthiest crime family, Castellano lived in a magnificent 17-room mansion on Staten Island. The blue-collar contingent of the Gambino family, ruled by Dellacroce, derisively referred to it as the White House and to Castellano as the Pope. The house stood elegantly on Todt Hill, the highest point of elevation on the east coast of the United States.

Castellano invariably held meetings with his Mob underlings in his kitchen as if it were a corporate boardroom with its long conference table; however, there were times when he refused to meet people in his home: those whom he considered beneath him, such as members of the notorious gang of Irish thugs, the Westies, who controlled the Hell's Kitchen area of Manhattan, west of Eighth Avenue and extending from West 34th Street to West 59th Street. The Westies were known for their involvement in a wide range of rackets, including bookmaking, assault, murder for hire, kidnapping, extortion, drug dealing, robbery, and loan-sharking. Their reputation for committing grisly murders and dismembering the bodies of their victims terrified anyone who got in their way.

Castellano had heard that Westies had killed a valuable Mob associate, a shylock named Charles "Ruby" Stein. He was the biggest Mob loan shark in New York City, who supposedly had no less than $1 million on the street at any time. The amount of money he collected from the vigorish (i.e., interest) was the envy of every banker in the city. He kept a little black book with the names of those to whom he had lent money and the amount of money they owed to him, along with payment schedules. Stein had made the mistake of hiring Jimmy Coonan, notorious boss of the Westies, as his bodyguard. Coonan and members of his gang owed a considerable amount of money to Stein and were looking for a way to renege on their loan payments. Because the Westies killed as casually as swatting flies and with the eagerness of serial killers, they decided to kill Stein. Coonan asked Stein to meet him at Club 596, a bar owned by Coonan that was located on Tenth Avenue and 43rd Street in Hell's Kitchen. Stein was taken into the back and then shot and killed; his body was dragged into a bathroom, where a pair of Westies, using a hacksaw and a boning knife, dismembered Stein and stuffed his body parts into a garbage bag. They dumped his torso into the Hudson River. The torso later washed ashore and was identified as Stein's. Word of this reached Castellano as well as the bosses of the Colombo and Genovese families, all of whom were furious that Stein had been killed. He was a major earner for those Mafia families, and someone would have to pay for the loss of money. In addition to Stein's murder, his black book disappeared. Castellano figured the book was worth millions of dollars. It was not until years later that Westie turncoat, Mickey Featherstone, revealed that Coonan wanted the book so that he could collect on the outstanding debts.

Something had to be done, so Castellano called Coonan and Featherstone to a meeting at Tommaso's Restaurant in the Bay Ridge section of Brooklyn. The restaurant was next door to a Gambino social club called Veterans and Friends. Apprehensive that they might be murdered, Coonan and Featherstone arranged for members of the Westies to be stationed down the street from the restaurant. The Westies were to keep out of sight, and if their two compatriots didn't show up in 3 hours or if they heard gunshots, they should come into the restaurant and blast away at the Italians.

Castellano, similarly not trusting the Westies, included in his entourage Gambino members, Aniello Dellacroce, Joe N. Gallo, Nino Gaggi, and Carmine Lombardozzi as well as a member of the Genovese family. Although they were all armed, Coonan and Featherstone had been warned to come unarmed, which they did. After interrogating the two Westies about Stein's death and being assured that the Westies knew nothing about the hit, Castellano told the Westies that they would now be working for him and the Gambino family. They could no longer kill without his permission; they could use the Gambino name in their racketeering enterprises to intimidate others if necessary, but they had to pay 10 percent of everything they made to Castellano. Coonan was also told that when any member of the Westies was called to a meeting with a Gambino capo or soldier, he had to drop everything and come immediately, just as made members had to. Coonan was delighted to be considered as an associate of the Gambinos and soon copied the way the Gambino capos dressed and imitated their various gestures. He was also relieved that he would not have to pay for Stein's death with his own life. The Gambino go-between for Coonan was Roy DeMeo, a prolific Mafia killer, whose homicidal behavior was equal to that of the Westies; Coonan was not to initiate contact with any other Gambino member.

Having reined in the Westies and increased his income, Castellano felt he could return to the comforts provided by his wealth. One such comfort was his maid Gloria Olarte; though Castellano had married his boyhood sweetheart, Nina Manno, in 1937, he had lost interest in her. The couple had three sons (Paul, Phillip, and Joseph) and one daughter (Constance). By the time Castellano hired Olarte as his maid, his children were adults. Castellano was 64 and Olarte was 30. Though Nina remained in the Todt Hill mansion,

Castellano initiated an affair with Olarte who regularly flattered her boss. Unfortunately, she could not flatter his sexual performance because he was impotent. John H. Davis, in *Mafia Dynasty*, writes,

> Still for all the fondling, petting, and gifts, Gloria became extremely confused over the fact that Mister Paul, as she called him, never tried to make love to her. It had become acutely frustrating for her. All the foreplay leading to nothing.
>
> Mister Paul had been afflicted with diabetes for many years and his constitution was of a type that suffered sexual impotence from the disease. By the time Gloria came into Big Paul's life, he had been unable to achieve an erection for almost four years.[4]

The solution for Castellano was to undergo a surgical procedure for a penile implant. The result was a permanent erection, which he had to keep strapped to his lower abdomen, so his pants would not tent. Castellano was embarrassed about it and tried to keep it secret. However, the FBI had bugged his mansion and soon thereafter learned of the implant. Somehow rumors of it also spread among members of Gotti's crew, who felt that it reflected badly on Castellano's manhood. They often asked one another: how can we be bossed by a man who can't get it up? Eventually, Mrs. Castellano felt so angry and humiliated by her husband's flagrant adultery that she moved from the Todt Hill mansion into an apartment. Olarte said she would live with her paramour for the rest of his life. She had no idea how short a period of time that would be.

Although surgery led to a happy bedroom life for Castellano, problems were brewing on the outside. Dellacroce died of cancer, and much to the disgust of his crew, Castellano did not make an appearance at either his wake or his funeral. Dellacroce had always leashed in Gotti's anger about Castellano because he did not want to see an intrafamily war. With Dellacroce's absence, however, a war became more of a probability than a possibility. Castellano further managed to pour fuel on Gotti's anger when he chose Thomas Bilotti, rather than Gotti, as the family's new underboss. In addition, Castellano had vehemently proscribed drug dealing, and a member of Gotti's crew, Angelo Ruggiero (known as "Quack Quack" for his inability to censor his conversations), had not only been dealing drugs, but he spoke freely with his associates about his drug dealing and the conversations were bugged by the FBI. Castellano demanded to hear those tapes, which had been turned over to Ruggiero's lawyer, but Dellacroce had been able to stall Castellano. Now that Dellacroce was dead, Castellano's insistence that the tapes be turned over to him became an adamant demand. Gotti knew that if Castellano heard the tapes, which also included insults about Castellano, Gotti would not only be demoted from capo to soldier with a lackluster crew, but he would probably be killed.

As angry as Castellano was, his anxiety level significantly increased when he was indicted for being the boss of a stolen car ring and taking large sums of tribute money from the actual thieves. Next, he was indicted in the famous Mafia Commission Trial. Castellano was 70 years old, and a guilty verdict in either case would, in effect, be a death sentence. There was apprehension in Gotti's crew that Castellano would flip to avoid a prison sentence and in the process give up Dellacroce's old *borgata*; Castellano would have to be killed.

The hurricane against which the Five Families had inadequate protection and that would ultimately shatter the structures of their families was just over the horizon, and when it made landfall, the bosses were shocked by its intensity. The hurricane came in the name of Rudolph Giuliani. Not since the days of Attorney General Robert Kennedy had there been such a zealous and persistent prosecutor of the Mob. As US Attorney for the Southern District of New York, Giuliani was the first Italian prosecutor determined to send the bosses of the Five Families to prison for the rest of their lives. He was completely uncompromising, and the Mob was stunned.

The bosses of the Five Families whom Giuliani indicted were Castellano, boss of the Gambino crime family; Anthony "Fat Tony" Salerno, boss of the Genovese crime family; Carmine "Junior" Persico, boss of the Colombo crime family; Anthony "Tony Ducks" Corallo, boss of the Lucchese crime family; and Philip "Rusty" Rastelli, boss of the Bonanno crime family.

Each of them had been bugged discussing criminal enterprises. A bug had been placed in Castellano's kitchen where he openly discussed the Concrete Club and payoffs from developers. Another bug was placed in Corallo's elegant Jaguar, where he discussed the operations of the Lucchese's criminal activities with his capo, Salvatore Avellino. A bug in the Palma Boys Social Club in East Harlem recorded the conversations of Salerno about the Genovese crime family's involvement in the construction industry. The Casa Storta restaurant, in Bensonhurst, Brooklyn, was where Gennaro Langella was recorded discussing Colombo family crime businesses. A fifth bug was placed in the union office of the Colombo family, where bribes and shakedowns were discussed. All the bosses were recorded discussing many of their rackets, such as loan-sharking, extortion, price-fixing, etc. When the recordings were played in court, the hurricane had succeeded in blowing away whatever defenses the bosses thought that they may have had.

One of those bugged conversations, though not providing criminal information, proved to be unintentionally prescient: Castellano stated without irony that, "This life of ours is a wonderful life. If you can get through life like this and get away with it, hey, that's great. But it's very, very unpredictable. There's so many ways you can screw it up."[5]

The Mafia Commission Trial, which ran from February 25, 1985 to November 19, 1986, not only included bosses but also soldiers and capos. All were tried under the Racketeer Influenced and Corrupt Organizations (RICO) Act on charges including extortion, labor racketeering, and murder for hire. When asked about the indictments, Giuliani stated, "Our approach is to wipe out the five families."[6]

At trial's end, the heads of four of the Five Families were convicted of all 151 counts of their indictments, and on January 13, 1987, each of the bosses was sentenced to 100 years in prison. Having been murdered prior to the trial, Castellano evaded conviction. Friends and relatives speculated that Castellano would have preferred to die, though not necessarily by gunfire, than to spend the remainder of his life in prison, where his carefully self-made image as a legitimate businessman would have been destroyed.

To many in the media, Giuliani had become a hero, a knight who slew the dragons of organized crime. Among mobsters, however, hatred for Giuliani was as hot as molten lava; as they had with Thomas Dewey and Robert Kennedy, the Mob considered assassinating him. According to an FBI memo, leaders of the Five Families voted in 1986 on whether to issue a contract for Giuliani's death. Heads of the Lucchese, Bonanno, and Genovese families rejected the idea because the wrath of the Justice Department would have been a holocaust for the Mob; yet, there are always hotheads (such as Dutch Schultz, who had wanted to assassinate Dewey), who wanted Giuliani killed; they were Colombo boss Carmine Persico and John Gotti, leader of the Gambinos.

In addition to those two bosses, there were many fearsome mobsters, who would have welcomed Giuliani's murder because their need for vengeance was undiminished. Even after Giuliani became mayor of New York, having run on a platform that he had destroyed the Mob, there were those scheming to kill him. Giuliani knew of the contract on his life and was heavily guarded. He asserted to the media that the Sicilian Mafia offered $800,000 for his death as late as 1994.[7]

As bad as the Mafia Commission Trial was for the Five Families, the murder of Castellano would prove particularly disastrous for what remained of the Gambino family. Having lived the life of a self-styled legitimate businessman, Castellano had created a world where he was insulated from the gripes, concerns, and difficulties of the street guys in Gotti's crew; he had no idea he was in their gun sites. He thought his problems were all legal. On his way to his final destination, he stopped to confer with his lawyer, James LaRossa, about his trials. After leaving his lawyer's office, Castellano had his driver and underboss, Bilotti, stop at a store where he bought a bottle of perfume as a Christmas present for his secretary. They then continued heading north to 46th Street, between Second and Third Avenues, where they had a dinner reservation at Sparks Steak House. Along that street, eight men, each dressed in a trench coat and each wearing a Russian fur hat, waited with concealed guns. Castellano's black Lincoln Town Car pulled into a parking space right in front of the restaurant. As he and Bilotti emerged from the car, the eight gunmen swarmed around them like a pride of murderous lions, their guns roaring as pedestrians scattered. Multiple bullets riddled Castellano and Bilotti's bodies. One gunman bent over Castellano's dead body and fired a single shot into his head. An angry coup de grâce. The shooters did not run from the murder scene; they just strode east to Second Avenue where they got into a waiting car that drove them through rush-hour traffic to safe havens. Minutes after the shooting, Gotti and his underboss, Sammy "the Bull" Gravano, drove by the dead bodies of their former boss and underboss, quickly looked at the corpses, assuring themselves that the hits had been successful, and drove on.

The Castellano family wanted the Catholic Church to provide a requiem mass for their deceased patriarch, who had been baptized and confirmed in the Catholic Church. John Cardinal O'Conner denied the Castellano family's request. On December 20, 1985, Castellano was buried in one of New York's oldest cemeteries, the Moravian Cemetery in Dongan Hills on Staten Island. A priest was permitted to say a graveside prayer. Castellano death marked the end of an important era for the Gambino crime family. Gotti would be its new boss, and he would be a lightning rod that attracted the full force of ambitious prosecutors. Carlo Gambino, clever, cagy, and always low profile, would have been appalled at the events that would crumble so much of what he had built. The decline of the Mafia, unbeknownst to Gotti, had been set in motion.

Meyer Lansky

Fernandez, Orlando, photographer. "[Meyer Lansky, three-quarter length portrait, facing slightly left, at 54th St. police station, New York City, being booked for vagrancy]" Photograph. N.Y. World Telegram & Sun c. 1958. From Library of Congress: Miscellaneous Items in High Demand. www.loc.gov/pictures/item/98506863/

Meyer Lanksy, a Free Man

Ravenna, Al, photographer. "Sharply dressed, [gangster/gambler], Meyer Lansky as he left court today" Photograph. N.Y. World Telegram & Sun c. 1958. From Library of Congress: Miscellaneous Items in High Demand. www.loc.gov/pictures/item/2011660014/

Frank Costello, Glowering at US Senate Committee

Aumuller, Al, photographer. "[Frank Costello, half-length portrait, seated, behind microphone, testifying before the Kefauver Committee investigating organized crime]" Photograph. World Telegram & Sun c. 1951. From Library of Congress: Miscellaneous Items in High Demand. www.loc.gov/pictures/item/98506867/

Wax Figure of Bugsy Siegel, Hollywood and Vegas Celebrity
Highsmith, Carol M., photographer. "Celebrities cloned at Madame Tussaud's Wax Museum inside the Venetian Hotel include the mobster Benjamin "Bugsy" Siegel, who built the Flamingo Hotel." Photograph. Las Vegas, Nevada. From Library of Congress: Highsmith (Carol M.) Archive. www.loc.gov/pictures/item/2011634441/

Ellsworth Raymond "Bumpy" Johnson, Harlem Mob Boss and Associate of Lucky Luciano
Pacific Sierra Region RG 129, Records of the Bureau of Prisons, Alcatraz Penitentiary.

Brick From the Newark Chop House Where Dutch Schultz Was Murdered
"Brick from Dutch Schultz Murder Location" Photograph. Federal Bureau of Investigations Multimedia. https://multimedia.fbi.gov/?q=dutch&perpage=50&page=1&searchType=image

Lepke Buchalter, Arrested
Aumuller, Al, photographer. "[Louis "Lepke" Buchalter, center, handcuffed to J. Edgar Hoover, on the left, with another man on the right, at entrance to courthouse]" Photograph. World Telegram c. 1939 or 1940. From Library of Congress: Miscellaneous Items in High Demand. www.loc.gov/pictures/item/2004676730/

Lepke Buchalter On His Way to Prison
Aumuller, Al, photographer. "[Louis "Lepke" Buchalter handcuffed to guard, getting into van]" Photograph. World Telegram & Sun c. 1939. From Library of Congress: Miscellaneous Items in High Demand. www.loc.gov/pictures/item/95511436/

Vincent "the Chin" Gigante, arrested for the shooting of Frank Costello
Stanziola, Phil, photographer. "[Vincent Gigante, three-quarter length portrait, seated, facing front]" Photograph. World Telegram & Sun c. 1957. From Library of Congress: Miscellaneous Items in High Demand. www.loc.gov/pictures/item/99471566/

Vito Genovese, boss of the Genovese Crime Family
Stanziola, Phil, photographer. "[Vito Genovese, half-length portrait, standing, facing right]" Photograph. World Telegram & Sun c. 1959. From Library of Congress: Miscellaneous Items in High Demand. www.loc.gov/pictures/item/99471743/

John Gotti, Strolling Outside His Social Club
"Surveillance photo of mobster John Gotti, walking down a street in 1980s in New York City." Photograph. New York, New York. Federal Bureau of Investigations Multimedia https://multimedia.fbi.gov/item?type=image&id=1751

Salvatore Sammy "the Bull" Gravano
"Mugshot of Salvtore Sammy "The Bull" Gravano, henchman of Gambino family's John Gotti, whose eventual cooperation with the FBI and NYPD helped build a case against the "Teflon Don."" Photograph. New York, New York. Federal Bureau of Investigations Multimedia c. 1990. https://multimedia.fbi.gov/item?type=image&id=807

Robert A. Santucci, Esq., Former Chief of the Rackets Bureau, Office of the District Attorney of Bronx County and Special Assistant United States Attorney for the Southern District of New York, Public Corruption Unit.
Permission from Robert A. Santucci

12

John Gotti: Media Star and Fashion Plate

N OT SINCE THE DAYS OF AL CAPONE had there been such a flashy gangster beloved by the media. John Gotti and the media had a symbiotic relationship; the more the media publicized Gotti, the more he became what they wanted of him. He dressed in bespoke $2,000 suits, had his hair professionally groomed and trimmed daily, wore $400 imported Italian shoes, looked tan and fit, and always had friendly words for his public. When passersby across a street would call out, "Hi, John," he would respond with a wave and a grin. In restaurants, he would sign autographs for dazzled fans. Although most Mob bosses kept a low profile, operating in the shadows, Gotti was always out there; he even engaged in walk-and-talks with his underboss, Sammy "the Bull" Gravano, and assorted capos. He was a star not only on Mulberry Street in Manhattan's Little Italy but also in fancy restaurants and night clubs on the Upper East Side. Wherever he went, he turned heads and caused fans either to murmur his name or to shout out greetings. And Gotti loved the attention. He referred to all those people as "my fans" or "my public."

It was not the world into which Gotti had been born. John Joseph Gotti Jr. was born on October 27, 1940, 1 of 13 children of John Joseph Sr., and Philomena, known as Fanny. The family was extremely poor, for John Sr. was often out of work, gambled away what little money he earned, and could barely support his family.

The alternative to the poor laborers in the neighborhood were the local Mafioso. John and his brothers were impressed by those neighborhood wise guys who always flashed large rolls of $100 bills, drove new Cadillacs, and wore expensive suits. By the time he was 16, Gotti had dropped out of

Franklin K. Lane High School and took to the streets. He became a member of a local gang, the Fulton-Rockaway Boys, which did favors and ran errands for local Mafioso. Gotti had worked at a couple of legitimate jobs (assistant to a truck driver and a pants presser in a garment factory) and found neither job to his liking. Robbery was his thing: it was exciting and profitable. A few years previously, he had attempted to steal a cement mixer that fell on his foot, crushing a couple of toes. Thereafter, he walked with a slight limp. He got caught robbing and served time in jail; his career as a mobster did not get off to a promising start. When he wasn't engaged in thefts, he would hang around with friends, Angelo Ruggiero and Wilfred "Willie Boy" Johnson (called "Indian" and "half-breed" because his father was part American Indian).

In 1958, while hanging out with his pals, Gotti met his future wife, Victoria DiGiorgio; her father was Italian, and her mother was a Russian Jew. John and Victoria married in 1962 and had five children (three sons and two daughters); their son John Angelo Jr. would be inducted into the Gambino family at his father's direction.

Gotti and his brothers all wanted to be made men, and Gotti got his opportunity by doing a favor for Carlo Gambino. The boss's nephew, Manny Gambino, had been kidnapped and held for ransom by a trio of thugs, two of whom had been caught by the FBI. Gotti and his cohorts, Ruggiero and Ralph Galione, were assigned to kill the remaining thug, James McBratney. Pretending to be detectives, the three gangsters entered a bar on Staten Island where McBratney had been drinking. They attempted to arrest him, but McBratney resisted, shouting that they weren't real cops. He put up a struggle, and Galione shot and killed him. Gotti was later identified as one of the killers, arrested, and indicted. Gambino hired Roy Cohn to defend Gotti. The high-profile lawyer worked out a plea deal in which Gotti agreed to accept a guilty plea for attempted manslaughter and was sentenced to 4 years in prison, of which he served 2 years.

Prior to his arrest, Gotti had done work for Carmine Fatico, a capo in what was then known as the Anastasia family. (Following the murder of Anastasia, Gambino took over as boss, and the family has since been known as the Gambino family.) While carrying out truck hijackings and collecting gambling debts for Fatico, Gotti was introduced to Aniello Dellacroce, a tough street gangster and member of the Anastasia family. Dellacroce admired Anastasia and regaled Gotti with tales of his hero's exploits, including murders and beatings. Anastasia became Gotti's role model, and Dellacroce became Gotti's mentor. Fatico was indicted and sentenced to prison for loan-sharking, and during his imprisonment, he put Gotti (not yet a made man) in charge of his Bergin Hunt and Fish Club's gambling operations. Part of Gotti's job consisted of delivering money and reporting his and the club's activities to Dellacroce at the Ravenite Social Club at 247 Mulberry Street in Little Italy.

Gotti had proven himself a loyal protégé of Dellacroce and a good earner for Fatico. Thus, following his release from prison for his part in the murder of McBratney, Gotti was rewarded by being inducted into the Gambino family. He felt as if he had realized a boyhood ambition. His brothers Gene, Peter, Richard, and Vincent also became members of the family, though only Gene preceded John. Shortly after being inducted into the family, Gotti was made a capo and put in charge of the Bergin Hunt and Fish Club.

Life as a gangster finally went into high gear for Gotti, and his high profile became a regular target for law enforcement. Remo Franceschini, former commander of the Queens District Attorney Squad and author of *A Matter of Honor: One Cop's Lifelong Pursuit of John Gotti and the Mob*, told the author that he began bugging the Bergin Hunt and Fish Club in 1981. Franceschini said that Gotti was alternately paranoid and Machiavellian. He was quick-witted, perceptive, and had a volatile temper. More than money, Gotti loved power: the power of life and death over other men. And he loved the movie *The Godfather* in which Vito and Michael Corleone exercised power like ancient Roman emperors.

However, not everything went according to script for Gotti; on March 18, 1980, Gotti's youngest son, Frank, who was 12 years old, was riding his bicycle. He rode out onto the street and was immediately struck and killed by a car driven by neighbor John Favara. Shortly afterward, Favara rang the Gottis's doorbell in an attempt to apologize, and even though the police had ruled the death an accident, Victoria went after Favara with a baseball bat. He retreated to the safety of his house, but he became the target of ongoing threatening phone calls. Someone spray painted the word "MURDERER" in large capital letters on his car. Favara, not being a member of any Mob, had no one to turn to; he realized his life was in danger, so he put his house up for sale, hoping he could sell it before someone actually tried to kill him. It did not sell fast enough. One day in July, when leaving the furniture company where he worked, Favara was abducted by several men who threw him onto the back seat of a car. According to Nat Hendley in *American Gangsters, Then and Now,*

> He disappeared and his body was never found. Rumor had it that he was murdered with a chain saw, and then placed in a car, which was, in turn, placed in a demolition machine that pounded it into a one-square foot block. John and Victoria Gotti made sure they were in Florida when their neighbor disappeared and claimed they knew nothing about Favara's disappearance when asked by the police.[1]

While Favara's fate at the hands of the Mafia was terminal, another man named Romual Piecyk came close to a similar fate. Although he had not killed anyone, Piecyk managed to get into a fist fight with one of Gotti's cohorts and then Gotti himself. Piecyk had been driving down a street in Maspeth, Queens, when his transit was blocked by a double-parked car. Piecyk leaned on his horn until Frank Colletta nearly flew out of the Crazy Corner Bar, where there was gambling in progress and, in a rage, punched Piecyk's face. Piecyk was still sitting in his car when Colletta reached in grabbed $325 that was in Piecyk's shirt pocket. Piecyk, at 6'2" and a relatively youthful 35 years old, flung open his car door and lunged at Colletta. The two men were trading punches when Gotti saw the fight from inside the bar and ran out to assist his friend. Gotti punched Piecyk's face and told him to beat it. Outnumbered and on the losing end of two severe punches to his face, Piecyk withdrew and went to a local police precinct, where he filed charges against Gotti and Colletta. The two were arrested for assault and theft. A year and half later, the two attackers went on trial. Meanwhile, Piecyk had received numerous threats. He also learned that Gotti was a notorious gangster who could easily have him killed. At trial, Piecyk claimed that he could no longer recall what his attacker looked like, and the case collapsed. Piecyk later said that any sensible person would lie to save his own life. The *New York Post* headlined the outcome: "I Forgotti!" Gotti, the head of the Gambino family, with murderous soldiers at his command, was not a man any sensible person wanted to cross. One only need look at the fate of Paul Castellano.

But a year later, Gotti faced another trial, one more serious than the assault case. He and his boss, Dellacroce, and members of the Bergin Hunt and Fish Club were indicted on racketeering charges by Assistant US Attorney Diane Giacalone. She would be battling Gotti's attorney Bruce Cutler, himself a former assistant US attorney, who knew both sides of the street far better than Giacalone.

> As for Cutler versus Diane Giacalone, it would be a contest between an apprentice and a master, between a sparring partner and a champion. . . . Cutler would repeatedly seize the initiative, often succeeding in turning prosecution witnesses into *his* witnesses, making Giacalone look like a fool. He dominated the courtroom upstaging everyone else with is flamboyant, combative style.[2]

The final humiliation for Giacalone occurred after she decided not to use Matthew Traynor as a prosecution witness. He was a bank robber and heroin dealer as well as an FBI informant who was in prison and had wanted to get his sentence reduced by testifying for the prosecution. However, after Giacalone discovered that he had lied to her, she chose not to call him to the stand. Traynor then contacted Cutler. On the stand for the defense, Traynor claimed that Giacalone provided him with drugs. He then told a tale that caused a jaw-dropping reaction from the jurors. During one of their meetings when Traynor was stoned on the drugs that he claimed Giacalone had provided, he told her that he wanted to get laid. He then said that Giacalone pulled out a pair of her panties from the bottom desk drawer and told him to make do with these. Giacalone was understandably furious and demanded that Traynor's testimony be stricken from the court record, but the judge refused to do so. The defendants were nearly gleeful.

Giacalone did not know that behind the scenes she had been set up to fail: early in the case, following jury selection, juror number 11, George Pape, reached out to Gravano and agreed to sell his vote for $60,000. A not-guilty verdict was in the bag long before the prosecutor and the defense attorneys turned the courtroom into a theater that the judge seemed unable to control.

A week after Traynor's outrageous testimony, the case went to the jury, and Gotti and his codefendants were found not guilty on all counts of the indictment. Gotti was thrilled and was now tagged with the sobriquet "the Teflon Don." One of Gotti's codefendants was not so sanguine; he was Gotti's boyhood pal Johnson, who Giacalone revealed (to the FBI's fury) was a government informant. Though offered an opportunity to enter the Witness Protection Program, Johnson refused, and on August 29, 1988, he was gunned down in front of his home in Brooklyn. He was shot 19 times by two Bonanno family hit men as a favor to Gotti. The gunmen threw spikes across the road to prevent police cars from pursuing them. Johnson, like many of his gangster cohorts, is buried in St. John's Cemetery in Middle Village, Queens, New York. Following Johnson's death, Gotti commented, "Everyone's gotta die sometime."

Of Gotti and his trial, Anthony Celano, a former New York Police Department Squad Commander working for Franceschini in the Queens District Attorney's office, told the author,

> Remo was concerned that Gotti might abscond to avoid further prosecutions. There was concern that Tony Roach [real name Anthony Rampino] might flip and testify against Gotti and members of his crew. So Remo sent me and my partner to keep an eye on Gotti. We parked across the avenue from Gotti's house in Howard Beach. A young guy in a Cadillac pulls up to the house, gets out, and delivers some clothes. A few minutes pass, he comes out, gets into his car, drives around the block, and then parks next to us. Out of his window, he yells at us "Mr. Gotti has something for you in the house, you sneaky bastards." My partner tells him to take a walk. The guy drives back to Gotti's house, goes inside, and a few minutes later Gotti comes charging out. He didn't look like himself: he was unshaven, his hair wasn't combed, and he was wearing a rumpled jogging suit. He looked like he just woke up. He sticks his head in our car window and

demands to know what we're doing here. Every muscle in his face is twitching. He's furious and cursing at us. We say nothing. I figure that when someone is screaming at you, it's best not to argue with that person. Eventually they're going to stop. They'll run out of words. However, he was boiling with rage, and my partner had his .38 revolver out of his holster and placed between his legs. I thought he might raise the gun and shoot Gotti. I could just see the headline in the *Post*: "Cops shoot John Gotti." That was the last thing I wanted. I placed my hand over my partner's hand, which was on the revolver. Gotti began to look surprised because we remained silent. He hadn't been able to suck us into an argument that only would have gotten out of hand. Finally, my partner, who was driving said something that calmed him, after which I leaned over and said to John that Remo sent us. It's our job to surveil you. Gotti shouted, "You tell Remo I know who he's fucking!" (That made no sense, since Remo didn't have a girlfriend and was a straight arrow.) Gotti continued his tirade against Remo, and when we told him that Remo takes his orders from DA Santucci, Gotti started a new tirade against Santucci. When Gotti finished yelling, I got out of the car and walked over to him. I said "I don't know what that kid told you, but we didn't mean any disrespect. We're just here sitting in our car and never tried to embarrass you or your family. We follow Remo's orders the way your people follow what you say. He would do what you would do." "I believe it," said Gotti, who swung around to the kid and pointed at him, while shouting, "He's an asshole, his brother's an asshole, and his father's the biggest asshole." Gotti then turned back to me, extended his arm and shook my hand. After which, he turned and walked back to his house.

Back at the office, I told Remo what had happened. When I mentioned the .38, he said it was too bad we hadn't shot Gotti. The next day Remo says we're going for a ride. We get into his Mercedes and drive to Gotti's Bergin Hunt and Fish Club. We get out of the car and head for the club. We stopped in front of the club, then walked among eight or ten guys who were hanging around in front of the club. We looked at the club, but didn't go in; we looked up at the building, and looked at the adjoining buildings like we had big plans or were perspective buyers. All of a sudden I wished I had brought a couple of guns with me. There are guys there that would just as soon kill us as look at us. They all know who Remo is. Nobody says a word. They don't talk to us. We don't talk to them. We left the club and left an implicit message with them: "We're not intimidated. Don't try to intimidate us." It was a message that was sure to reach Gotti's ears when he was told that we had been at his club. And it was a message he would respect.

Remo respected Gotti as a tough guy who had the allegiance of his crew, and Gotti respected Remo for the same reasons. Gotti, said Remo, was intelligent, quick-witted, perceptive, and could strategize his ambitions. He also had a volatile temper and could frighten anyone who got in his way, including members of his own crew. During the trial, you saw Gotti giving his lawyer instructions. He was the boss and everyone did what he ordered. He never personally killed anyone, as far as I know. He had others do it for him. Nobody in his crew would ever disobey him. He was a natural born leader, a very smart man, however misguided. No one of limited intelligence could have gotten a Frank DeCicco and a Sammy Gravano to go along with killing Paul Castellano. Gotti was a flamboyant guy but that was his personality. He was a product of his times: Joe Colombo was flamboyant, Muhammad Ali was flamboyant, Norman Mailer was flamboyant, Mick Jagger was flamboyant. In the 1920s, '30s and '40s, gang bosses kept low profiles, and athletes like Joe Louis and entertainers like Bing Crosby were always polite and respectful.[3]

The flamboyance continued. Gotti delivered the image that the public expected. The media referred to him as the "Dapper Don." He had a movie star's persona, assured by his carefully coifed hair, his perpetual tan, and an elegant wardrobe that would have been the envy of Cary Grant.

Vincent "the Chin" Gigante, the boss of the Genovese crime family, was no fan of the flamboyant Gotti as media star. Gigante exhibited a different kind of flamboyance than Gotti: Gigante shuffled around Greenwich Village in a bathrobe, accompanied by two minders. He would mumble to himself, putting on a superb performance of someone who was mentally ill and so couldn't possibly be the boss of a Mafia family. In private, however, he was outraged that Gotti had assassinated Paul Castellano because Gigante believed that Gotti had no right to kill his boss. Castellano had been the most prominent member of the commission. In addition, Gotti's flamboyance, his playing a role for the media, was attracting too much government attention. It was bad for all Mob families. The Mafia is supposed to be a secret society and not a made-for-television movie. Gotti, for all the world to see, had thumbed his nose at the government by beating it at trial, and furious and embarrassed prosecutors were intent on convicting him. They wanted a judge and jury to give him a one-way ticket to a life sentence. Ironically the FBI wound up protecting Gotti because the agency had learned that Gigante (the man who had shot Frank Costello) was plotting to have Gotti killed. Yet, the FBI wanted to get Gotti on its own terms, and not blow him up or shoot him down in the street. They found a way: learning that Gotti oversaw meetings in an apartment above the Ravenite Social Club at 247 Mulberry Street, the FBI was able to plant a bug in the apartment while its resident, Nettie Cirelli, was away for Thanksgiving. She was the wife of a former Gambino soldier and so dutifully accommodated Gotti: whenever he wanted to hold a meeting, she left the apartment to shop or to visit friends. It was in that apartment that Gotti made the most self-incriminating comments about his involvement in racketeering and murder. On December 11, 1990, the FBI surprised Gotti when they burst into the Ravenite Club as he was holding a meeting. An annoyed Gotti was arrested, along with underboss Gravano and Frank Locascio. All three were charged with 13 counts under the Racketeer Influenced and

Corrupt Organizations (RICO) Act. The charges included murder, income tax evasion, loan-sharking, and obstruction of justice. Included in the murder indictment was Gotti's participation in Castellano's killing. Although Gotti thought he would be granted bail, the FBI foiled that plan by playing tapes of Gotti's incriminating conversations that were recorded in Cirelli's apartment. Judge Leo Glasser denied Gotti bail. Gotti was incensed that he had been denied bail and then was further outraged that his lawyer, Bruce Cutler, was not permitted to defend him. On the tapes, prosecutors had played conversations in which Cutler gave Gotti advice. The prosecutors said that Cutler could be called as a witness and that would create a conflict of interest.

Next to be disappointed was Gravano. On the tapes, Gotti can be heard complaining that Gravano had not given him enough of his earning, though Gravano had been giving Gotti $2 million a year. The more Gravano listened to the tapes, the more he began to believe that Gotti was setting him up as a fall guy. Deciding to save himself, Gravano agreed to testify against his boss. On November 8, 1991, Gravano was taken from prison and put in protective custody. He had an excellent memory and was able to tell agents the full scope of Gambino family activities and even filled them in on the meaning of various Mafia slang words and expressions.

Because Cutler had been barred from defending Gotti, Albert Krieger (who had defended Mafia boss Joseph Bonanno) came on board. He was not only a prominent criminal defense attorney, but he was also recognized as a premier expert on cross-examinations.

The trial began in January 1992, and Gravano proved to be a remarkable witness. He had a meticulous memory and was able to recount in detail the crimes of the Gambino family and those of his boss Gotti. Krieger was unable to shake Gravano from his testimony, and Gravano proved to be a devastating prosecutorial witness as he grippingly testified for 9 days, during which he elicited angry comments from Gotti. Gravano was unshaken by those comments, and the fury in Gotti's eyes had no effect on the advancement of his testimony. As part of his deal with the government, Gravano also had to confess publicly to all the murders he had committed, which were 19. Gotti believed that there were more murders than those Gravano described. One woman who attended the trial told the author that she was shocked when she heard Gravano testify that he had murdered her brother, for she had thought they were good friends.

The tapes of Gotti's conversations and Gravano's testimony proved to be insurmountable obstacles to an acquittal, though Krieger proved to be an otherwise resourceful courtroom advocate for Gotti. It was obvious to all that Gotti would be found guilty. There was no juror to fix as in a previous trial because the judge had sequestered the jury so attempts at bribery could not be effected.

More than in previous trials, this one was a spectacle, not only attracting hordes of fascinated spectators who took time off from their jobs to attend the trial but also attracting celebrities, such as Anthony Quinn and Mickey Rourke, who played supporting roles for the TV news cameras. On April 2, Gotti and Locascio, as expected, were found guilty of all charges. Jim Fox, the highest-ranking FBI agent in New York, stated at a press conference following the conclusion of the trial, "The Teflon is gone. The don is covered with Velcro, and all the charges stuck."[4]

Two months after the verdict, Gotti and Locascio were sentenced to multiple life sentences. Gotti's fans, who numbered in the hundreds, had gathered outside the courthouse and were stunned. They rioted, overturned cars, scuffled with police, and screamed their support for Gotti and demanded his release. Police were called from precincts all over the city to contain the mayhem.

> John Joseph Gotti, who had previously refused to fly because of his fear of airplane crashes, was put aboard a small government jet plane. His hands and feet shackled in irons, and surrounded by U.S. marshals, he was flown to a maximum security penitentiary in Marion, Illinois, then the harshest prison in the federal penal system.[5]

From the morning of June 24, 1992, until his final illness, Gotti was locked into an oppressively small cell for 22 hours each day. His only source of escapist entertainment was a small black-and-white television. He was regularly visited by family and lawyers. His seat of operations, the Ravenite Social Club, was seized by the government, which claimed it was a hotbed for racketeering. It was put up for auction, and a new landlord took it over and converted it into a store.

In 2002, Gotti died from neck and head cancer. His body was taken back to Queens, New York, for a spectacularly old-fashioned Mob funeral. It supposedly cost $200,000. The hearse that carried Gotti's coffin to St. John's Cemetery (resting place and holy ground for many Mafioso) was followed by 19 vehicles, each one overflowing with gorgeous arrangements of flowers. Twenty-two limos also followed, and hundreds of cars carrying friends, neighbors, and admirers created a motorcade fit for a movie star or conquering hero. None of the other Mafia families sent representatives to the funeral. (This was interpreted as a sign of their disdain for the man who brought down the wrath of government prosecutors.) The parade to the cemetery not only marked the end of the one of the most colorful gangsters in the history of the Big Apple, but it also marked the beginning of the decline of the Gambino family.

13

Sammy "the Bull" Gravano

THOUGH VINCENT "THE CHIN" GIGANTE had wanted to kill John Gotti, it was Salvatore (aka Sammy "the Bull") Gravano who ended the Mob boss's reign and not with a gun or a bomb but with his testimony. At the time, Gravano, an underboss in the Gambino family, was the highest-ranking mobster to flip and testify against a boss. His testimony resulted in a Mob contract on his life and reams of newspaper print referring to him as "King Rat." When the circumstances governing his testimony became apparent, the sobriquet, "King Rat," may have been unjustified.

Gravano did not spring from the terrible poverty that his boss, Gotti, did. Born on March 12, 1945, to Giorlando and Caterina Gravano in Bensonhurst, Brooklyn, the youngest of three children, young Gravano and his two sisters grew up in relative comfort. Their father owned a successful dress-manufacturing company, and the family owned a small country house in upstate New York. Salvatore was nicknamed Sammy because he closely resembled his uncle Sammy. By the age of 7, Sammy, for reasons unknown, began stealing. He stole small items, such as cupcakes from a local store, and the stealing excited him. By age 13, he was a member of a local gang, the Rampers. It was around this time that some neighborhood kids stole Sammy's new bicycle. Sammy was furious and determined to find the thieves and teach them that no one stole from him. He scouted his neighborhood like an Indian tracker and soon spotted his bicycle in the hands of some young neighborhood thieves. They were taking turns riding it in circles and laughing at their hijinks. Gravano was furious and propelled by that fury, he charged into the group like a lion into a herd of gazelles. He tackled one boy, got up, threw several punches at another boy, head-butted a third, and left them stunned. One boy was left on the ground, blood streaming from his nose. The bicycle wasn't worth the punishment, and the thieves let Gravano ride away. "Take your bike and get outta here," one boy yelled at him. As Gravano rode his bike toward home, he passed a number of mobsters hanging out in front of a local bar. They had watched the little demon attack the pack of thieves and were impressed with the ferocity of his attack. One of the mobsters commented that Gravano was like an angry bull, and the sobriquet became part of his name. From that day onward, he would be referred to as Sammy "the Bull" Gravano. He learned a lesson that accompanied his new nickname: never back down from a fight. Challenged, he would fight until his opponent either gave up or could no longer defend himself.

School was not the streets, and Gravano, who suffered from undiagnosed dyslexia, proved to be a poor student. It led to him being held back two grades. Other kids called him a dummy, taunting his lack of scholastic abilities. It was a mistake they came to regret because Gravano answered their taunts with a few roundhouse punches that left them with bloody noses and lips. He was a genuine tough kid and his reputation spread like a warning through the neighborhood. No one wanted to mess with him. He was short for his age and would remain short as an adult, but he was powerfully muscled and used those muscles to intimidate those who got in his way. The name Sammy the Bull fit, for it was said of him that he was built like a bull and even had a neck that was as thick as a bull's. His fighting and lack of interest in scholastics led to his being expelled from school when he was 16, which was the legal age in New York for dropping out of school.

He had enjoyed being a member of the Rampers and proved himself an adept young delinquent. But when Gravano turned 20, he got a respite from the mean streets and the wild life of a young hoodlum. It was 1964, and Lyndon B. Johnson was running for president as the peace candidate against the alleged war hawk, Barry Goldwater. Johnson had promised voters that he would not send US boys to fight in foreign lands; Goldwater said he would bomb the Vietnamese communists back to the Stone Age. And so the country elected the peace candidate, who then sent tens of thousands of boys to their deaths in a foreign land.

The draft went into high gear, roping in thousands of boys who were eligible for the draft. Gravano was listed 1A by his draft board, but then heard nothing for 2 years; no invitations arrived for him to have one of the army's perfunctory medical examinations, no telegrams, no registered letters, no phone calls, nothing. The draft board in its bureaucratic slumber apparently did not take notice of Gravano. It was, indeed, as if its workers were asleep at their desks. That is, until the Pentagon wanted more men in uniform. The trumpet call to arms blared, the drums of war loudly beat, and the awakened members of the once-somnolent local draft board summoned Gravano to appear. There was a new quota to fill, and Gravano was one digit added to the roll call of new recruits. He was fortunate not to have been sent to Southeast Asia, where US soldiers encountered fiercely determined Viet Cong soldiers who wanted the invaders of their land either dead or gone. As the war heated up, the body bags of dead US soldiers began arriving by the plane loads at military air bases. By the time the war was over there would be more than 50,000 US soldiers who had died in a war that the United States lost. Gravano was one of the fortunate ones: instead of facing the grim realities of combat, he served his 2 years as a cook and was promoted to the rank of corporal. He proved to be a good soldier and was given an honorable discharge. But other than being a cook, Gravano had no professional skills. He returned to the streets of Bensonhurst, where only the life of a mobster beckoned. Gravano responded to its siren call. It was a far more seductive song of recruitment than the US government ever sang.

Being a gangster seemed to be Gravano's most ardent ambition. He first became associated with the Colombo crime family through Anthony Spero and Anthony's uncle Thomas "Shorty" Spero, who paved the way for Gravano to become a full-fledged gangster. Shorty had heard of Gravano's take-no-prisoners, tough-guy reputation and wanted to size him up as a possible recruit. Shorty briefly became a mentor to Gravano and instructed him to carry out a series of crimes. In 1970, the crimes escalated to murder: Shorty ordered Gravano to kill Joseph Colucci (one of Gravano's friends whose wife was having an affair with Shorty's nephew, Anthony). Gravano believed that Colucci was planning to kill him; Gravano, therefore, believed he would be justified in killing Colucci. Here's how Gravano described the hit which took place in a car. Gravano was sitting in the backseat just behind Colucci:

As the Beatles song played, I became a killer. Joe Colucci was going to die. I was going to kill him because I had been ordered to do it and because he was plotting to kill me. I felt the rage inside me. "You fucking cocksucker," I thought. Even if I wasn't directly behind him, I felt invisible. I pointed the gun at the back of his head. Everything went into slow motion. I could almost feel the bullet leaving the gun and entering his skull. It was strange. I didn't hear the first shot. I didn't seem to see any blood. His head didn't seem to move, like it was a blank instead of a real bullet. I knew I couldn't have missed, the gun was only inches from his head, but I felt like I was a million miles away, like this was all a dream.

I shot a second time in the same spot. This time everything was different. I saw the flash. I smelt the gunpowder. The noise was deafening. Now I saw his head jerk back, his body convulse and slip sideways. I saw blood. Joe Colucci was dead. He looked like he was sleeping. He looked peaceful. "You going to blow me away now?" I thought.[1]

Shorty was so impressed with the efficient way Gravano carried out the murder that he told him he would soon be eligible to become a made man, just as soon as the La Cosa Nostra's books were reopened. The books had been closed since 1957, the year of Albert "Mad Hatter" Anastasia's assassination.

Gravano was eager to join; he was strongly motivated by his ambition to become a made man, and he was also motivated by greed. His ambition fed his ruthlessness, which led him higher and higher in the ranks of the Mob. Along the way, he became a mentor to Jack Colucci, the son of the man whom he had murdered.

Gravano was such a highly regarded eager beaver with the Colombo family that he even participated in one of Joe Colombo's picketing demonstrations of FBI headquarters in Manhattan. The demonstration was ostensibly for the agency's alleged anti-Italian persecution of men who had been falsely accused of being Mafia members. Colombo and future boss of the Colombo family Carmine "Junior" Persico thought that Gravano would have a great future in the Mob.

Gravano was on such a fast track in the Colombo family that he aroused the envy of other up-and-coming gangsters. Shorty, in an effort to avoid unnecessary bloodshed between those who were close to him and those who resented Gravano's rapid rise, decided that his protégé should leave the Colombo family and join the Gambinos, which Gravano did. It was a bigger and wealthier family and offered Gravano the kind of largesse that may not have been available with a smaller family.

Although a good portion of Gravano's time was spent pursuing criminal opportunities, including shakedowns, loan-sharking and hijackings, he also devoted himself to weight lifting and boxing. He developed a powerfully muscular physique that was enhanced by steroids. Speaking of Gravano's boxing, Bruce Silverglade, owner of the world famous Gleason's Gym in Brooklyn, said, "Sammy paid for his locker right away. Right on time." Asked if Gravano was a good boxer, he said,

> You have to put him in perspective. He was a businessman. He wasn't a fighter. He was a tough guy. But tough guys aren't going to win fights. . . . You could be a mean, tough guy, it doesn't mean you're a good fighter. . . . My amateurs at his weight are gonna beat him. My pros at his weight are gonna beat him. [With] another business guy, he'd probably hold his own.[2]

In the Gambino family, Gravano found a mentor who taught him how to be a smart gangster, how to think things through and strategize. Anyone could be a hothead and resort to violence to accomplish his goals. But Todd Aurello, who was a capo in his 60s, was like the Vito Corleone figure in *The Godfather*, who understood the value of listening and arriving at a smart decision. He warned Gravano not to take the character of hotheaded Sonny Corleone as a role model. His impulsive reactions got him killed. Gravano was impressed by Aurello, who reminded Gravano of his own father. Gravano stated,

> I really enjoyed being with him. What made me love him more than anything, is that he just reminded me of my father. He had all the same mannerisms. He was small, like my father. The same build, same height. My father was one billion percent legitimate. Todd was a mobster, but the most honorable guy you ever wanted to meet in your life.[3]

Things were going smoothly for Gravano, until another mobster, Michael Hardy, accused Gravano and another mobster, Alley Boy Cuomo, of murdering the Dunn brothers. Now Gravano had to focus on acquitting himself of the murder. To pay the ever-mounting bills of a defense lawyer and an investigator, Gravano went on a robbery spree. "Me and Alley went on a robbing rampage for a year and a half that was unbelievable. We robbed everything that wasn't nailed down."[4]

Aurello was so impressed by Gravano's robberies that he arranged for his protégé to be quickly inducted into the Gambino family. He was one of the first men to be inducted in the newly opened La Cosa Nostra books. Gravano was truly on his way to the top. He was no longer an associate: he was a soldier and looked forward to the day he would be a capo.

As a made man, Gravano had to obey his boss. No matter who he was ordered to kill, he had to do it. If he argued, or refused, he would be the one killed. Gravano, however, faced a dilemma that not many in the mob had to face: Paul Castellano ordered him to kill his brother-in-law Nick Scibetta, who was a cocaine addict and heavy drinker. Scibetta's behavior was often impulsive and violent; he could not be controlled. The Gambino hierarchy believed he posed a potential problem. He couldn't be dishonorably discharged, as in the army. He had to be permanently silenced. Gravano had previously saved Scibetta from being killed by smoothing over situations before they escalated. But smoothing things over was no longer an accepted solution. Scibetta had insulted the daughter of George DeCico, who was the uncle of Gambino member Frank DeCico. George complained to Castellano, who ordered Frank to kill Scibetta. Frank gave the contract to two of Gravano's friends, Louie Milito and Stymie D'Angelo Sr. They told DeCico they could not carry out the hit without first telling Gravano. So DeCico went back to Castellano and got permission to inform Gravano; however, if Gravano objected to the hit, then he would be killed, too. On being told of the contract, Gravano threatened to kill Castellano. DeCico warned him that such an act would not only result in Gravano's death, but also Scibetta's, so why bother. Regardless of what Gravano decided, Scibetta was a dead man.

The bottom line is that I let it happen. That makes me just as guilty. I didn't know his body would be chopped up afterwards.

The cops found his hand somewhere. There was a memorial. I figured my job was to comfort the family as much as possible. What else could I do?[5]

As a made man, the ambitious Gravano moved beyond street crimes and into more lucrative avenues of money making; in particular, he expanded his operations to include numerous aspects of the construction industry, such as plumbing, drywall, cement, and demolition. He was so successful at these enterprises that he rapidly became a multimillionaire. Nevertheless, he continued murdering people. When a motorcycle gang attempted to trash an after-hours club that Gravano owned in Brooklyn, he tracked down the gang's leader and seriously wounded him but not before killing another member of the gang. (The incident is said to have inspired the scene in the movie *A Bronx Tale*, when a motorcycle gang attempts to trash a Mafia bar in the Bronx.)

One of the most infamous murders occurred outside the Plaza Suite Disco. The disco was originally built and opened by Victor Giannini and three other businessmen in Bensonhurst, Brooklyn. It was incorporated under the name Enjoy Yourself, by Victor's son, Joe Giannini, a friend of the author. Joe is a criminal defense attorney and former boxing manager. He said,

It was the biggest club in Brooklyn during the 1970s when the Hustle was popular. It accommodated several hundred people. In a matter of weeks of its opening, Sammy Gravano came in and took the club from my dad. I never met Sammy, though we both used to train and spar at Gleason's Gym: he went in the morning, and I went in the afternoon. My dad told me that Sammy just came in and said he was taking it over. I went to see a client of mine, Jerry Pappa, who ran a crew in Bay Ridge. [Jerry Pappa had been a member of the Rampers with Gravano. He was a fearsome street fighter and known as one of the "baddest bad asses" in Brooklyn.] Two of his crew blindfolded me and drove me to a meeting with Pappa. It took place in a kitchen. He said he would look into it, and I was blindfolded again and driven back to Brooklyn. He came back and told me that Gravano was there. I next went to see Big Al Visconti, the consigliere of the Lucchese Family; he was one of my clients. I met with him every week for sixteen years. He had a sit down with Gravano. Afterward, he told me that I should have come to him earlier. There was nothing he could do, but he did arrange for my dad to get his original investment back. I think it was around thirty thousand.[6]

In *Underboss*, Peter Maas writes,

The disco, housed in a building belonging to Sammy, was originally owned by four businessmen, who formed a corporation in 1979 called Enjoy Yourself, Inc., and obtained a liquor license. Two of them immediately had silent partners, a soldier in the Genovese family whose street name was Salty and a captain in the Colombo family, Vinnie Sicilian. Intimidated by this turn of events, the other two shareholders brought in Sammy for protection and support. This, in effect, granted him a fifty-percent interest in the disco.

Unhappy with what he considered to be sloppy management, Sammy decided to take over the whole operation and got rid of the four original owners. "I just bullied my way in. I said I was going to make them an offer they couldn't refuse."[7]

It all turned sour in 1982 after Frank Fiala decided to rent the disco for a "surprise" party for himself. He was a multimillionaire who owned a garage of expensive cars, a hangar with his private airplane, and a dock for his 41-foot yacht. He also turned out to be a major cocaine dealer and murderer. His check for the rental of the disco bounced and had to be replaced. On the night of the party, Fiala and his partygoers made a mess of the disco, and Gravano told him to leave at 2 a.m. Fiala was insulted but departed. Two days later, he offered to buy the disco. He said he would pay $1 million. He wrote a check for $100,000 as a deposit. He would pay $650,000 in cash under the table, and the rest he promised to pay by check at the closing. The cash would remain undeclared. Before the closing, Fiala took possession of the building and started renovations. Walls came down, holes were drilled, furniture was removed. When Gravano saw what Fiala had done before the closing could take place, he was furious. He confronted Fiala in the office of the disco and told him to leave. Fiala pulled out an Uzi from a desk drawer and called Gravano a greaseball, loudly instructing him to get out. Gravano left his office and waited, along with several of his cohorts on the sidewalk outside of the disco. When Fiala appeared, Gravano called out, "Hey Frank" as a signal for his men to take action. One of Gravano's gunmen fired a bullet into Fiala's head, who slumped to the ground. The gunman then shot out each of Fiala's eyes. Gravano stood over Fiala's body and spit on him. Though the police arrived shortly after the shooting, no one identified the shooters. To make sure he would not be charged, Gravano paid $5,000 to crooked cop Louis Eppolito. However, the notoriety that ensued following the murder caused the IRS to launch an investigation into Gravano's finances. The agency had discovered a cashiers' check for $650,000 that that had been funneled into the account of an armored car company, which deposited it with a bank that gave Gravano the money in $100 bills. At trial, Gravano was represented by famed criminal defense attorney, Gerald Shargel, who won an acquittal for his client. Gravano returned the $100,000 deposit to Faila's widow but kept the cash he had received from the bank.

Gravano's next problem consisted of having to placate his boss, Castellano, who was furious that Gravano had committed an unsanctioned murder. Under Mafia rules, Gravano needed permission to kill someone. If he hadn't been so impatient to hit Fiala, he probably would have been given the go-ahead. He managed to talk his way out of his problem by telling Castellano that he did not say anything because he did not want to involve Castellano in case something went wrong. If Castellano knew about the hit before it went down and it somehow failed, Castellano could be considered complicit. Castellano begrudgingly let Gravano off the hook. Neither Castellano nor Gotti would again interfere with Gravano's murderous activities.

Following Castellano's pardon, Gravano not only continued killing business partners and fellow mobsters, but more importantly for him, he was free to keep enlarging his construction empire. He would come to own one of the most successful construction and cement companies in New York City. He claimed that no big building could be erected without his cement, and those included Donald Trump's buildings. In a 1997 interview on ABC-TV with Diane Sawyer, Gravano stated,

> I literally marvel at the sight of Manhattan when I see it, because I controlled it. I literally controlled Manhattan. When I see it at night—those lights and everything about it—I think of Donald Trump and Tishman and everybody else who couldn't build a building if I didn't want them to build it. That got me off. Plus, I made a lot of money with it.[8]

In a *Page 6* story in the *New York Post* titled "Sammy the Bull Thinks the President Should be a Mob Boss," Gravano was quoted as saying "The country doesn't need a bookworm as president, it needs a mob boss." The former hit man, who confessed to his involvement in 19 murders, said President Trump has to deal with the leaders of North Korea, Iran, and Russia. "You don't need a Harvard graduate to deal with these people. These guys are real gangsters. You need a F**king gangster to deal with these people."[9]

Oliver Coleman and Denis Slattery, in a *New York Daily News* story, reported,

> The daughter of mob rat Sammy (Sammy Bull) Gravano hopes Donald Trump ends up in the White House and makes her dad an offer he certainly wouldn't refuse. Karen Gravano, talking about the GOP front-runner's alleged ties to organized crime, said Tuesday her father would be happy to see Trump call 1600 Pennsylvania Ave. home. "All I can say is maybe he can give his old friend Sammy a f---in' pardon," the VH1 "Mob Wives" star told the *Daily News*.[10]

Trump denied that he was friends with Gravano, and added that, as a far as he could remember, he never met him.

Regardless of who admitted knowing him, Gravano continued to make millions of dollars from his construction and cement business right up until the time he was arrested along with John Gotti and Frank Locascio. After months in jail, Gravano got word to the FBI that he "wanted to change governments." He signed a cooperation agreement with the government that required him to confess to all his previous crimes, including all the murders that he had committed. The government promised him that he would not have to serve more than 20 years, whereas Gotti and Locascio would each get life in prison. Gravano also requested that he not be required to testify against members of his crew and relatives. Though it wasn't part of the formal agreement, it became de facto because he was never required to testify against them. When word got out to the Mob that Gravano had flipped and was sure to testify against Gotti, there was stunned disbelief: Gravano was the highest-ranking mobster to testify against a boss. When the media got hold of the story, they couldn't get enough. Day after day, there were stories in the tabloids about "King Rat" driving nails into the coffin of Gotti's career. Local TV news stories kept showing clips of Castellano's corpse on the ground outside of Spark's Steak House. There were also clips of Gravano and Gotti entering the Ravenite Social Club on Mulberry Street. There was a clip of the two engaged in a walk-and-talk in the rain, Gravano holding an umbrella over the two of them like a Marine protecting the president of the United States against the elements while escorting him to and from Air Force One. Locascio, who was also indicted and subsequently convicted with Gotti, seemed almost an afterthought to the news media.

The FBI had wanted to get Gotti, the "Teflon Don," who had put his thumb in the eye of past prosecution attempts, so badly that they were willing to excuse the 19 murders to which Gravano confessed. At trial, jurors and reporters were riveted, hearing FBI bugged conversations of Gotti confessing to crimes. They were even more enthralled by Gravano's story about how Gotti planned Castellano's murder. No one had previously heard the details of the murderous plot, and the media extensively reported what Gravano had told the court. Gravano testified for 9 days. His memory for details was extraordinary, nearly encyclopedic. For the jury and spectators, it was the best drama in town, better than anything on Broadway, and it attracted a host of celebrities, reporters, and Mob buffs.

During Gravano's testimony, he and Gotti often coldly stared at one another, neither one turning away from the other. They were like two antagonists in a school yard, each trying to outstare the other. The trial lasted 6 weeks, and Gotti began to look defeated as Gravano's testimony went on. The combination of testimony and the FBI bugged conversations were sure to result in a conviction. The jury required only 14 hours to reach guilty verdicts.

Although the men whom Gravano testified against were imprisoned for the rest of their lives, Gravano got a mere 5-year sentence, but because he had already served that amount of time, he was set free. Upon his release, he went into the Witness Protection Program and testified against many members of the Gambino family, resulting in dozens of convictions and additional time added onto already existing prison terms. In addition, Gravano testified against members of the Colombo, DeCavalcante, and Genovese families. Again, his testimony resulted in convictions. In addition, labor union officials, a corrupt cop, and a paid-off juror were all convicted on Gravano's testimony and given prison sentences of varying lengths. He was the best weapon in the government's arsenal for destroying the Mob.

One of the few lawyers who successfully cross-examined Gravano was prominent criminal defense attorney Jay Goldberg, who told the author that he was able to cast such doubt on Gravano's veracity as a witness that jurors discounted his testimony and acquitted his client, Joseph Gambino. In his book, *The Courtroom Is My Theater*, Goldberg quotes law professor John Iannuzzi who wrote in *Cross Examinations: The Mosaic Art*, "If not for defense attorney Jay Goldberg's methodical destruction of Mr. Gravano showing that he was not telling even the same story, no less the truth, then Mr. Gravano would still be selling his versions in the way that 'professional anti-Communists' created testimony to order in the 1950s. Goldberg's client was acquitted."[11] It was one of the few times when Gravano failed to deliver for the prosecution.

Though Gravano continued to say he was finished with crime while in the Witness Protection Program, he returned to a criminal life after leaving the program. He had grown tired of being Jimmy Moran of Tempe, Arizona, operating as a pizza parlor owner and an installer of swimming pools. Gravano missed the life of big money. In 1997, he wrote the story of his life with Peter Maas in a book titled *Underboss*. The families of his murder victims sued him for $25 million; they believed that he should not be able to profit from his crimes by publishing a book about those crimes. At the same time, New York State filed another legal action to seize the profits from *Underboss*, based on a law known as the Son-of-Sam law that prohibits criminals from profiting from their crimes.

Those lawsuits did not dissuade Gravano from criminal activities. Crime had been his life and to it he returned. He partnered with a youth gang, the Devil Dogs, and began selling Ecstasy pills. He was soon caught, and he, his son, his daughter, and 47 gang members were tried and convicted of drug trafficking. Gravano was sentenced to 19 years in prison; his son Gerard received a 9-year sentence, and his wife, Debra, and his daughter, Karen, were each put on probation. Gravano was sentenced to 20 years in a New York State Court, but the sentence was to run concurrent with the one in Arizona. While in prison, Gravano contracted Graves disease, a thyroid disease that results in hair loss as well as fatigue and weight loss. While serving time on the drug charge, Gravano was indicted for a previously undisclosed murder of New York City cop Peter Calabro. The witness who claimed that Gravano gave him the contract was professional hitman, Richard Kurlinksi (aka the Iceman). However, the charges against Gravano were dismissed, following Kurlinski's death because there was no one else to testify against him. Gravano was released from prison on September 18, 2017, which was 18 months before his sentence was supposed to end.

Whatever one might think or say about Gravano, one cannot deny his extraordinary resilience and will to go on living. He has now devoted himself to a legitimate career in the entertainment business. His criminality has come to an end.

14

Vincent "the Chin" Gigante

HE ATTENDED CATHOLIC MASS EVERY SUNDAY; he was a professional boxer in the light heavyweight division and had 25 bouts, losing only four times; and he turned from boxing to crime. But looking at Vincent "the Chin" Gigante, one would not have known that he was the boss of the biggest Mafia family in the United States. To dissuade prosecutors of the likelihood of bringing him to trial, he pretended to be insane, walking around in his Greenwich Village neighborhood, wearing a ratty bathrobe, old bathroom slippers, and mumbling to himself. Nevertheless, federal agents were always looking for indications of Gigante's sanity. One day, without notice, federal agents came calling with a subpoena; they found Gigante in the bathroom of his mother's apartment; he was standing in the bathtub, under a shower of hot water, wearing a bathrobe, galoshes, and holding an umbrella over his head. He smiled at the baffled agents. Yet, his brother Father Louis Gigante, a priest and former New York City Councilman, declared that Vincent was, indeed, crazy. If so, he was as crazy as a fox. Marlon Brando could not have given a more convincing performance of insanity. It was a performance that had federal and local prosecutors befuddled for many years. The performance won him the sobriquet, the "Oddfather." He was the most accomplished method actor in organized crime.

Gigante was born on Sullivan Street in Manhattan's Little Italy on March 29, 1928. His parents, Salvatore and Yolanda, were immigrants from Naples, Italy, who originally settled on Thompson Street. Salvatore made a modest living as a jewelry engraver, and Yolanda was a traditional housewife. Vincent had four brothers: Mario, Pasquale, Ralph, and Louis. All but Louis followed Vincent into the Mob. Louis became a high-profile Catholic priest and was a pastor at St. Athanasius Church in the South Bronx. He had graduated from Georgetown University on a scholarship and shortly thereafter was ordained. As a city councilman and parish priest, he worked diligently on behalf of tenant rights and founded the South East Bronx Community Organization (SEBCO). Father Gigante created 100 jobs and constructed or renovated 1,100 federally subsidized apartments in the Hunts Point section of the Bronx. He stated, "I brought the neighborhood up from ashes to help the people in the South Bronx. There isn't one other organization that can take credit."[1]

To affirm Father Gigante's role in reducing slum conditions in the South Bronx and making the neighborhood livable for thousands of residents, John Cardinal O'Conner, the Archbishop of New York, acclaimed Gigante as a "master builder." Father Gigante's roles as priest, elected member of the New York City Council, and builder never deterred him from vigorously defending his older brother Vincent. He even went so far as to opine that the media defamed Italian Americans by attributing a criminal status to them. In pursuit of his mission to undo what he considered an unjustified and fallacious prejudice against Italians, he appeared at Joseph Colombo's Italian-American Civil Rights demonstration in Columbus Circle in 1971. On the day of the demonstration, Colombo was assassinated. Colombo's assassin was quickly executed by Colombo's bodyguards as mayhem erupted. Seizing control of the moment, Gigante ran to the podium, raised his arms to quiet the crowd, and announced through a microphone that he would lead them in prayers. His actions calmed the crowd as police and ambulances arrived on the scene.

Vincent "the Chin" Gigante could not have had a more vigorous defender of his reputation than Father Gigante. All of Vincent's family rallied to his defense, but it was just that Father Gigante in his various roles had a bigger megaphone than other family members. From his mother, Vincent received a quiet protective love that never ceased. From the time he was a baby, she referred to him as "Chinzeeno," an Italian diminutive of the name Vincenzo. When his boyhood friends heard Vincent's mother call him Chinzeeno (or Cinzeno), they shortened it to "Chin," a name never to be uttered by anyone in the Mafia. If a made man ever referred to him as "Chin," he would be killed. Instead, when referring to him one had either to point to one's chin or make the letter C by curving one's index finger and thumb.

But before he became a big-time gangster, Gigante did small crimes and was often apprehended and either released on probation or served brief stints in jail. It was not until he became a protégé of Vito Genovese that Gigante began making his upward moves in the Mob. His boxing manager, Thomas

"Tommy Ryan" Eboli, had previously opened doors that led Gigante into the presence of the man who wanted to take over the Luciano crime family. Gigante's big opportunity to prove himself to Genovese arrived on the night of May 2, 1957. To prepare for his big night, Gigante packed on the weight, going from muscular 175 pounds to a blubbery 300 pounds. It was a disguise worthy of a character played by Brando or by Robert DeNiro in his role as Jake LaMotta in *Raging Bull*.

Frank Costello, the boss that Genovese wanted to eliminate, was returning to his apartment in the Majestic apartment building on Central Park West. He was followed into the lobby by the bulky hulking assassin, who pointed a .38-caliber revolver at Costello then called out to him, "This is for you, Frank." The invitation caused Costello to turn to his greeter as a bullet grazed one side of his scalp. Thinking that he had succeeded in killing Costello, Gigante ran as quickly as his overweight body was able to move and got into a waiting car. Costello was rushed to Roosevelt Hospital, where he quickly recovered from his superficial but bloody wound. News of the attempted assassination spread as quickly and as suddenly as a lightning strike, so there were reporters en masse at the hospital. Like a pack of hungry wolves, they bayed at Costello, asking if he knew who had shot him. Costello tersely claimed he didn't know. He was devoted to his oath as a made man to maintain omerta.

Shortly after the shooting, Gigante went into hiding in upstate New York. He was fortunate that Genovese didn't have him killed because such a bungled attempt on the life of a Mafia don is usually followed by a death sentence. Genovese did not go into hiding, but he barricaded himself into his home in Atlantic Highlands, New Jersey, where he was guarded round the clock by soldiers in his *borgata*. In addition to bungling the assassination, Gigante made another mistake: he used his own car for his getaway; the license number was noted by a witness; and there were numerous outstanding parking tickets for the vehicle. There was no doubt that Gigante had been the gunman.

However, his fat man's disguise served him well because the doorman of the Majestic described the shooter as immensely fat. The tabloid headlines thereafter began referring to Gigante (who had been identified by his car's registration and parking tickets by the motor vehicle bureau) as the "Waddler" and the "Fat Man." He was also called a "washed-up pug," "fat hanger on," and "low-level criminal."

On August 17, which was 3 months and 15 days after he fired his .38-caliber revolver at Costello's head, a slimmed-down Gigante, clean shaven with his long hair neatly trimmed to a crew cut, walked into a police precinct (known as the Midtown North Precinct) on West 54th Street in Manhattan and asked if he was wanted for questioning in the shooting of Costello. He smiled nonchalantly at the desk sergeant.

At trial, Gigante was represented by a brilliant criminal defense attorney, Maurice Edelbaum. He had previously represented Sonny Franzese, a member of the Colombo family, on a bank robbery indictment, and he later represented Anthony "Tony Pro" Provenzano, a member of the Genovese crime family as well as a member of the Teamsters Union and golfing partner of Richard Nixon.

Gigante's trial was anticlimactic because the doorman could not identify the slimmed-down Gigante. When Edelbaum asked Costello if he knew who had shot him, Costello turned the question around and asked Edelbaum if he knew who shot him. Then added that he didn't know. (Edelbaum revealed to a colleague that if Costello had answered in the affirmative, he would have had a heart attack right on the spot.) As Costello left the witness stand and strode up the aisle to exit the courtroom, Gigante called out to him in a stage whisper, "Thanks a lot, Frank." Shortly after that, Costello decided to retire but was permitted to keep his income from various gambling enterprises he owned in partnership with other mobsters. Gigante was now on his way to the top. However, before he could reach the pinnacle, he and Genovese would be sentenced to prison as heroin drug traffickers. Gigante was sentenced to 7 years in prison but had 2 years shaved off his sentence for good behavior. Genovese was not so fortunate: on April 17, 1959, he was given a term of 15 years in prison and died in the 10th year of his incarceration. He was 71 years old, and his death left a vacuum that brought Gigante closer to sitting on the throne.

Before that could happen other more senior members had to be seated in the position of ultimate power. Following Genovese's death in 1969, Gerard "Jerry" Catena became the boss of the Genovese family. His position didn't last long because in 1970, he was indicted and jailed. In his absence, Thomas "Tommy Ryan" Eboli, who had once been Gigante's boxing manager, became the boss. He owned a number of touristy night clubs and gay bars in New York City. In addition, he owned and distributed jukeboxes and cigarette vending machines. As successful and powerful as he was, Eboli was just fronting for the real bosses: underboss Michele "Big Mike" Miranda and capo Phillip Lombardo. However, Eboli did not like being a mere front man—a straw boss. He was too ambitious to settle for being a goat for the feds; he wanted to be the tiger in charge. To obtain that position, he decided he needed control of a large-scale drug operation. However, he could not finance it on his own and so borrowed $4 million from Carlo Gambino. Eboli acted without sufficient caution, and the FBI got wind of what he was about to accomplish. The feds swooped in and arrested most of Eboli's crew. Learning that Eboli's enterprise had collapsed, Gambino demanded the return of his money. Eboli stalled and ultimately refused to repay the money—a suicidal move. On the night of July 16, 1972, Eboli left his girlfriend's apartment in Crown Heights, Brooklyn at 1 a.m. Eboli strolled to his chauffeur-driven Cadillac.

Driver Joseph Sternfeld held the car door open for his boss, but Eboli never made it inside.

A lone assassin was waiting inside the cab of a red-and-yellow truck, and he sprang into action at the sight of the mobster. His aim was true: Eboli took five bullets in the head. Blood poured from his wounds, red covering the gold crucifix hanging from his neck.

Sternfeld told cops that he dove for cover after the first shot, and never laid eyes on the killer—although later reports indicated he gave up the names of some possible suspects. The hot-headed Eboli was gone. The murder was never solved, with Genovese bigwig Frank "Funzi" Tieri and boss Carlo Gambino—reportedly irate over an unpaid debt—cited as the possible forces behind the hit.[2]

To show their lack of respect for Eboli, none of the bosses or capos from other families attended his funeral at George Washington Memorial Park in Paramus, New Jersey.

Gigante may not have wanted Eboli's death, but it greased the wheels for his ascension from soldier to capo to boss. His power was assured, and he would not let it slip through his fingers. He would not make the same mistakes as his predecessors. He would keep such a low profile that he hoped it would make him nearly invisible. He would secretly meet his capos in any of the three social clubs where he held highly structured meetings. No one could mention his name: each man could either point to his chin when referring to their boss or make the letter C by curving an index finger and thumb. The three clubs that Gigante used for his meetings were the Triangle Social Club at 208 Sullivan Street, the Dante Social Club at 81 Macdougal Street, and the Panel Social Club at 208 Thompson Street, which were all located in Greenwich Village. If those locations did not work out for Gigante, he would meet with associates in his mother's apartment at 225 Sullivan Street.

While Gigante remained an habitué of Greenwich Village, he decided to move his wife and children to a large, comfortable house in Old Tappan, New Jersey. He divided his time between the Village and Old Tappan, and in a move to ensure his safety and that of his family, he regularly sent Christmas gifts of small amounts of money to the local police officers: $20 to one, $15 to another, and each donation enclosed in a Christmas card. Eventually, the gifts were discovered and a hue and cry went up about corrupting the local cops. Gigante was indicted for attempting to bribe the local cops, but it was a flimsy accusation. The donations, his lawyers declared, were comparable to giving the mailman or the garbage man a Christmas gift. Gigante walked away from the indictment without going to trial as he affected the persona of someone who was mentally unstable. It was the beginning of what the FBI called his crazy act, and he became known as the "Oddfather." The chief of police and the four officers to whom Gigante had sent his modest Christmas gifts were all fired.

While Gigante's wife Olympia raised their children in the suburban comforts of Old Tappan, Gigante established another family in an elegant townhouse on the Upper East Side of Manhattan. His paramour was also named Olympia. Gigante would spend nights there, following his daytime meetings in the Village. He would be chauffeured there late at night, often arriving at 2 or 3 a.m. His driver, Vito Palmieri, in an effort to make sure they weren't being followed, drove as if he were a getaway wheelman eluding cops. He drove through red lights, turned the wrong way down one-way streets, and crossed double yellow lines, heading against traffic. He never got in an accident, and Gigante always arrived with no one tailing him.

Gigante also spent a great deal of time with pal and Mob business associate Morris Levy, who owned 900 businesses in the music industry that included Roulette Records, 10 additional labels, the Birdland nightclub and Roulette Room, a chain of 81 record stores, record-pressing and distribution companies, and the contracts of top recording artists. He was known for not paying millions of dollars in royalties to singers he had under contract as well as adding his name to the copyrights for numerous song lyrics that others had written and his singers recorded. Among those who claimed that Levy stole millions of dollars from them were Tommy James of the Shondells, Frankie Lymon of the Teenagers, and Jimmie Rodgers. When popular singers, who were under contract to him, threatened to leave his labels, Levy would threaten them or some cases have them badly assaulted as happened to Jimmie Rodgers. The character of Hesh Rabkin, in *The Sopranos*, was supposedly based on Levy. In December 1988, Levy was convicted of conspiracy to commit extortion; he died of cancer on May 20, 1990, which was 2 months before he was to enter jail.

The recording industry was not the only industry that Gigante and the Genovese family had its hand in: it controlled labor unions, the Fulton Fish Market, the Javits Center, the Coliseum, gambling, and with Sammy Gravano, the Concrete Club and the Waste Paper Association and the Association of Trade Waste Removers of Greater New York. The private carting business was widely known as being controlled by the Mob, and it did so with threats and violence.

Any maverick carter who defied the associations' rulings on carving up routes, selling "stops" to each other, and setting prices would be confronted by teamsters' union headaches and threats of violence and vandalism to equipment. An illegal but ironclad monopolistic regulation by the associations forbade companies from competing with other members for the same customer. All bids and prices for highly profitable "stops" were rigged.[3]

While he controlled so much of the city's industries, Gigante did all that he could to remain under the radar of law enforcement. He was secretive, manipulative, and deceitful; he moved like a shadow in a dark alley. He not only extended his crazy act by periodically checking himself into mental institutions for what his capos called "tune-ups," but he also craftily pushed Fat Tony Salerno into pretending to be the boss of the Genovese crime family. Salerno followed previous Genovese front boss, Frank "Funzi" Tieri. Salerno, who controlled a numbers racket in Harlem worth millions of dollars, was a financial backer for the first heavyweight title fight between Ingemar Johansson and Floyd Patterson in 1959. He was a true Mafioso, who never violated the rules of omerta of La Cosa Nostra. When arrested, he did not say he was just a front for the real boss; Salerno accepted his lot, a stand-up guy, who died in prison on July 27, 1992.

Gigante did not rely on just the silence of members of his *borgata*. To ensure that the government believed he was genuinely mentally unstable and could not possibly be the boss of the wealthiest crime family in the United States, Gigante had numerous highly respected psychiatrists from six major medical schools attest to his condition; they said Gigante suffered from schizophrenia, dementia, and psychosis. And because it was noted that he had been a professional boxer, it was also said that he may have suffered from dementia pugilistica (DP) more commonly known as "punch-drunk syndrome" or "boxer's dementia." It is a form of dementia that results from repeated concussions caused by traumatic blows to the head. It may take up to a decade before a boxer begins showing signs of such dementia and 15 to 20 percent of all boxers develop the condition.

That wasn't all that Gigante relied on. According to Selwyn Raab in his book, *Five Families,*

> Gigante cultivated his penchant for constant vigilance and covertness. He instituted longer testing periods or apprenticeships before inducting members, and he instructed capos and soldiers to conceal as long as possible the identities of prospective soldiers from other families. The secrecy, he thought, would prevent investigators learning from informers about new and possibly vulnerable Genovese inductees. Concealing rookie soldiers from the other *borgatas* would also camouflage the actual strength of the Genovese family in the event of a violent showdown. In another directive, capos were urged to keep a low profile, to avoid being seen in public with him, and to forward all messages through two trusted lieutenants, Quiet Dom Cirillo and Benny Eggs Mangano.[4]

While the FBI was unable to garner information from the social clubs where Gigante did business, they were able to bug his mistress's town house at 67 East 77th Street on the Upper East Side. The feds were able to rent space in an adjoining building and succeeded at placing several bugs in the town house; however, no incriminating talk was ever recorded. But it was ascertained by the lucidity of Gigante's conversations that he wasn't insane.

Then something occurred that Gigante, as clever and secretive as he was, did not anticipate and could not control: it began in 1978, when four of the five Mafia families agreed to take control of the window-replacement business that was worth millions of dollars. The racket that the families put together consisted of winning contracts from the New York City Housing Authority to replace windows in apartment buildings throughout New York City. Each of the four families designated a representative to carry out the scheme. The Lucchese family was central to the scheme because it had control of Local 580 of the Iron Workers Union, whose members were essential to the tasks ahead. The Mob, through bribery, extortion attempts, and sweetheart deals was able to control the scheme. Those who could not be bought off were threatened or beaten into submission. If a window company refused to acquiesce, its property was damaged or completely destroyed. Once all the elements of the operation were in place, the Mob was able to charge a tax of $1 to $2 for each window sold and replaced and that included windows in publicly owned housing as well as those in privately owned buildings. Eventually the mob had won $150 million in contracts from the New York City Housing Authority. It was an impressive outcome.

While he gave directions to his top capos in private, Gigante continued to act like a crazy man when out on the streets of his neighborhood. To make sure the windows racket continued to operate smoothly, he had chosen three members of his *borgata* to oversee the family's interest in the operation: they were underboss Venero Mangano, soldier Gerard Pappa (formerly a Colombo family associate), and associate Peter Savino. Gigante believed he could rely on all three without having to worry about their loyalty and discretion, but he had made a fatal mistake; Savino was confronted by FBI agents who presented him with incontrovertible evidence that he had participated in six murders, and when convicted, he would no doubt spend the rest of his life in prison. If, however, he agreed to cooperate and testify, he would be granted leniency. Savino decided to save himself and agreed to become an informant. For the next 2 years, Savino ingratiated himself with Gigante, becoming an ever more trusted associate; during that time, he wore a wire, recording all of his transactions with his boss. While some Genovese capos did not trust Savino and warned Gigante to stay away from him, Gigante ignored their warnings. He completely trusted Savino, who continued to wear a wire.

Gigante was indicted for racketeering, murder, and conspiracy. He went on trial and Savino was called to testify. Savino kept his side of the bargain with the feds. He testified after being placed in the Witness Protection Program. He was dying of cancer and in considerable pain, yet he continued with devastating testimony.

When he testified in July at the trial of Mr. Gigante, who was convicted of murder-conspiracy and racketeering charges, Mr. Savino was reported to be gravely ill with cancer—so ill that the judge, Jack B. Weinstein, ruled that Mr. Savino did not have to testify at the Federal courthouse in Brooklyn, where the trial was held, but could testify through closed-circuit television from an undisclosed location in another state. In some of the most dramatic moments of the month long trial, participants and spectators in the downtown Brooklyn courtroom watched the gaunt, often profusely sweating figure as he appeared on television screens in the courtroom.

"I need to stop a minute now, guys," he said at one point, leading to one of several recesses he requested. "I got to take a break, please," he said at another point, and a prosecutor who was with him said, "The witness is in a lot of pain."

But Mr. Savino's voice was loud and clear as, for a day and a half, he told of dealings with Mr. Gigante that he said went back to at least 1980 and lasted until 1987. That is when Mr. Savino agreed to become an informer for the Government.

One of the charges on which Mr. Gigante was convicted was conspiring to kill Mr. Savino after he agreed to help the Government.

Mr. Savino's most important testimony, in the Gigante trial and in earlier trials, had to do with a lucrative, decade long racket: Prosecutors said Mr. Gigante and the bosses of other Mafia groups led a scheme in which the mob skimmed millions of dollars in Government funds from window-installation contracts in New York City public housing. Mr. Savino was a central figure in the bid-rigging scheme, in which, he testified, he represented Mr. Gigante's Genovese crime family.[5]

Savino's testimony was amplified and confirmed by Salvatore "Sammy the Bull" Gravano, former underboss and consigliere of the Gambino crime family; Alphonse "Little Al" D'Arco, former boss of the Lucchese family; and Phil Leonetti, former underboss of the Philadelphia Mob. All three averred that Gigante never would have been considered a boss if he were truly insane. On July 25, 1997, Gigante was found guilty of racketeering and conspiracy. He was sentenced to 12 years in prison by Judge Weinstein, who defined Gigante's reign in the Genovese family as "decades of vicious criminal tyranny."

The law, however, was not finished with Gigante: in 2002, he was indicted for still leading the Genovese family from prison and for delaying his previous trial for 7 years by feigning insanity, an act that he continued to perform in prison. Gigante's son Andrew was also indicted for being a courier of his father's messages to mobsters in New York. On April 7, 2003, Gigante surprised the court by lucidly confessing that he had conned doctors and others into believing he was insane. As a result, the government dropped a racketeering indictment for running the family business from prison and imposed an additional 3 years on his prison sentence, rather than the 20 years that could have been imposed. His son, Andrew, pled guilty to racketeering and agreed to a plea bargain. He was sentenced to 2 years in prison and ordered to pay a $2 million fine. Gigante's plea deal not only won a reduced sentence for his son but also exempted all of his relatives from prosecution for helping him in his insanity charade.

Gigante died in prison on December 19, 2005. His funeral service took place at Church of St. Anthony of Padua, which is appropriately located at 155 Sullivan Street, just down the street in Greenwich Village, where Gigante spent all his years other than his nights on East 77th Street. The Village had been his home, and it was appropriate he be returned there. His ashes are interred in the National Historic Landmark Green-Wood Cemetery in Brooklyn, the final resting place of many the city's luminaries, good and bad, including Leonard Bernstein, Joey Gallo, and Boss Tweed.

15

Crazy Joey Gallo: Counterculture's Romanticized Gangster

Joey Gallo inspired both admiration and satire. Bob Dylan and Jacques Levy wrote a paean of a song titled "Joey" that won both plaudits and harsh criticism. Lester Bangs, called America's Greatest Rock Critic by Jim DeRogatis, said that the song was "repellent romanticist bullshit."[1]

Legions of others, however, have loved the song and regard it as a lasting tribute to a misunderstood man who attempted to reform his life but was gunned down before he could prove himself.

Jimmy Breslin took another tack and wrote a satirical novel titled *The Gang That Couldn't Shoot Straight*. Its satirical protagonist is a character based on Gallo and named Kid Sally Palumbo. The book was the basis of a movie with the same title, and Jerry Orbach played Palumbo and Robert DeNiro played conman Mario Tratino. Palumbo's portrayal in the movie annoyed Gallo because it not only presented him as inept, but the name Palumbo sounded too similar to Colombo, and Joseph Colombo was one of Gallo's most hated enemies. Peter "Pete the Greek" Diapoulas, Gallo's bodyguard and boyhood pal, sarcastically commented, "The whole thing was funny. The Profaci war was just a bunch of laughs. Well, Breslin should have spent one night with us, found out what it would feel like if some Profaci clipped him in the ass. Even with a small Baretta, he wouldn't be fucking laughing."[2]

Gallo was born April 7, 1929 to Umberto and Mary Gallo in the Red Hook section of Brooklyn. During the Great Depression, it was one of the grimmest neighborhoods in Brooklyn, beset by poverty and crime. It had originally been a neighborhood of Irish families whose men worked on the docks as longshoremen. The longshoremen were called in each day for "shape-up" during which they would be chosen to load and unload cargo ships. The work was hard, and the pay was minimal. Over the years, the Irish achieved greater financial security and began to leave the neighborhood. As they moved out, the Italians, many of whom were immigrants, moved in. The Gallos were one of the families that followed in the wake of the departing Irish. The Red Hook neighborhood became a criminal training ground for Joey and his two brothers, Larry and Albert "Kid Blast," but not for the boys' only sister Carmella. During Prohibition, their father had been a bootlegger with limited success, and he encouraged his sons to be mobsters, to never back down from a fight, and to eliminate whatever competition they encountered.

Other than his father, Gallo found inspiration and a role model in the career of Albert "Mad Hatter" Anastasia, who as cohead of Murder Inc., left a trail of dozens of bloody corpses throughout New York. Anastasia's brother Anthony "Tough Tony" Anastasio (he spelled his last name with an o) controlled the Brooklyn waterfront docks through the International Longshoreman's Association (ILA). Tough Tony's power and presence were known to all throughout Red Hook and wherever ships were loaded and unloaded of cargo on the East coast. No one who wanted to work on the docks rebelled against him. He may not have been a role model for Gallo, but his power was undeniable and Gallo respected it.

Gallo's other inspiration was a fictional movie character portrayed by Richard Widmark in the movie *Kiss of Death*. The character is named Tommy Udo, a psychopathic killer who maniacally laughs at his own acts of cruelty. Gallo memorized many of Udo's lines and enjoyed repeating them to friends. Two of Udo's more memorable lines: "I wouldn't give you the skin off a grape," and "You know what I do to squealers? I let 'em have it in the belly, so they can roll around for a long time thinkin' it over. You're worse than him, tellin' me he's comin' back? Ya lyin' old hag!" This last utterance was following by Widmark's maniacal laugh.

In 1950, following one of his arrests, Gallo was sent to Kings County Hospital Center where he was diagnosed as being schizophrenic. According to Anthony Colella, who grew up in Red Hook and knew the Gallo brothers; they were a wild bunch. Colella was about 15 years younger than the Gallos but watched them much as the young boy Colagero in *A Bronx Tale*, watches the gangster named Sonny, played by Chazz Palminteri. Colella said,

> The Gallos had a social club on President Street called Longshore Rest; I think it was owned by Umberto, who his sons used to call the Old Man. The guys in the neighborhood used to go in there and gamble. The Gallo boys were known as the big boys. We were little guys, and we all aspired to be the big boys one day. And some of the neighborhood kids did, in fact, go into the gangs. I worked in a pastry shop after school, and I would deliver pastries to the guys in the Long-

shore Rest, and they would tip me. One of the guys in the neighborhood, who went into the mob, was Bobby Boriello. He started out with the Gallos then went into the Gambino Family and became John Gotti's driver. His younger brother, Stevie, was a friend of Joey's.

I think that Joey was a paranoid schizophrenic, but his paranoia only became evident if strangers came into the neighborhood. I remember once there was a shout-out on the corner of Columbia and Union Streets between local guys and guys who had invaded the neighborhood. It was territorial. In our neighborhood, Joey seemed normal. He and his brother used to buy me and the other younger kids pizzas and ice cream. They were very nice to us, and the kids liked them, looked up to them. Joey and his brother owned a lounge, where there was a bar and dancing. It had a juke box with all the latest songs. In fact, Joey was called Joey Juke Box because he controlled all the juke boxes in the neighborhood. Not only juke boxes, but also cigarette, candy, and gum vending machines. He made the merchants take his machines; they had no choice.[3]

Joey graduated from neighborhood mobster to enforcer and hit man for Joe Profaci, boss of the Profaci crime family. Profaci founded his family in 1928 and reigned as its leader for 30 years; following his death, it became known as the Colombo crime family. While Profaci made millions of dollars through typical Mafia enterprises, such as loan-sharking, extortion, and protection rackets, he also had a highly successful olive oil business. In fact, it was so successful that he became known as the Olive Oil King. The business also provided him with an opportunity to file federal tax returns from a legitimate business, so he wouldn't wind up like Al Capone, who was nailed for income tax evasion. Nevertheless, the IRS sued Profaci in 1953 for $1.5 million in unpaid taxes. Nine years later, Profaci died and his taxes remained unpaid.

In 1957, Carlo Gambino, who wanted to take over the Anastasia family, gave Profaci the contract to kill his boss, Anastasia. Profaci, who had come to rely on the Gallos as efficient hit men, was so impressed by their abilities that he gave them the contract. The Gallos, in turn, were joined in their endeavor by Carmine Persico. Anastasia was assassinated while sitting in a barber's chair in the Park Sheraton Hotel; soon thereafter, Gallo referred to his hit team as the barbershop quintet.

Though Profaci was grateful the deed was carried out, he remained miserly when it came to rewarding the Gallos. Nevertheless, the Gallos agreed to carry out another hit for Profaci. Frank Abbatemarco, a Profaci bookmaker, stopped paying tribute to his boss. Profaci demanded payment of $50,000. Abbatemarco refused. Profaci then told the Gallos that if they killed the bookmaker, they would inherit his rackets. Following the murder, Profaci refused to keep his promise and the Gallos received nothing.

Infuriated by Profaci's miserliness and duplicity, the Gallos decided that there was only one way to get even: they would kidnap and hold for ransom the top echelon of the Profaci family. Their victims were Joe Magliocco, underboss and Profaci's brother-in-law; capo Colombo, and three other capos. Profaci, fearing he might also be targeted, retreated to a hospital in Miami, Florida. Eager to have his men released, Profaci agreed to share more of the family's wealth with the Gallos, who then released their hostages. Profaci's promise, however, was written on water. Not trusting the Gallos and deciding to eliminate them as a possible threat, Profaci enticed Persico back into the family with promises of greater wealth. Persico then asked Larry Gallo to meet him at the Sahara Lounge, a Brooklyn bar. While sitting at the bar, Larry was set upon by two men who attempted to strangle him. They would have succeeded, but just as the cord was closing off Gallo's windpipe, a cop entered the bar and surprised the two thugs. They immediately let go of the rope and fled out a back door. Larry was left with a scar on his neck but still breathing.

Bullets would now fly as the two sides declared war on one another. One of the more dramatic events occurred after Joseph "Joe Jelly" Gioiello, Joey's bodyguard, was last seen heading to a fishing boat in Sheepshead Bay. Later that day, Joe Jelly's clothing was thrown from a car and landed with a thud in front of a restaurant where the Gallos were dining. Joe Jelly's clothing was stuffed with dead fish, a resonant symbol from *The Godfather* when Sonny and crew learned that Luca Brasi was sleeping with the fishes. (When it comes to the Mob, life imitates art and art imitates life.)

The Gallo war would continue unabated, taking the lives of gangsters on both sides. Finally outnumbered and outgunned, the Gallos lost the largest number of soldiers. Carlo Gambino and Thomas "Three-Finger Brown" Lucchese attempted to convince Profaci to make peace with the Gallos, but Profaci thought that the two big crime bosses were attempting to take over his family with the possible help of the Gallos. He refused to cooperate, so Lucchese and Gambino went back to their own enterprises, even though the battles that raged were hurting their business and bringing too much attention to what was supposed to be a secret society.

The war was a financial drain on the Gallo faction; the gang needed new sources of income. Determined to generate a regular flow of cash wherever possible, Gallo finagled some no-show jobs for his crew at several small Brooklyn businesses. One was a bowling alley, where the owner was induced to provide a weekly stipend for several of the Gallo men.

During this period Gallo married a former Las Vegas showgirl named Jeffie Lee Boyd. But that didn't get in the way of him organizing a new money-producing racket: he pretended to represent a union of bartenders and went around to local bars, demanding $30 a week to prevent damage and possible injury. He extorted numerous bars in Brooklyn and then branched out to

Manhattan. There, one owner defied Joey and reported the threats to the district attorney's office. The owner was subsequently wired and then met with Gallo in a restaurant in Little Italy. As soon as Gallo issued his threats, cops descended on the surprised mobster. They cuffed Gallo and led him off to jail. He was arraigned and eventually tried. With evidence against him on tape, Gallo was convicted of extortion and sentenced to 10 years in prison. That same year Profaci died of liver cancer and was buried in St. John Cemetery in Middle Village, Queens, New York, a popular resting place for numerous gangsters. With the two belligerents no longer on the field of battle, a truce went into effect, ending the Gallo-Profaci War.

Gallo would serve his time in three prisons: Green Haven Correctional Facility in Beekman, New York; Attica Correctional Facility in Attica, New York; and Auburn Correctional Facility in Auburn, New York. At Auburn, Gallo embarked on a course of self-education, reading many of the great books in the Western Canon, including works by Franz Kafka, Ernest Hemingway, Albert Camus, Jean-Paul Sartre, and most importantly for him, Machiavelli's *The Prince*. In addition to his readings, Gallo began to paint watercolors, and many of his paintings still hang in the offices at Auburn.

While incarcerated at Attica, Gallo had befriended and tutored a number of African American criminals, one of whom was Nicky Leroy Barnes. Following his release from prison, Gallo wanted to have a presence in the Harlem drug trade, and so he tutored Barnes about how to run a drug-trafficking enterprise. He also asked Barnes to assemble the necessary personnel to run such an operation. He told Barnes that on his own release from prison, he would hire a lawyer to get Barnes's conviction overturned, which is exactly what happened. Gallo also made sure that numerous African American criminals were brought into his crew by Albert "Kid Blast" Gallo, following his brother Larry's death from cancer.

Upon his release from prison on April 11, 1971, Gallo was invited to meet with Colombo, the new head of what had been the Profaci family, which was now named the Colombo family. In attendance was Joseph "Joe Yac" Yacovelli, the family's consigliere. Gallo said he never agreed to the peace between the Gallos and Profaci (thus implying a threat of renewed warfare) and now felt he was entitled to a $100,000 settlement of their dispute and for the years he had spent in prison. (His additional implication was that the $100,000 would buy a permanent cease-fire.) Colombo regarded Gallo as a has-been with no gang to back him up. So instead of the $100,000, Colombo offered Gallo $1,000 to pay for a welcoming-home party. Gallo scorned the offer as an insult to his status as a feared gangster.

Though Colombo didn't think that Gallo represented much of a threat, he was not going to take any chances because Joey was still known as Crazy Joey

Gallo and could be reckless in pursuit of his goals. So just to be on the safe side, Colombo issued a contract on Gallo's life but still hoped that Gallo's new persona as a budding intellectual would lesson Gallo's drive to do something crazy.

Gallo's new persona was a credible façade that hid the reality of what being a gangster meant. He developed friendships among admirers in show business, such as Jerry Orbach and David Steinberg. Orbach had played the role of Palumbo in *The Gang That Couldn't Shoot Straight*, and though Gallo hated the movie, he enjoyed speaking with Orbach about acting on Broadway and in the movies. He also became friends with Orbach's wife, Marta, to whom he confessed that he was completely reformed and writing a memoir. His celebrity friends regarded him as if he were a character out of Damon Runyon's *Guys and Dolls*, a charming rascal who had learned to live in the straight world and shed his Mafia past. After seeing the movie *The Godfather*, Joey felt that show business offered a new opportunity to enrich himself by selling his story to Hollywood. As an aspiring Hollywood entrepreneur, he began hanging out in such celebrity haunts as Elaine's on the Upper East Side. There, one could see Woody Allen, Mia Farrow, Norman Mailer, Mario Puzo, Clint Eastwood, Mick Jagger, Willie Nelson, Leonard Bernstein, Jackie Kennedy Onassis, and many others. To rub shoulders with such luminaries never would have happened in Gallo's preprison days in Red Hook. Celebrity was an irresistible siren call for Gallo, and he fell under its considerable charms. He was as much a seducer as one who is seduced. He could charm the brightest luminaries to shine their radiance on him and then reflect it back to them. He envisioned all the benefits that could possibly accrue to him for as long he could keep the world fascinated in the persona of the reformed gangster.

How could such a celebrity endanger his new role in society by continuing to be a Mafia hit man? It was absurd, and so Colombo continued to be out in public as if there were no threats to his life. Colombo must have felt further assured that Gallo no longer thought of himself as a Red Hook gangster when Gallo moved from his old stomping grounds to an apartment in Greenwich Village and began hanging out at the Eighth Street Bookshop. In addition to attending celebrity parties, Gallo seemed more interested in philosophy than Mob activities. If this new role was mere window dressing, then Gallo was a convincing actor. Mobsters all over the city could finally believe that the Gallo-Profaci Wars were history, and—as a result—there would be no more negative publicity.

Negative publicity, however, could rear its ugly head at any moment, and on June 28, 1971, Italian-American shopkeepers throughout the city were instructed to close their stores for a celebratory Italian-American Unity event. Angelo Parisi's widowed mother owned a pizza parlor in Queens and refused to close her store for the day. Her family relied on the income from the store, and she could not afford to close it. When Colombo's people learned she was a widow working hard to make ends meet, they permitted her store to remain open. Other Italian-Americans would pour into Columbus Circle to raise their voices in support of the Italian-American Civil Rights League and its leader, Colombo.

The underworld, however, got a rude shock on that sunny June day. And the publicity that followed caused a certain amount of agita. There, in Columbus Circle, Colombo was mixing with the crowd, shaking hands and greeting well-wishers. As he approached the podium to speak to the crowd, a poor African American named Jerome Johnson, who had been posing as a newspaper photographer, pulled out an automatic pistol and shot Colombo three times, hitting him in the neck and head. Mayhem ensued, and Johnson was rapidly brought down by bullets fired by one of Colombo's bodyguards. Colombo would linger in a vegetative state until May 22, 1978, when he died of a heart attack that doctors said resulted from his original wounds.

Almost immediately afterward, the Colombo family concluded that Gallo had been responsible for the hit. After all, he not only did not accept the peace that was supposed to have ended the Gallo-Profaci Wars, but he had befriended African American criminals while in prison and then recruited them into his gang. He was also sufficiently reckless to have engineered such a hit, they said. It was likely that he offered money and a promise of a position in his rackets to Johnson for taking out Colombo. The police agreed with the Colombos that Gallo was responsible for the hit.

> The hit on Colombo, detectives theorized, was intended to clear the way for Gallo's comeback. A pariah in the Colombo family, Gallo had much to gain from the boss's elimination, and [Chief of Detectives Albert] Seedman believed that the assassination attempt bore Crazy Joe's peculiar trademark. "Gallo had earned his nickname by striking when his victims least expected," Seedman stressed. "He was also right in character by going for the top of the same family he had attacked in 1960, when Joe Profaci was the don."
> Called in for questioning, Gallo maintained he had no knowledge about Johnson or about the shooting, insisting that he had straightened out his life. While appearing carefree, Gallo nevertheless kept a bodyguard close by, usually the burly Peter "Pete the Greek" Diapoulas, a crony since their schoolboy days.[4]

Many Mob historians and insiders didn't go along with the theory that Gallo was responsible for the hit. It was well-known in Mob circles that Carlo Gambino, though he had originally supported Colombo as boss of the Profaci family, was appalled at all the publicity that Colombo and his Italian-American Civil Rights League was generating. The Mafia is supposed to be a secret organization, and its bosses should operate in the shadows and not in the beam of a spotlight, which was all right for movie stars, singers, and co-medians but not for Mob bosses. Gambino had called Colombo to a meeting and told him to disband the league and call off all demonstrations and rallies. Colombo refused, turning his back on Gambino. Shortly thereafter, Johnson supposedly visited one of the Gambino social clubs and was given the con-tract to hit Colombo. That an African American had hit Colombo would lead everyone to believe that Gallo had organized the hit. If true, it was typical of Gambino's clever and deceptive tactics. However, it's just a theory and no one has ever proved it.

The theory didn't matter to the Colombo hierarchy: Yacovelli, Persico, and other members. A contract was issued on Gallo's life.

On the night of April 7, 1972, Gallo threw a 43rd birthday party for him-self at the famed Copacabana Nightclub, which was once owned by Frank Costello. Accompanying Gallo was his wife of 3 weeks, Sina Essary and her daughter Lisa; his sister Carmella; Jerry and Marta Orbach; David Steinberg and his date; and Broadway columnist Earl Wilson. On stage, Don Rickles mercilessly ribbed Gallo, who laughed at jokes that others may have found in-sulting. The comedian and the gangster even toasted one another. The Copa closed at 4:00 a.m., and Gallo invited everyone to continue the party down-town; he was still hungry and wanted to get something to eat in Chinatown. The Orbachs, Steinberg and his date, and Rickles begged off. So Gallo, his wife and her daughter, his sister, his bodyguard "Pete the Greek," and Pete's date piled into Gallo's Cadillac and drove to Chinatown. There, they couldn't find a restaurant that was still open at that time, so they drove to Little Italy, just a few blocks away. On Mulberry Street, the lights of Umberto's Clam House were bright in the dark night. The Cadillac pulled up in front of the restau-rant, which was owned by Genovese capo Matthew "Matty the Horse" Ian-niello. The Gallo party got out of the car, entered the nearly empty restaurant, where only one man was having a drink at the bar. The Gallo party sat at one of the restaurant's butcher block tables. Gallo and Diapoulas sat with their backs to the door, an unusual arrangement, especially for mobsters who could at any moment be targets for assassination. Gallo, however, was arrogantly self-confident, believing that no one would venture to kill such as high-profile celebrity gangster, especially in Little Italy. Gallo ordered shrimps and clams and a bottle of Chianti.

The man at the bar was unknown to Gallo and his bodyguard. He was Jo-seph Luparelli, a Mob wannabe and sometime associate and gofer. Luparelli immediately recognized Gallo and quickly finished his drink. He left the bar and strode to a nearby Colombo family hangout just a few blocks away. There, he found four Colombo soldiers. He told them that the crazy one and his family were eating at Umberto's. One of the Colombo men phoned Yacovelli, who allegedly gave the order to whack Gallo. The four Colombo soldiers and Luparelli drove in two cars to Umberto's. One of the men quickly exited a car, walked to the restaurant, and flung open the door. He then began firing at Gallo with an automatic pistol. The women screamed and everyone dove to the floor. Gallo quickly overturned the butcher block table, providing a shield to his wife, her daughter, and his sister. He drew his own gun and began firing at the gunman, but Gallo was hit in one elbow and a bullet lodged in one cheek of his ass. As the gunman turned and left the restaurant, Gallo ran toward the door. Out on the street, he collapsed on the sidewalk, having been hit in the back by a third bullet that severed an artery. Diapoulas, who had once sarcastically told a reporter it would be no fun to be shot in the ass, even with a small Baretta, was shot in the ass. Yet, he too managed to stagger out onto the sidewalk where he fired several shots at the getaway car as it sped north on Mulberry Street.

Police cars soon arrived and Gallo was placed on a stretcher and delivered to a nearby hospital. He died in the emergency room from a loss of blood.

Luparelli and the four Colombo men drove to Yacovelli's apartment on the East Side and from there to a safe house in Nyack, New York. The five hid out there, but Luparelli grew increasingly uneasy, believing that as a witness he would eventually be silenced. After 5 days of hiding, Luparelli left the house, drove to Newark airport, where he boarded a plane to southern California; there, he spent some time with relatives. He realized that the Mob, if they wanted to, would track him down and kill him. He decided that the only way he could save himself was to contact the FBI, offer to be a witness, and then go into the Witness Protection Program. He disappeared into the program, shedding his previous identity, and he was never heard of again. No one was ever prosecuted for the Gallo killing. The district attorney figured that Luparelli's testimony, uncorroborated, would be insufficient to win a conviction. The four Colombo men and Yacovelli were never charged. Yacovelli moved to Florida, and Gallo's surviving brother, Albert, became a member of the Genovese family. The Catholic Church denied Gallo a funeral mass, so his wife arranged for a priest to be flown in from Cleveland, and he performed the burial service. The funeral could have been staged for a Hollywood movie:

> The scene there had an authenticity that was almost theatrical. From the brownstones along Clinton Avenue, old women stared in black shawls. Men in working clothes muttered to one another in Old World accents. Inside, under a lithograph of Christ, rested a $55,000 burnished bronze casket festooned with flowers and surrounded by heavy, silently angry men and weeping women. Within it lay Joey Gallo, assassinated three days before as he celebrated his 43rd

birthday in a Lower East Side clam house called Umberto's. His mother keened: "My Joey! What did they do to my Joey!"

The cortege, led part of the way by a police car with a flashing dome light, slowly toured Gallo's old President Street neighborhood, then drove to Brooklyn's Greenwood Cemetery. Police and federal agents were among the spectators. An unusually large number of gravediggers and an out-of-place olive-drab telephone van were on hand. The mourners filed by, dropping single roses onto the casket and crying: "Take him, Big Boy! You've got him now, Big Boy!" Big Boy meant God.

In its baroque atmospherics, the Gallo assassination was more than merely an episode of gangster nostalgia. As Gallo lay in his open casket, his face a mask of mortuary perfection, his sister Carmella promised: "The streets are going to run red with blood, Joey."[5]

Albert A. Seedman, the head of New York's detective bureau, called Gallo "That little guy with steel balls."[6]

16

Harlem Nights

W HEN ONE REFERS TO MOBSTERS, one thinks of Italian and Jewish gangsters. But African Americans were also some of the most colorful gangsters of the 20th century. Several became celebrities, and their stories were told in books and romanticized movies. Among the most colorful and high-profile ones were Stephanie St. Clair, known as "Queenie" for being Harlem's Queen of Numbers or the Numbers Queen of Harlem; Ellsworth Raymond "Bumpy" (named for the bump on the back of his head) Johnson; Frank Lucas, innovative international drug smuggler; and Leroy Nicholas Barnes, the drug king of Harlem and other neighborhoods. In addition to being drug traffickers, Johnson and Barnes became poets while serving prison terms.

Madame Stephanie St. Clair (invariably referred to as "Madame") was the toughest female racketeer in Harlem. She was a resourceful woman who would not give in to the insatiably greedy demands of the notorious gangster Dutch "the Dutchman" Schultz, who wanted to take over her numbers operation. Schultz, who had made millions as a bootlegger during Prohibition, needed a new racket when Prohibition ended in 1933. Through threats and violence, he forced all of the men who controlled numbers in Harlem to work for him; they became mere vassals. He not only paid each of them meager salaries of $200 a week, instead of the thousands that they had previously been making, but he also cheated them out of their commissions. St. Clair, however, remained beyond Schultz's grasp. She refused to knuckle under: one time, when Schultz sent some of his thugs to beat up St. Clair, she hid in a coal cellar until the threat passed. She emerged covered in coal dust, but she maintained control of her numbers operation. Shortly thereafter, St. Clair tipped off the cops to the locations of the Schultz's illegal betting operations, and the cops seized more than $12 million of his receipts. How much went into their pockets and how much wound up as government property has never been ascertained, but St. Clair believed the cops personally profited from their raids. She and Schultz made paying off the cops their cost of doing business. After Schultz was gunned down in a chop house in Newark, New Jersey, in 1935 on the orders of the National Crime Commission and lay dying in a hospital, he received a telegram from St. Clair that contained a brief message from Galatians: "As ye sow, so shall ye reap."

St. Clair retired shortly after that and in the late 1930s, she married Sufi Abdul Hamid, who was known as the Black Hitler because of his pro-Nazi activities and his vitriolic anti-Semitism. Their marriage foundered after St. Clair learned that Hamid was having an affair with a fortune-teller who used the name Fu Futam and that Hamid was embezzling some of St. Clair's money. Hamid was shot to death, and St. Clair was convicted of shooting him. Tried and found guilty, she served a 10-year sentence in the Bedford Hills Correctional Facility for Women. Following her release from prison, she became an ardent civil rights activist.

St. Clair lived a tough, colorful life and was esteemed by many of her Harlem neighbors, who admired her entrepreneurial capacity to maintain her numbers business while refusing to submit to Schultz, a detested white gangster, who was regarded as an invader of Harlem territory. She was also admired for standing up for the civil rights of her community and criticizing the police for acts of brutality. St. Clair, much to her community's sadness, died in 1969, at age 73. It was noted in some obituaries that she had been a vital member of the community, and some said it was too bad that the woman who had been born on Christmas Eve didn't die on Christmas day. She is buried in the historic cemetery of Trinity Church in Manhattan, the same church burial site where Alexander Hamilton was laid to rest; they were both born in the West Indies.

Ellsworth "Bumpy" Johnson would one day encounter St. Clair and their lives would periodically intertwine. Johnson was born in the historically picturesque town of Charleston, South Carolina, in 1905. His family, like many other poor black families, was treated with humiliating condescension by most of the white populace. Blacks knew their place in that society, and if they acted uppity, they could be beaten or lynched. It is little wonder, then, that Johnson, who refused to bow down to the Jim Crow customs of the time, became an insolent and often belligerent teenager. He frequently got into fights with white kids, and his behavior so worried his parents that they thought young Johnson would be better off in a more tolerant society than the one in Charleston. As far as his parents knew, there was no Jim Crow prejudice in Harlem. They figured that once settled in Harlem, Johnson's hot temper would cool and his quick resort to violence would mellow. Johnson's parents believed that Harlem was a community where blacks could live side by side and undisturbed. At the very least, Johnson would not be a potential target for lynching while living in Harlem. So the family scraped together the fare for their 14-year-old son to go north to live with his older sister, Mabel.

Removed from the restrictive environment of the south, Johnson felt free to pursue new opportunities, and without parental rules, there was no net to curtail his actions; he became a free-wheeling boy of the streets. By 15, he was a member of a gang that committed burglaries. It didn't take long for Johnson to meet St. Clair. The woman took a liking to rough-hewn Johnson, and within a few years, he became her employee.

An aspiring gangster, Johnson could not have had a better teacher than St. Clair. As he learned the ropes of the numbers racket and displayed an intimidating capacity to use violence, he was promoted to be St. Clair's enforcer. Anyone who threatened St. Claire would either be battered into bloody surrender or cut up with a straight razor. Wherever he went, Johnson never left home without his razor. During her conflict with Schultz, St. Clair sent Johnson to break up the store fronts where Harlem's former independent numbers racketeers were now operating as Schultz's employees. A war ensued between the factions, and it did not end before Schultz died.

When St. Clair decided to retire, rumors on the street were that Johnson had forced her out of the numbers business. It was a palace coup, and he had proven tougher than his patron. Others thought she had grown tired of the racket and turned it over to Johnson, who promised to pay her a percentage of the business for the rest of her life. Because there were no IRS audits of her books and no corporate minutes, there was no clarification.

St. Clair's retirement provided an auspicious beginning for Johnson's ambitions. Johnson found a more agreeable partner in Lucky Luciano than St. Clair would have found in Schultz, assuming the two could have ever come to an agreement. Having taken over some of Schultz's rackets, Luciano decided that the gambling income from Harlem should be shared by the Mob. Meyer Lansky approved. Lansky and Luciano had always been partners in gambling ventures, and the large number of Harlem customers was too inviting to pass up. Luciano offered Johnson a deal he couldn't refuse, and the two embarked on a de facto partnership. Luciano provided expansion funds, muscle to keep other mobsters out of Harlem, and political and judicial connections through Frank Costello. No one would interfere with their operation. But numbers wasn't the only action in Harlem. The place proved to be a dealer's haven for distributing heroin and marijuana, and the Mob, ever opportunistic, was happy to satisfy the growing appetite for drugs.

As Johnson's power and wealth grew, his prestige shot up in the neighborhood. He became so well known in Harlem that he was profiled in local media as a gangster celebrity, such as in a summer 1952 issue of *Jet* magazine. Such publicity for mobsters often has negative results, and Johnson was no exception. He was arrested, indicted, and sentenced to prison for selling heroin. He was given a 15-year sentence, which he served in Alcatraz Prison. While there, he began to write poetry, some of which was published in a poetry journal. He was released in 1963. Altogether, Johnson had been arrested more than 40 times, but not all of his arrests resulted in prison time. When he got out, he was still a Harlem celebrity. He proudly strolled down 125th Street as if he owned it, and most people smiled their good wishes or called out their greetings.

Prior to being convicted, Johnson had lived the high life as a local godfather.

In the throes of a torrid love affair with sultry *Vanity Fair* editor Helen Lawrenson, the almond-eyed 5-foot-7 Bumpy looked every part the crime boss. At her direction, he had suits custom made while purchasing shirts and ties from elite haberdasher Sulka. In her book, *Stranger at the Party*, Lawrenson writes about the time he left a steak dinner for a shootout on the street. She sat nervously while hearing gunshots. Two minutes later, Bumpy returned and Lawrenson, a nervous wreck, asked what had happened. "Nothin'," replied Bumpy. "We both missed. Now I'm gonna have a banana split. How about you?"[1]

By the time of his release from Alcatraz in 1963, much of Johnson's illegal operations had been taken over by others. However, a successful gangster will always be on the alert for new opportunities. And so Johnson became an ally of the charismatic black leader Malcolm X. And that certainly added to his aura as a celebrity hero. It also gave him cover to operate an extermination company named Palmetto Chemical that allegedly distributed heroin.

The year was 1968, and Johnson's life was winding down. He was still treated as a respected mobster, almost as an elder statesman, in the community. But his health and stamina had diminished. He moved in with his former employer and partner, St. Clair, and continued writing poetry. It was not a good year for Johnson because in addition to having to bear the burdens of his declining health, he was under indictment for drug dealing. He was free on a $50,000 bail. His freedom was short-lived because not long after moving in with St. Clair, Johnson died of a heart attack, the result of congestive heart failure. At the time of his death, "Johnson was eating a breakfast of fried chicken and eggs at Wells Restaurant in Harlem when cholesterol accomplished what his adversaries could not." He is buried in Woodlawn Cemetery in the Bronx.[2]

While Johnson had to cut in the Mafia to be a successful drug dealer, the innovative Frank Lucas found a more profitable alternative. No Italian mobsters and no middlemen was Lucas's operating credo. He bought his drugs directly from the source: he went to the Golden Triangle in Southeast Asia. The Golden Triangle is the area where the borders of Thailand, Laos, and Myanmar meet at the confluence of the Ruak and Mekong rivers. The name was coined by the Central Intelligence Agency (CIA). Along with Afghanistan, it has been one of the largest opium-producing areas of the world, accounting for nearly a quarter of the world's opium. This makes the Golden Triangle the second-largest opium producer. Most of the world's heroin came from the Golden Triangle until early in the 21st century when Afghanistan became the world's largest producer. In addition to going directly to the growers of opium, Lucas's second innovation was his delivery method. He claimed to hide the heroin in the coffins of dead US soldiers whose bodies were about to be shipped back to the states. Others said that heroin was hidden in pieces of furniture or in pallets beneath the coffins or underneath the false bottoms of coffins. Regardless of how it was hidden, the heroin arrived at US military bases. Lucas had confederates who then off-loaded the heroin and brought it to him for cutting and distribution. His scheme worked throughout the 1960s and well into the 1970s, making him many millions of dollars.

Like Johnson, Lucas was born in the Jim Crow south. His first home was in La Grange, North Carolina, and then in Greensboro. It was there that he saw a 12-year-old boy lynched by the Ku Klux Klan, and that set the tone of his angry, rebellious life. After getting into a fight, he was advised by his mother to move to Harlem. And like Johnson, Lucas indulged himself in a life of petty crime, including burglaries, street hustles, and small-time scams. Eventually, his activities brought him to Johnson's attention, who saw in Lucas a younger version of himself. He regarded the young Lucas as street smart and resourceful, an ambitious young hustler. He became Lucas's employer and mentor. Lucas learned a great deal about the gangster life from Johnson, learned its limits and its possibilities, some of which had escaped Johnson's ability. Shortly after Johnson's death, Lucas realized that he could make an immense fortune if he cut the Mafia out of his drug ambitions. He brought an old Carolinian neighbor into his budding enterprise. Lucas traveled to Bangkok, where he met with Leslie "Ike" Atkinson, who was married to a Lucas cousin. One night while drinking in Jack's American Star bar, a hangout for black soldiers, the two men hatched their scheme for exporting heroin back to the United States.

He called his dope Blue Magic and set up a makeshift store on 116th Street.

He was perhaps the biggest heroin dealer in Harlem, Frank Lucas would sit at the corner of 116th Street and Eighth Avenue in a beat-up Chevrolet he called Nellybelle. [But he lived] in a suite at the Regency Hotel with 100 custom-made, multi-hued suits in the closet; Lucas owned several cars. He had a Rolls, a Mercedes, a Corvette Sting Ray.[3]

On the street, he was just a neighborhood drug dealer, but in the rest of the Big Apple, he was a big, bad, black gangster. Asked by Mark Jacobson during a *New York Magazine* interview why he turned to the drug trade, Lucas said that he wanted to be rich, to be as rich as Donald Trump. He claimed that he achieved his goal. He said he was worth $52 million. Most of which was squirreled away in banks on Grand Cayman Island. In imitation of Trump, Lucas bought numerous office buildings in Detroit and several apartment buildings in Miami, Los Angeles, and New York. Yet, he never cut his roots to North Carolina, where he bought a 1,000-acre ranch and raised a herd of 300 Black Angus cows. And like the Sicilian Mafia, he only trusted family members and those who grew up in and around the areas in North Carolina where Lucas had lived when a young boy. He called his operatives the "Country Boys," and their dealings made Lucas the biggest drug trafficker in Harlem and beyond. Federal Judge Sterling Johnson Jr. said that the gang was one of the most outrageous international dope-smuggling gangs ever. He also said that Lucas was vicious, violent, and illiterate. But that didn't stop him from strutting his wealth at the 1971 bout between Muhammad Ali and Joe Frazier, where he wore a $100,000 chinchilla coat and matching chinchilla hat. His eye-catching getup caught the attention of detectives who began an investigation that would have its results in January 1975.

A task force of agents from the federal Drug Enforcement Administration (DEA) and detectives from New York Police Department's Organized Crime Control Bureau raided Lucas's home in Teaneck, New Jersey. Two witnesses who subsequently testified against him before a grand jury were murdered. The following year, Lucas was convicted of drug trafficking and sentenced to 70 years in prison, which consisted of a 40-year federal sentence and a 30-year New Jersey sentence. Not willing to spend what could have been the rest of his life in a small prison cell, Lucas agreed to become a cooperating witness against other drug dealers. He testified in 100 drug cases and was offered placement in the Witness Protection Program. In 1981, his sentence was reduced to time served. However, in 1984, he violated his lifetime parole in another drug case and was sentenced again to prison. He was finally released in 1991.

Lucas, who was married to Puerto Rican beauty queen Julianna Farrait-Rodriguez, had seven children. His wife served brief jail terms for drug-related crimes. The two were married for more than 40 years. Lucas claimed that the government took all of his money, including what he had stashed in offshore banks. His last years were relatively quiet because he was out of the drug business and confined to a wheelchair following an auto accident, during which his legs were broken. He died on May 30, 2019, at the age of 88.

Nicky Barnes, who was 3 years Frank Lucas's junior, took a different route to being a Harlem drug kingpin. Rather than avoiding the Mafia, Barnes would partner with them, and as if in imitation of a Mafia commission, Barnes formed a seven-member council in 1972 that was to control the drug trafficking in Harlem. All of the council's members were African American drug dealers. While the Mafia commission had tentacles that stretched across the United States, the council's authority was limited to drug dealers and their disputes in Harlem and nearby environs. Barnes's invitation to partner with the Mafia came after he had been schooled in the ways of mob drug dealing by Joey Gallo, while both were serving prison terms. Gallo had been Barnes's map maker and navigator, and Barnes followed the route that Gallo had laid out for him. Gallo supplied heroin to Barnes, who then arranged for its distribution primarily through Harlem street dealers, all whom worked for Barnes. Gallo was the wholesaler; Barnes was both the middleman and the large store. As part of their deal, Barnes would supply thugs who would carry out hits and beatings for Gallo. When Gallo was assassinated in 1972, his demise had no effect on Barnes's business. Gallo was not irreplaceable. Barnes quickly and efficiently continued working with the Mafia. It was too lucrative an operation to let the demise of one man ruin a smooth-running, multimillion-dollar drug business. Barnes and the Mob made millions.

Gallo had also taught Barnes how to insulate himself and delegate responsibilities; the DEA noted that Barnes had seven lieutenants working for him, and each of them controlled 12 distributors, who had 40 dealers to sell drugs on the streets of Harlem. In just a few years, he extended his operation throughout New York state and as far north as Canada. He was like a large corporation with subsidiaries and satellite offices.

Barnes also realized that so many Mob bosses, such as Al Capone, were prosecuted for failing to pay income taxes on undeclared income. Barnes, however, paid taxes on $250,000 in annual miscellaneous income. The IRS claimed that he owed additional sums, but they were unable to prove their claim. After he beat the IRS, he made sure that his admirers knew he had won; his celebrity status in Harlem skyrocketed.

He was rich, stylish, and a role model for aspiring African American gangsters. The accoutrements of his life dazzled those who wanted to be like him, to be another Nicky Barnes. Residents of Harlem would see Barnes motor down 125th Street or Lenox Avenue in his Citroen-Maserati or his Mercedes; other times, he would be seen driving Lincolns, Cadillacs, and other expensive cars. To keep the tax men at bay, Barnes kept the ownership of his cars hidden by setting up paper-leasing companies from which he supposedly leased the cars. He also owned numerous apartments in New York and New Jersey. Wherever he went, he made a splash that elicited admiration from those who wanted to be like him. He was the man!

His Harlem celebrity was soon noticed by the *New York Times*. In 1976, it featured him on the cover of its Sunday magazine section. There was Barnes looking proud and arrogant under the title "Mr. Untouchable." The story so angered President Jimmy Carter that he instructed his Justice Department to nail Barnes. In 1978, he and 10 associates were tried in federal court and charged with drug trafficking. After 9 weeks of testimony, all were found guilty. Barnes was sentenced to life in prison. *Time* magazine reported in a story titled "The Law Finally Touches Mr. Untouchable" that,

> his friends claimed he was just a wealthy real estate investor who was harassed by overzealous, even jealous white authorities. Police contended he was the biggest heroin dealer in New York City, maybe in the country. To blacks in his old Harlem neighborhood, Leroy ("Nicky") Barnes, 45, was a legend of defiance and success. What he had he flaunted, and he had a great deal: 300 custom-tailored suits, a string of glamorous women and powerful friends in show business and politics. He drove two Citroën-Maseratis and four Mercedes.[4]

The fall from drug kingpin to common prison convict was steep and dispiriting. Deprived of all the accoutrements of luxury that he had enjoyed on the outside, Barnes decided to best way to beat the rap was to become a snitch, or in Mob lingo, a rat or a stool pigeon. He was not only motivated by his depressing surroundings, but also because he believed that he was being cheated by his lawyers and those members of the council who were free and still operating his drug business. As if that were not enough to turn up the flames of his anger, Barnes also believed that his mistress was having an affair with one of the council's members. The best way to lash out was to get even. Having elicited incriminating information while behind bars, Barnes became a prosecution witness in 1984. During his testimony,

> Even the judge was shocked. After listening to hours of testimony about a multi-million-dollar drug-distribution network involving hired killers with a penchant for chain saws, US District Judge Milton Pollack marveled that such iniquities "could be so cold bloodedly related." Yet the tales so coolly told in court helped indict 44 major traffickers and convict 16.[5]

All of those indictments impressed the lords of law. Barnes sang aria after aria, putting away some of the most violent and vicious drug dealers. It was certainly more than sufficient reason for US Attorney Rudolph Giuliani to try to get Barnes's sentence reduced, but his appeal was rejected. Then US Attorney Otto Obermaier also asked that Barnes's sentence be reduced.

Still nothing happened. Then in 1998 the sun finally shone on Barnes as he breathed the air of a free man. He was placed in the Witness Protection Program, which was certainly a big improvement over his tiny cell. The Mob, however, was not smiling: it placed a $1 million bounty on Barnes. Had the Mob found him, they would not have recognized him. He was not the same Leroy Nicky Barnes who had appeared on the cover of the *New York Times Magazine* section:

> The 74-year-old man who used to be Leroy Nicholas Barnes, owner of 60 pairs of custom-made shoes, 27 full-length leather coats and more than one Mercedes-Benz, wears baggy Lee dungarees these days and drives to work in a used car he bought five years ago.
>
> With his slight limp and mostly bald pate, he seems the antithesis of his former persona as Mr. Untouchable, the dashing Harlem heroin dealer who posed 30 years ago on a magazine cover in a blue denim suit and a red, white and blue tie.
>
> The dapper Nicky Barnes that audiences will see bears little resemblance to the man he says he has become, a grandfather who puts in solid 40-hour weeks at an undisclosed job, who lives in a white neighborhood in an undisclosed state, and who matter-of-factly takes home doggie bags from restaurants.
>
> "Nicky Barnes is not around anymore," he said. "Nicky Barnes's lifestyle and his value system is extinct. I left Nicky Barnes behind."
>
> Money is a common denominator between his lives past and present. Once he made so much that he worried about how to dispose of it. Now, he says he needs more to survive.
>
> "I live within my paycheck," he said. "I want to get up every day and get in the car and go to work and be a respected member of my community. And I am respected. I know I am. I'm not looking in the rear view mirror to see if anyone is tailing me anymore. I don't turn on the blender when I'm at home so I can talk. That is not a part of my life. Sure, I'd love to have more money, but I am not willing to do anything but go to my job to get it."
>
> The millions he made and squandered, he said, are gone.
>
> "I miss it," he said. "There was glamour, money, influence, attractive women. I didn't have any financial concerns, and I do have them now. I'm concerned about being able to retire at some point comfortably. That's my principal concern."[6]

While in prison, Barnes earned a college degree and wrote poetry. Following his release into the Witness Protection Program, Barnes worked at a Walmart store and told neighbors that was a bankrupt businessman. He lived a modest life and died on June 18, 2012. His death was not revealed until 7 years later. While he was justifiably condemned for flooding his neighborhood with heroin that addicted thousands of African Americans, he may best be remembered for the Jim Croce song, *Bad, Bad Leroy Brown*.

17

The Grim Reaper

H E WAS A KILLING MACHINE, probably one of the most violent Mafioso of the 20th century. No one knows for sure the number of people he killed: the outside numbers are between 80 and 120. He so enjoyed killing that he reportedly said that he wanted to dig up one of his victims and shoot him again. To protect himself from law enforcement agencies, he became an FBI informant, providing information about his enemies, while earning immunity for his crimes—and many of those crimes included murder. When his relationship with the FBI was eventually revealed, the agency's reputation was besmirched. Yet, Gregory Scarpa Sr. did one heroic deed that inspired a movie. He was also a beloved family man who showered his children with love and protection and inspired their undying love. They were the only ones who were safe from his homicidal fury; others never wanted Scarpa as an enemy.

Scarpa, born on May 8, 1928, was the son of Salvatore and Mary Scarpa, immigrants from a small town on the outskirts of Venice, Italy. His family moved to Bensonhurst, Brooklyn, where Salvatore worked as a coal delivery man, earning just enough to keep a roof over his family and food on the table. By 1935, young man Scarpa was helping his father deliver coal. It was monotonous, repetitive work that offered no prospects for earning a decent living. By the time he was a teenager, he was fascinated and then attracted by the lives of the local mobsters in his neighborhood; they were sharp dressers, drove fancy cars, flashed large rolls of money, and were often accompanied by beautiful babes. Their major occupations seemed to be enjoying their lives of leisure and pleasure. Those lives were a far cry from the life of one pouring coal down basement chutes. At day's end, coal dust covered his hands and face and occasionally got into his eyes and, even worse, into his lungs. Scarpa rebelled against the work and decided he wanted to be one of the neighborhood mobsters; and a few years later, his older brother, Salvatore Jr. introduced him to members of the Profaci family (later renamed the Colombo family). Scarpa was mentored by Calogero "Charlie the Sidge" LoCicero, the family's consigliere. He hired the 6-foot, muscular Scarpa as an enforcer who collected the vigorish due on shylock debts and had him shake down local shopkeepers so that their stores wouldn't be firebombed or otherwise damaged and extort small manufacturers with threats of unionization and endless strikes. Scarpa was exceedingly good at the tasks that LoCicero had set for him. He was tough and fearless and did not tolerate arguments; his intimidating attitude was sufficient to generate stomach spasms of fear in his victims. His temper was explosive and came with a short fuse or, in some cases, no fuse. Violence, not charm, was his métier. He knew that peremptory strikes result in submission. No sensible person argued with Scarpa. LoCicero was deeply pleased by the success of his protégé. He had all the ingredients necessary to be a successful Mafia soldier. The trajectory of Scarpa's life was now in place; he was adept at doing more than just beating people into submission. The alacrity and celerity at which he carried out hits additionally impressed LoCicero as well as other capos in the family. Scarpa's eagerness to commit murders even made him a suspect in the slaying of his mentor, who was killed in 1968 while drinking a strawberry milkshake at Carlisi's Luncheonette in Borough Park, Brooklyn. The motive for the killing remains unknown, but the contract for the hit must have come from the family's boss. No one else had the authority to issue a hit on LoCicero. Scarpa's lack of loyalty did not block his rise in the Mob; in fact, betrayal was an integral feature of his life in crime.

For his love and eagerness of killing and the number of murders he committed, Scarpa became known as "the Grim Reaper." With such a reputation, he was soon invited to become a made man of the Profaci family. For the family, he was not only the best hired gunslinger in town, but he was also a top earner. From truck hijacking and extortion to loan-sharking and murder for hire, he was a bright star in the family firmament of ambitious criminals. He would ascend from soldier to capo, and only a few would stand in his way. He had all the necessary ingredients for success: he obeyed, no boundaries, moral, or ethical codes, only his own highly flexible and opportunistic rules.

Though a killer gangster who took obsessive pride in his work, he was also a ladies' man, a womanizer who thought of himself as irresistible. He had a perpetual tan, a neatly trimmed black mustache, an expensive toupee that matched the remainder of his black hair, and elegantly tailored expensive suits and sports jackets. He always carried a roll of $100 bills totaling $5,000.

When not wearing a colorful tie, he wore a thick gold chain around his neck. He carried himself as if he owned the world. His diction was not that of an uneducated, street thug. He spoke as well as any impassioned trial lawyer to a jury, or dictator whipping up the emotions of his followers: lucid, logical, and lusty. In restaurants and nightclubs, he was accompanied by beautiful women whose sex appeal magnetized all the eyes in a room. His love of beautiful women did not prevent Scarpa from getting married to Connie Forrest in the early 1950s. The couple settled in Bay Ridge, Brooklyn, and had four children, three boys and a girl. One son, Greg Scarpa Jr., was inducted into what became known as the Colombo family and is now serving a 40-year prison sentence. Greg Sr. and Connie separated in the 1970s, although they never divorced. Scarpa then had a 30-year relationship with Linda Schiro, and they had a son and a daughter. Their son Joey was shot and killed during a drug deal.

Jay Goldberg, a prominent attorney who successfully defended numerous organized crime figures, met Greg Scarpa when representing the gangster's girlfriend, Lili Dajani, winner of the 1960 Miss Israel Beauty Contest. (Though not divorced from his wife, Scarpa married Dajani in 1975 in Las Vegas.) Goldberg and his wife, Rema, met Scarpa and Dajani for dinner at the Sea Fare of the Aegean restaurant on West 56th Street in Manhattan. In his book, *The Courtroom Is My Theater*, Goldberg writes,

> When Greg walked in, it was apparent to me that he was a person of class. He dressed impeccably, wore a well and expensive toupee, and had a deep suntan. [Goldberg informed the author that the two couples, over a 6-month period, had about 15 subsequent dinner dates.] Greg, apparently when with me, wearing his toupee, was a person of class, but when he returned to Brooklyn to support a crime family boss [Carmine Persico], he removed the toupee and became a notorious killing machine—supposedly aided, shockingly, by members of the FBI.[1]

To protect himself from prosecution and to ensure that his rackets would continue to operate profitably, Scarpa became an FBI informant; in return, the FBI gave him carte blanche to commit crimes, even murders, though the agency later denied this.

Goldberg told the author that Scarpa was very well spoken, was knowledgeable about current events, and could speak with some authority about topical political issues. He was charming but also a con man.

Goldberg writes,

> One morning I received a call from Greg Scarpa Jr. that his father had been arrested by the District Attorney's Office in Kings County for involvement in a massive gambling enterprise. I went to the detention center on Court Street in

Brooklyn and I could not find Greg. When I spoke to the prosecutor, she did not know what had happened, but only that federal authorities had taken custody of Greg. Just who was he really?

Whenever Scarpa was arrested an FBI agent would submit a confidential memo to the judge setting forth all of Scarpa's contributions to the FBI.[2]

Years earlier, Scarpa had been indicted for controlling a massive credit card scam. He pled guilty; but after prosecutors asked the judge to hand down a substantial prison sentence, Scarpa was sentenced to just 5 years of probation with no time in prison and fined $10,000. Before his final prison sentence, just before he died, Scarpa served 30 days in jail in 1976 for attempting to bribe two police officers. Throughout the world of the Five Families, Scarpa's reputation for his ability during a 40-year period to evade convictions and jail inspired doubts and awe. Some people doubted his adherence to the code of omerta. Most others, however, refused to believe that Scarpa had made a deal with the FBI because the agency had made it known that they would not permit an informant to commit murder; yet a criminal defense lawyer told the author that no one could have evaded prison so effectively without being aided by the feds. Scarpa did not have a get-out-of-jail card: he had a no-jail-in-my-future card. Though members of his own *borgata* wondered about Scarpa's ability to avoid the clutches of the law, none of them would voice their doubts to him. They knew better than to question the Grim Reaper about why he was never convicted of crime. Instead, they enjoyed the profits and camaraderie of Mafia life, while hanging out in their ironically named private club, The Wimpy Boys Social Club on 13th Avenue in Brooklyn. Scarpa regarded the club as another one of his homes, though he had residences in Brooklyn, Staten Island, Las Vegas, and on toney Sutton Place in Manhattan. The club was also the site of the murder of a young woman whom his *borgata* feared had become an informant. The woman was shot in the head, rolled up in a carpet, driven away, and dumped far away from the club. A few days later, a dog that often accompanied a member to the club was discovered to be chewing on the woman's ear.

Away from Brooklyn and his social club, Scarpa's involvement with the FBI had one salutary benefit: on June 24, 1964, three civil rights workers were murdered in Mississippi. They were Andrew Goodman, James Chaney, and Michael Schwerner. They had gone to Mississippi to register African Americans to vote during what was known as Freedom Summer. There existed in the state an organization with the bland name of the Mississippi State Sovereignty Commission, which was determined to thwart the efforts of civil rights workers, whom the commission described as "outside agitators." The commission did so by paying spies to infiltrate groups of civil rights workers. Spies provided names, license plate numbers, and descriptions of civil rights workers to the commission, which passed along the information to local authorities. In the case of Goodman, Chaney, and Schwerner, the information was given to the Neshoba County Sheriff, who was later implicated in the murders of the three, all of whom had earlier gone to Philadelphia, in Neshoba County, Mississippi, to investigate the burning of a church that had been a site for voter registration. After they left the church in their station wagon, they were stopped by Ku Klux Klan members and deputy sheriff Cecil Price. They were arrested for exceeding the speed limit by 5 miles per hour and taken to jail. Chaney paid a $20 fine, and all three were released from jail. Driving out of town, the boys were stopped again by Deputy Price, who ordered them to get into his car. Followed by two carloads of Klansmen, Price drove the three workers to a deserted area and ordered them out of the car. Chaney was viciously beaten and then shot in the head and abdomen. Seeing the gruesome murder of Chaney, Goodman and Schwerner knew they were next. "Are you a nigger lover?" shouted one of the Klansmen at Schwerner and then shot him; Goodman met the same fate. Their bodies were buried in an earthen dam. After their bodies were discovered, autopsies were performed, and the medical examiner determined that Goodman was still alive at the time of his burial.

When the FBI agents entered the case, they were unable to get any cooperation from local residents who may have known about the murders. To find the bodies and identify the killers, the FBI decided to hire Scarpa because they figured that Scarpa's rough methods would produce results that they were forbidden by law to employ. Upon his arrival in Mississippi, Scarpa was given a gun and more than $100,000 by the FBI. He quickly located a likely squealer, a Klansman named Lawrence Byrd, who ran an appliance store. Scarpa entered the store and purchased a TV; he asked Byrd to help him load the TV into his car. As Byrd entered an alley with the TV, Scarpa put a pistol to Byrd's head and pushed him into the car. He drove Byrd to a local army base called Camp Shelby. Though Scarpa pistol-whipped Byrd, demanding to know where the three civil rights workers were buried, Byrd refused to provide the information. Scarpa pulled off Byrd's pants and underpants, took out a razor, and told Byrd that he had 5 seconds to provide Scarpa with the information he wanted or his balls would be cut off. The whimpering Byrd quickly told Scarpa of the location of the burials. Without any public fanfare, Scarpa became the hero of Mississippi Burning. Only the FBI and Scarpa's lawyer knew of his accomplishment. The FBI was so impressed with Scarpa's results that they hired him again in 1966 to help obtain evidence in the case of the murder of Vernon Dahmer, who had been president of the NAACP in Hattiesburg, Mississippi, and who had been killed in a fire set by Klansmen. FBI agent Damon Taylor commented about Scapa, "He was the crown jewel, for all his faults."[3]

Scarpa's relationship with the FBI proved extremely valuable to him during the third Colombo war, a bloody Mob war that lasted from 1991 to 1993 and that left more than a dozen bodies scattered on streets of various Brooklyn neighborhoods. (The first Colombo war raged from 1961 to 1963, and the second from 1971 to 1974.) The boss of the Colombo family, Carmine (nicknamed "Junior" or the "Snake," depending on one's point of view) Persico, was sitting in prison and issuing orders to his son, Alphonse "Allie Boy" Persico, whom he had appointed acting boss of the family. However, Allie Boy was indicted for loan-sharking and went AWOL. His absence didn't last long; he was soon taken in and convicted. He was sent to prison, and while there, his father appointed Vittorio "Little Vic" Orena as the acting boss of the Colombo family. He grew the family's business and power. Money flowed into its coffers from multiple sources. Orena proved to be a successful and resourceful boss; but he was not satisfied with merely being the acting boss: he wanted to be the permanent boss. He appealed to the Mafia Commission for their consent that he should replace Persico. Instead, the commission told him to poll his capos for their decision. Orena laid it out to his consigliere Carmine Sessa, who—in turn—informed Persico of Orena's plans. Persico was furious about Orena's betrayal and issued a hit on him. A five-man hit team lay in wait for Orena to arrive at his home; however, as the ever-watchful and suspicious Orena drove toward his home, he spotted the team parked in a nearby car and sped away. Orena suspected that the hit team had been organized by Scarpa, who was Persico's top warrior. Five months later, Orena organized his own hit team to kill Scarpa, who was determined to kill all of Persico's enemies within the family. On November 18, 1991, Scarpa had just escorted his daughter to her car; she was carrying her infant son. Scarpa got into his Mercedes and drove off; his daughter followed in her BMW. A white van suddenly blocked their way, and gunmen emerged blasting away with automatic weapons at Scarpa's car. He and his daughter sped off, driving up on the sidewalk, and managed to escape unscathed. The war was now going at full throttle. Though the war was only taking the lives of Colombo family members, it was a threat to the safety of those in proximity to the killers. Bullets flew wildly and police were worried that innocent people could be counted as collateral damage. The Brooklyn district attorney Charles Hynes commented, "I have no problem letting these folks [the Colombos] blow each other away. It's good for us ultimately. The problem is most of them don't get annual firing practice, so when they begin to miss, they end up killing innocent people." (After an innocent man was shot and killed at a Brooklyn bagel store, Hynes issued 41 grand jury subpoenas to Colombo associates, capos, and soldiers): "It stopped the war," he said, "because when they're under subpoena they can't shoot. They all hide."[4]

The one man who wouldn't lay down his arms was, of course, Scarpa. The Grim Reaper was on a mission—undeterred by subpoenas, possible indictments, and bullets from Orena's associates. He was undeterred because he believed he had a deal with the FBI that would protect him. Lyn DeVecchio, who headed the FBI's squad for surveilling the Colombo family, was also Scarpa's handler. He was alleged to be the first FBI agent who aided a gangster in the commission of crimes (allegations that proved to be false). Though the FBI conducted a 2-year investigation of DeVecchio, it was unable to come up with evidence that would have led to a conviction. He was cleared of any wrongdoing.

> DeVecchio vehemently denied that he had spilled secrets to Scarpa or had undermined investigations of the Colombo family. An agent with a distinguished record, he retired from his $105,000-a-year job soon after the Justice Department found insufficient cause to prosecute him for misconduct. "The bottom line is that I never gave Scarpa any confidential information about the [Colombo] war or any other matter," DeVecchio insisted in an interview. He attributed the agitation over his relationship with Scarpa to agents and prosecutors inexperienced in organized-crime investigations, and who misinterpreted justified and legal techniques in dealing with informers.[5]

When it was finally revealed that Scarpa had been an informant for the FBI, he had a more immediate and dangerous problem. For many years, Scarpa had eaten aspirin as if munching on peanuts. Eventually, the aspirin ate a hole in his gut, and he suffered from serious internal bleeding. Emergency surgery was scheduled to stop the bleeding. In Victory Memorial Hospital, Scarpa told doctors that he did not want blood transfusions from unknown donors; he would only accept blood from his own crew. One of those chosen to donate blood was mobster Paul Mele, a dedicated weightlifter who regularly injected himself with steroids. Unfortunately, he used dirty needles (as did thousands of other others), and contracted HIV before unknowingly passing it on to Scarpa, who underwent emergency surgery at the hospital. Following surgery, Scarpa developed a high fever and wavered between consciousness and unconsciousness.

In an article in *The New Yorker* on December 16, 1996, Fredric Dannen writes,

> Linda Shiro [Scarpa's mistress] claimed that the resident surgeon who had performed the operation, a Filipino named Angelito Sebollena, insisted that everything was all right, but she was unnerved one day when she caught him shaving Scarpa's face, in order to, as the doctor put it, "make him look nice." She had Scarpa transferred to Mt. Sinai Hospital, in Manhattan. There his

stomach, which was hemorrhaging beyond repair, was removed. Scarpa finally went home in October, with the aid of a walker.

Scarpa blamed Sebollena for making a faulty decision, and Victory Hospital for exposing him to AIDS. He filed a law suit. Before long Sebollena was in further trouble. In 1991, he injected two male patients with the drug Versed, a central nervous system depressant that leaves a person conscious but immobile, and performed oral sex on them. Gary Pilledsdorf, the lawyer who represented Scarpa at the medical-malpractice trial, in August 1992, recalls that on the morning of the opening statements the judge motioned him to the bench and said, "Let me get this straight. You're representing a hit man with AIDS against a doctor who sodomizes his patients. Am I on the right page?"[6]

Scarpa won his lawsuit against the hospital and doctor. Though jurors said after the trial that they were prepared to award Scarpa more than $1 million, Scarpa had called for a settlement; he was too weak to continue. The insurers settled and paid Scarpa $200,000 for the hospital and $100,000 for the doctor. Scarpa had successfully claimed that the hospital should have warned him of the risks involved in accepting unscreened blood from friends and family. He claimed that a hospital nurse suggested that he only accept blood from family and friends. Scarpa commented at a news conference, "I wasn't given ample warning. It was never something that should have been left to the prerogative of the patient."[7]

Scarpa would not accept a check in settlement; he wanted the $300,000 in cash. He sent one of his associates to pick up the money from a Manhattan Citibank branch. He warned a bank employee that all of the money that he tossed into a duffle bag better all be there. Or he would return.

During an interview on *60 Minutes*, conducted by Harold Dow, Scarpa stated,

> This is the hand that was dealt to me. I'll play the hand. If I could out-bluff the opponent, which is death—fine. If I can't, I lose the hand. [Speaking of friends and enemies, he said] "I'll show the courage I've displayed all this time, the bravado. I will show them—hey—this is still me. There isn't anything on earth that I'll hide from or back up from. And I certainly won't do it with this [the AIDS virus] either. It's a killer, no question about it. It's a killer, and I accept it. Maybe I'll get lucky, and get a heart attack. A heart attack. Bango. It's all over."[8]

While suffering from AIDS, Scarpa continued to kill dissident members of the Colombo family who wanted to oust Persico and install Orena. A high-level member of the Colombo family told Dow that Scarpa, while dying of AIDS, wanted to settle scores and had nothing to lose. He added that Scapa was "no candy store gangster." During the last months of his life Scarpa personally murdered four men. He was placed under house arrest and had to wear an electronic anklet so that government agents would know of his whereabouts 24 hours a day.

One day, Scarpa's son, Joey, came home after a failed drug deal and told his father that two mobsters had threatened to kill him, and one of them pointed a gun at him. Scarpa had his son accompany him as he drove through the neighborhood looking for the guys that had threatened Joey. Scarpa found his targets and shot them. One man fired at Scarpa, wounding him in his left eye. When Scarpa arrived back at his home, blood was pouring out of his left eye socket. He poured a glass of scotch into the wound and answered a phone call from the FBI. The agent wanted to know why the electronic anklet was beeping. Scarpa said everything was all right. He had just stepped out for a moment but was back home. Nothing to worry about. He was then taken to a hospital.

Not long afterward, Scarpa, blind in one eye, badly emaciated, and dying of AIDS, decided the easiest route to follow for the brief time he had left was to plead guilty to committing three murders and conspiracy to murder several others. Would a brief time in a prison hospital be any worse than a civilian hospital? He knew he would die soon, and did not want to be a burden on his family. On December 15, 1993, he was sentenced to 10 years in prison and fined $200,000. On June 4, 1994, the Grim Reaper sowed what he had reaped and died of AIDS in the Federal Medical Center for prisoners in Rochester, Minnesota. He was 66 years old.

18

Gangster Cops

EDDIE LINO WAS DRIVING HIS MERCEDES S-CLASS. He didn't notice the unmarked police car following him. He was not speeding, had not violated any traffic laws. Yet, on the police car's dashboard there was a spinning red light accompanied by a few brief blares of a strident siren that warned him to stop. He pulled over on the service road as two detectives exited from their unmarked car. Was this just another one of those rousting of mobsters by cops? Would a $50 bill be sufficient to send them on their way? Lino recognized one of the cops as the cop approached the driver's side of the Mercedes. He was Louis Eppolito. He greeted him, and Eppolito began chatting. Eppolito asked what was that on the passenger side floor. Lino bent forward to examine that object as Stephen Caracappa, standing on the passenger side of the car, fired a bullet into the back of Lino's head. Lino had left the gear shift in drive, while his left foot pressed the brake pedal. After being shot, his foot came off the pedal, and the Mercedes rolled into nearby bushes. The two cops returned to their car and drove off. The hit had been profitable: they split $75,000 for just a few minutes of work. Their paymaster was Anthony "Gaspipe" Casso, underboss of the Lucchese crime family. He had ordered Lino killed as a threatening message to John Gotti for his unsanctioned hit of Paul Castellano. Lino had been one of the shooters of Castellano outside of Sparks Steak House in 1985.

Who were Eppolito and Caracappa? Gangsters who became cops, or cops who became gangsters?

Louis Eppolito was born on July 22, 1948, in Flatbush, Brooklyn. His grandfather Louie made diamond watches for Lucky Luciano and newly made members of the Luciano crime family. Eppolito's father, Ralph, was a member of the Gambino family, as were his uncle James and cousin James Jr.; both were murdered on Castellano's orders. Ralph died of a heart attack at age 52 but not before teaching his son the ways of the Mob. Louis became a weight lifter in high school and developed a powerfully muscular body. He could not have been more proud of himself than when he won the Mr. New York City Contest for bodybuilders in 1967. The award further advanced his need for attention, and Eppolito became the loudest person in any room he entered. He acted as if there was always a spotlight on him. He had an ego as big as Hollywood and an insatiable appetite for self-glorification. He regularly called attention to himself, telling people how smart, talented, and resourceful he was.

One would not have thought that a man groomed to be a mobster would join the New York Police Department (NYPD). But that's what he did, after quitting a job as a mail sorter in the Post Office. A postal supervisor had asked Eppolito to get him coffee, and Eppolito responded that he wasn't a gofer; the proud son of the Mob father walked out. The NYPD looked like a better place to make his mark in 1969. So why did the NYPD hire a guy whose family members were in the Mob? Retired detective Anthony Celano told the author that Eppolito should never have been permitted to join, but he aced the entrance exam and easily passed the physical exam. At that time, there were tens of thousands of young men fighting in Vietnam, crime was rampant in big cities, and riots and demonstrations were occurring regularly. Many of the soldiers in Vietnam would have been likely candidates for the Police Academy, and their absence created a deficit. There were not enough cops to deal with widespread and unbridled crime, torrents of riots, and zealous antiwar demonstrators whose actions occasionally turned violent. Eppolito was accepted because he filled a need. "[Police officials] knew that Louis Eppolito had come from a mob family, that three members of the Eppolito Family had been murdered in mob hits. They knew that he liked playing the role of a wiseguy."[1]

Eppolito found a niche in the NYPD that permitted him to act out his role as a Mafia Cop, which is what he titled his memoir. And though required to wear a uniform, he dressed like a mobster when not on duty: he sported a black shirt, wide white tie, and gold chains around his neck and on one wrist. He also wore a large bejeweled ring.

In April 1984, Eppolito finally had an opportunity to be of assistance to a mobster: Rosario Gambino, a mobster and heroin dealer in New Jersey. Cops had raided Gambino's home, and in the process of rummaging through his home, they discovered—hidden in a dropped ceiling—a batch of confidential police reports about Gambino's activities and investigations into those activities. The reports had come from the precinct in which Eppolito worked. When analyzed by forensics, the reports had Eppolito's fingerprints. The information was turned over to the internal affairs bureau, and Eppolito was suspended and faced a departmental trial. The fact that he had grown up in a Mob family and had passed along confidential information to a mobster should have been sufficient cause to end his career and perhaps bring forth a criminal indictment. However, the judge determined that the fingerprints were Xerox copies of fingerprints, and there was insufficient evidence that Eppolito had turned over the reports to Gambino. (Michael Vecchione, who was in charge of the Rackets Division of the Brooklyn District Attorney's office told the author that he thought the departmental judge was wrong.) Eppolito subsequently claimed that he had been framed by his enemies. He was reinstalled as a cop and later promoted. According to an article in the *New York Times*, "A federal judge later took the opposite view criticizing police officials in a harsh ruling for what he called their 'inexplicable failure to discipline' Mr. Eppolito in 1985 'after he was caught red-handed passing confidential police documents' to Mr. Gambino."[2]

Though Eppolito's partner in crime, Stephen Caracappa, played no role in the Gambino matter, he also had a background in crime. As an 18-year-old man, he had organized a burglary of a warehouse and also arranged with a fence to unload the stolen merchandise, known as "swag." Caracappa was caught and, after a plea bargain, pled guilty to a misdemeanor charge. It should have been enough to keep him off the police force; but in 1969, he, too, was accepted by the New York City Police Academy. To say that scrutiny of young applicants was slipshod would be an understatement in the case of the two gangster cops.

Retired New York organized crime detective Anthony Celano told the author that he interacted with Caracappa and, at that time, had no suspicions about his being a criminal. His fellow officers regarded him as a conscientious cop who worked hard to solve cases. He was professional, discreet, and seemed somewhat removed. He was always well dressed and well spoken; however, if talking freely traces of a street guy would surface: he would say, for example, "tree" instead of "three." Celano said that when he had been working in the Queen's District Attorney's Office Squad he got a call from Caracappa, asking if Celano was working on anything new, in reference to organized crime cases. Celano found that call odd but not odd enough to raise suspicions. He later came to realize that Caracappa was, in all likelihood, hunting for information for his paymaster, Casso. This turned into hard realities after Caracappa and Eppolito had been arrested, convicted, and sent to prison. Years later after Caracappa had retired and moved to Las Vegas, Celano, who owned an investigative firm in midtown Manhattan, thought enough of Caracappa to consider him a business resource in Vegas. After Celano called him to see if he would be available for work, Caracappa offered to provide anything that Celano might need.

Caracappa was born in 1941 and raised in Staten Island. He dropped out of high school and at age 18 robbed a warehouse. His life seemed to be going nowhere. Without a promising future, he joined the army in 1966. His career was undistinguished. When he was discharged, he took the exam to enter the New York Police Academy. He easily passed and was accepted. When he met and was partnered with Eppolito in a robbery squad, it was as if two jagged pieces of a puzzle had suddenly fit together. It didn't matter that Eppolito was loud and brash and abrasive and that Caracappa was quiet, reserved, and seemingly cold. Placed side by side they were physical opposites: Caracappa was trim with a long, narrow face and a neatly trimmed mustache, and his expression was often dour. Eppolito had a round, fleshy face and a fat torso. He too had a mustache, but it looked slightly askew as if he had stuck it on with glue. In appearance, the duo was in the tradition of Laurel and Hardy, but there was nothing funny about them.

No one knows how they came to trust one another and embark on their careers as police criminals. They never spoke about it; in fact, they never even admitted their guilt, claiming until the time of their deaths that they were innocent men who had been framed. It was so hard for their fellow officers to believe that two cops would so viciously betray their roles as protectors of their communities that many cops refused to believe that they were gangsters.

The two were in the robbery squad for only a year, and then they were split up. Eppolito went to a precinct in Brooklyn that was based in Mob territory, and Caracappa was sent to the Major Case Squad that investigated many Mob activities. It was an ideal position for a Mafia spy. He could look at reams of information about wise guys, see who was being investigated, what evidence had been collected, and the placement of bugs. To the Mob, it would be a treasure trove, but it took a fortuitous link to bring it all together.

And there were two people who linked the cops to the Mob: Frank Santora Jr. and Burt Kaplan, who met while serving time in Allenwood, a low-security prison for white-collar criminals. Kaplan was serving a 3-year sentence for selling Quaaludes. Santora was serving time for a scam to rip off the estate of restaurateur Frederick Lundy for $12 million. While in prison, Santora told Kaplan that he had a cousin (i.e., Eppolito) who was a cop who partnered with another cop, and for a price, they could get inside information for him. And for an even bigger price, they might be willing to murder people. Kaplan, who was an associate of the Lucchese crime family and its underboss, Casso, was interested. This could be an opportunity for Kaplan to make some money and perhaps get rid of some enemies. It would also be an opportunity for Eppolito and Caracappa to make even more money. It looked like a win-win deal for all parties.

Shortly after his release from Allenwood, Kaplan called on Santora. He had some work for the two rogue detectives: Kaplan had conspired with a jeweler named Israel Greenwald to sell $500,000 of stolen Treasury Bonds. Kaplan believed that Greenwald had cheated him and might rat him out to federal authorities. Kaplan wanted the cops to kill Greenwald. The two cops got Greenwald's address and make of car. They followed him, then flashed a spinning red police light, and sounded their siren. When asked why he had been stopped, Greenwald was told that he was wanted for a lineup. He reluctantly agreed to be put in the lineup, but was driven to a garage, where his hands and feet were bound with rope; while kneeling on the garage floor, he was shot in the head by Frank Santora. The garage owner was told to dig a grave in the garage floor and roll Greenwald's body into it. Lye was poured over the body; the grave was filled with dirt, and cement was poured over the dirt. Kaplan gave Santora $30,000 to give to the cops. Santora kept $5,000 of that payoff for himself.

When Kaplan told Casso what the cops had done and what they could do for him, Casso was hooked. He wanted to meet the cops, but Kaplan refused. By remaining the middleman, he protected himself and could direct the deeds of the cops.

In September 1986, three men shot at Casso, who ran into a Chinese restaurant where he hid. When he finally emerged, he was furious and determined to get the shooters. He told Kaplan that he wanted revenge on the guys who had tried to assassinate him. The attempt had taken place in the environs of the 63rd Precinct in Brooklyn, where Eppolito worked. He was able to get all the investigation files on the case as well as a photo, the name, and address of James Hydell, the chief suspect in the case.

Eppolito and Caracappa were given the assignment of delivering Hydell to Casso, who would personally take his revenge by slowly torturing Hydell. The two cops staked out the home where Hydell lived with his mother, Betty, and his brother, Frankie. They saw Frankie coming out of the house and grabbed him. They quickly realized he wasn't the man in the photo, and so let him go. Frankie went inside and told his mother what had happened. Betty got in her car and went looking for the two cops. She found them around the corner, still sitting in their Ford Crown Victoria. She parked alongside their car and asked what they wanted with her son. Eppolito lowered the driver's side window, flashed his detective's shield at her, and said it was police business, and it was none of her business. She responded that her son was her business and that they better leave him alone. She then drove back to her house. The same day that the cops picked up and released Frankie, they also found James. It would be his last day alive.

Years later, when Eppolito was promoting his autobiography, *Mafia Cop*, on the *Sally Jesse Raphael Show*, Betty recognized Eppolito as the cop who had attempted to kidnap her son. She first relayed that information to the FBI, which didn't do anything about it. She later revealed it to New York Detective Tommy Dades, who became her friend, promising to bring the people responsible for her son's death to justice.

Prior to his being picked up by Eppolito and Caracappa, Hydell had gotten word that Casso was looking for him and that his life was in danger. Hydell was standing in Dyker Park in Brooklyn when Eppolito and Caracappa arrived in their unmarked car. Hydell was happy to see them because he believed they would protect him from Casso. Hydell got into their car and was driven to a parking lot; there, he exited the car only to be tossed into the car's trunk. He was then driven to a house, tied up, and placed in a chair. He was confronted by Casso, who demanded to know who ordered the hit on him and who Hydell's accomplices were. As he asked his questions, Casso shot Hydell in various parts of his body: knees, elbows, hands, groin. The torture went on for hours. Hydell knew he would eventually be killed and begged Casso to please leave his body in the street, so that it could be identified and his mother would receive an insurance benefit. Casso agreed. He then shot Hydell, killing him. Having delivered the coup de grâce, Casso felt no obligation to deliver on his promise. James Hydell's body was never found. For their work, finding and delivering Hydell, Eppolito and Caracappa were paid $50,000. Thereafter, they were given a monthly retainer that began at $4,000.

Next on Casso's hit list was Nicky Guido, who was one of the men who had attempted to assassinate Casso. Casso wanted the cops to locate and deliver him as they had Hydell. However, the cops wanted an additional $4,000. Casso balked at that, complaining to Kaplan that the cops were getting too greedy. Casso decided to get the information himself. He contacted someone he knew at the Brooklyn Union Gas Company, who provided an address for Guido. However, it was the wrong Nicky Guido, though this one was within in the same age range as the shooter and lived in a Mafia neighborhood. Casso figured he had located the right Nicky Guido. On Christmas day 1986, the wrong Guido was proudly showing off his brand-new red Nissan Maxima to his uncle. The two men were sitting on the front seats chatting about the car. Suddenly a car drove alongside of them and gunmen released a fusillade of bullets. As the shooters blasted away, Guido threw himself on his uncle's body to protect him from the gunfire. Guido was hit numerous times and died in his car. The shooters quickly drove off, believing they had executed their target; the uncle survived. Casso was furious that the wrong man had been killed and the cops complained to Kaplan that if Casso had paid them what they had demanded the right Guido would be dead.

Guido was not the only wrong victim: the other was Eppolito's cousin and Kaplan friend, Santora Jr. He was with another mobster, a man who was on Casso's lengthy hit list, when both were shot and killed by Casso's hit men. Casso later regretted the mistake, but those things happen when mobsters are out to kill each other.

Lino, who had been shot on a service road of the Belt Parkway, was not killed because he had attempted to kill Casso. It was a preemptive killing: Casso had been worried that that if he had succeeded in killing Gotti, then Lino (who was in Gotti's crew) would have come gunning for him. Better to eliminate Lino. So Casso paid the two cops $75,000 for Lino's murder. When testifying about the murder during the trial of the two cops, Kaplan said that he had asked Eppolito who shot Lino. Eppolito said that Caracappa had pulled the trigger "Why not you?" asked Kaplan. "[Caracappa] is a better shot," replied Eppolito.

As the cops committed murder after murder and provided classified information to Casso, they did not think their lives were in jeopardy—certainly not from prosecutors. However, their paymaster suddenly went on the lam in 1990. He was about to be arrested in what became known as the Windows Case, which was about how the Mob collected payoffs for the installation of millions of windows in New York public housing apartment buildings. Without their paymaster and now eligible for their pensions, the cops retired. Eppolito bought a house in a gated community in Las Vegas and Caracappa soon followed, buying a house directly across the street from his partner in crime. Eppolito published his autobiography, *Mafia Cop*, which contained a photo of him and Caracappa. The caption under the photo read "The Two Godfathers of the NYPD." The circumspect and reserved Caracappa was furious; the book would be sure to attract investigators, who Caracappa feared were already looking into their activities.

While evading capture, Casso stayed in touch with Kaplan, using him to receive and relay information. Kaplan also drove Casso's wife to and from her husband's hideouts. Casso was so paranoid that at one point, he suspected Kaplan of betraying him and ordered him hit, but then Casso was captured in 1993; so the hit never took place. Then, learning that prosecutors also wanted to nab him, Kaplan took off, going first to California and then to Mexico. In Mexico, Kaplan supported himself by exporting marijuana into the United States. Kaplan learned that Casso, after a year in prison, had flipped and was blabbing to the feds. Kaplan was disappointed, for he profoundly believed in omerta. He was a more of a die-hard, stand-up Mafioso than most made men. By 1996, Kaplan figured that it was safe for him to return to Brooklyn;

he was wrong. Cops were waiting for him and arrested him for drug dealing. He was convicted at trial and sentenced to 27 years in prison. Offered a deal to testify against the cops, he refused to cooperate. He was 63 years old and knew that he would die in prison. Still, he refused to flip. Though Casso had squealed about the cops and Kaplan, his stories were punctuated with so many lies and distortions that feds not only discounted his testimony, but they also rescinded their offer to release him into the Witness Protection Program. Casso would be imprisoned for the remainder of his life. Meanwhile, prosecutors kept meeting with Kaplan, attempting to get him to testify against the cops. He refused to do so. Then in late 2004, he finally changed his mind. Detective Dades told the author that Joseph Ponzi, Chief Investigator of the Brooklyn District Attorney's office, was attempting to get Kaplan to break his commitment to the code of omerta. But Kaplan wouldn't capitulate; he absolutely refused to cooperate. Then, just as the session was about to end, Ponzi confronted Kaplan about the murder of the wrong Nicky Guido, a young man completely innocent of Mob connections. Kaplan suddenly changed his mind. He didn't mind that mobsters killed one another, but that an innocent young man was gunned down stirred his conscience. That's when he agreed to cooperate. Ponzi had persuaded Kaplan to flip, without promising him a reduced sentence for his cooperation.

> Kaplan was moved to New Jersey. His debriefing began in early October 2004 and lasted six months. Day after day, week after week, Burt Kaplan matter-of-factly described in incredible detail the greatest betrayal in the history of the New York City Police Department. . . . Nobody, not even Casso, knew more about Eppolito and Caracappa than Kaplan. He was their contact; he relayed Casso's requests to them and reported the information they provided to Casso.[3]

During questioning, Kaplan admitted that he had been part of a conspiracy with the two cops to kill Hydell, Lino, and Greenwald. He claimed that over a 7-year period, the cops had been paid $375,000 for committing murders and providing information to the Mob, which came to $26,785.70 a year for each of the two cops. It was hardly bounteous pay for committing murders and other many criminal acts.

Thirty-four witnesses, including Kaplan, testified against the corrupt cops. At trial's end, Eppolito and Caracappa were convicted under the Racketeer Influenced and Corrupt Organization (RICO) Act as well as for eight murders and other crimes.

Upon the announcement of the guilty verdicts,

> [Eppolito] reaches under his jacket and pulls out his belt and throws it on the defense table. No guard needs to tell him about prisoners hanging themselves.

... He takes off his gold-yellow tie and throws it on his desk. He takes the gold chain from around his neck and drops that. Then a watch, a ring, a wallet and still more items.

Down the table, Caracappa has his tie off without anybody noticing it.[4]

As the cops are being led away, a man named Barry Gibbs leapt to his feet and shouted at Eppolito, "I had a family, too. You remember what you did to my family? You don't remember what you did to my family and me? Remember what you did to me? Me. Do you remember? You framed me."[5]

Gibbs had served 19 years in prison for a murder he had not committed. Eppolito had threatened a witness to lie that he saw Gibbs strangle a prostitute. The terrified witness testified as instructed at Gibbs's trial. Barry Scheck and Peter Neufeld of the Innocence Project were able to win Gibbs's freedom. Eppolito denied that he had interviewed the witness who had testified against Gibbs. New York City paid Gibbs $19,900,000 for the 19 years he served in prison.

On March 6, 2009, Eppolito was sentenced to life plus 100 years in prison, and Caracappa to life plus 80 years in prison. Each of them was fined more than $4 million. New York City agreed to pay $18,400,000 to seven families whose members the cops had murdered. Caracappa died of cancer in prison on April 8, 2017, and Eppolito died on November 3, 2019. The cause of his death has not been revealed. Following his retirement, Eppolito had wanted to be a screenwriter, an actor, and a movie producer. All that remains are the bit parts he had in several movies: *Goodfellas*, *Predator 2*, and *Lost Highway*. In *Goodfellas*, true to character, he was portrayed as a gangster.

Kaplan had his sentence of 25 years reduced to 9, which he had already served and so was released into the Witness Protection Program. He died at age 75 of prostate cancer. His daughter, Deborah, is a highly respected New York Supreme Court Judge.

Former Detective Dades told the author that he got a lot of satisfaction for his work bringing Eppolito and Caracappa to justice. The case had started after Betty Hydell saw Eppolito on the *Sally Jessy Raphael Show* and notified the police that Eppolito had harassed her son, Frankie, on the same day that her other son, Jimmy, disappeared. If it hadn't been for her, the case may never have gotten started. Dades said he was glad that he was able to provide some closure to Betty.

19

Goodbye to the Old-Time Bosses

F OR YEARS, Mob bosses were able to insulate themselves from zealous prosecutors. Even the two most successful prosecutors, Thomas Dewey and Robert Kennedy, although succeeding in sentencing many mobsters to prison, were unable to curtail the activities of Mafia families. The two prosecutors convicted numerous Mob bosses, but the bosses were quickly replaced. No matter what district attorneys and US Attorneys in many US cities achieved—and their achievements were often impressive—businesses run by the Mob continued thriving through the 1930s, 1940s, 1950s, 1960s, 1970s, and into the 1980s. But then something new happened: smoothly run racketeering operations were suddenly derailed by hard-charging prosecutors who decided that the Racketeering Influenced and Corruption Organizations (RICO) Act could be used to dismantle the tried-and-true tracks on which mobsters ran their businesses.

RICO provides for penalties for any ongoing criminal organization and its enterprises. The law permits prosecutors to indict the leaders of criminal organizations, such as the bosses and underbosses of Mafia families, for the crimes that they ordered others to commit. Prior to the passage of RICO, bosses were able to insulate themselves from being prosecuted for the acts committed by their subordinates. In Mafia families the subordinates were soldiers and associates and to a lesser extent the capos. RICO plugged a commonly employed loop hole.

The man responsible for developing RICO was G. Robert Blakey. He drafted the law while working with Senator John McClellan, who headed the Senate Government Operations Committee. It was signed into law in 1970 by

President Richard Nixon. Under RICO, a person who has committed two acts of racketeering (defined from a list of 27 federal crimes and 8 state crimes) over a 10-year period of time could be charged with racketeering, if those crimes were woven together as part of a racketeering enterprise. Those found guilty of racketeering can be fined up to $25,000 and sentenced to 20 years in prison for each racketeering count. On a multiple-count conviction, a defendant could be sentenced to more than 100 years in prison. Prior to RICO, it was not unusual for a mobster to be sentenced to periods in prison for a number of years that were regarded as the downside price of doing business. Brash mobsters would brag that they could endure short sentences standing on their heads. RICO not only eliminated that slogan, it also eliminated another common one: commit the crime, do the time. Under RICO, nobody was prepared to spend his lifetime upside down.

When defense attorneys explained the consequences of a RICO conviction to their clients, they caused stomach-churning bouts of anxiety. Defendants quickly learned that RICO charges would be easy to prove because those charges were based on patterns of behavior. Mafia bosses were exemplars of patterns of illicit behavior. A gloomy sense of doom followed their lives like an eager grim reaper.

Although RICO proved to be a popular and effective tool for prosecutors, many others found the acronym offensive because it implied that criminals were of Italian descent. Numerous Italian luminaries noted that the word *Rico* has been an Italian nickname for Enrico for centuries. As a further insult, Rico is the name of the gangster protagonist in the movie *Little Caesar*. The insult that many Italians perceived was certainly understandable.

No matter, the name stuck. And Blakey, the creator of RICO, made speeches in which he denied that the law was aimed solely at Italian gangsters. White-collar criminals of various ethnicities as well as white Anglo Saxons were also targeted by the RICO Act. Blakey stated that "We don't want one set of rules for people whose collars are blue or whose names end in vowels, and another set for those whose collars are white and have Ivy League diplomas."[1]

Blakey had been a man with a mission, and he was not going to be deterred by the sensitivities of politicians and mobsters, especially by those who declared there was no such thing as the Mafia. He had been a student of organized crime while pursuing his studies at Notre Dame University, where he wrote about the infamous Apalachin Conference. Shortly after earning his undergraduate degree, he was accepted at Notre Dame's law school, where he proved to be an outstanding student. With his Juris Doctorate degree under his belt, he was invited to join to the US Department of Justice under its Honor Program. It was inevitable that he would become a Special Attorney in the Organized Crime and Racketeering Section of the Department. Under Attorney General Robert Kennedy, the Justice Department went after gangsters the way beagles on a hunt in the English countryside go after foxes: within 2 years, Kennedy had indicted more than 300 gangsters. Blakey was integral to Kennedy's mission to nail the Mob and proved to be a brilliant attorney. He continued to play an important role at the Justice Department until his departure in 1964.

Though there had a been a RICO case brought against labor leader Anthony Scotto in January 17, 1979, it was not until Rudolph Giuliani began the famous Commission Trial that it was apparent that prosecutors could use RICO as an axe to chop off the heads of Mafia families. Scotto, who headed the International Longshoreman's Association, was convicted of racketeering, which included charges of accepting unlawful labor payments and income tax evasion. On November 16, 1979, Scotto was convicted of all charges brought against him.

With that trial under its belt, the government was able to foresee the benefits of RICO in going after the Mafia. Under the leadership of US Attorney Giuliani, the government brought indictments against New York Mafia bosses in what was known in the media as the Mafia Commission Trial, but was officially known as the *United States v. Anthony Salerno et al.* Those indicted included bosses, underbosses, and soldiers: Paul Castellano, boss of the Gambino crime family; Anthony "Fat Tony" Salerno, boss of the Genovese crime family; Carmine "Junior" Persico, boss of the Colombo crime family; Anthony "Tony Ducks" Corallo, boss of the Lucchese crime family; Philip "Rusty" Rastelli, boss of the Bonanno crime family; Aniello Dellacroce, underboss of the Gambino crime family; Gennaro "Gerry Lang" Langella, acting boss and underboss of the Colombo crime family; Salvatore "Tom Mix" Santoro, underboss of the Lucchese crime family; Christopher "Christy Tick" Furnari, consigliere of the Lucchese crime family; Anthony "Bruno" Indelicato, Bonanno crime family soldier; and Ralph "Little Ralphie" Scopo, Colombo crime family soldier.

Before bringing indictments, the governments had placed numerous bugs in locations that were sure to produce evidence necessary for convictions. The first bug was placed in Castellano's home, which recorded conversations about the Concrete Club, the Mafia entity that controlled the supply and price of concrete used in all large New York City construction projects. Another bug was installed in the Jaguar of Corallo , who spoke freely about Mafia enterprises as he was being driven around the city by his capo, Salvatore Avellino. A third bug was placed in the Palma Boys Social Club in East Harlem. The club was the headquarters for Salerno, who issued orders from his seat of power and discussed payoffs for construction projects. Another bug was placed in the ceiling of the Casa Storta restaurant in Bensonhurst,

Brooklyn. The bug was directly over Langella's favorite table. The fifth bug was place in Scopo's union office, where the details of the Concrete Club deals were worked out. All the bugs provided a cornucopia of information not only about crooked construction projects but also about labor rackets, loan-sharking, extortion, and gambling. Most troubling for some of the defendants in the Mafia Commission Trial were their discussions about hits they had ordered.

The Mafia Commission Trial began on February 25 1985, and generated ribbons of banner headlines through the trial's end on November 19, 1986. Giuliani had been determined to obliterate the five Mafia families and send their bosses and underbosses to long prison terms that would deter other ambitious gangsters from wanting to take their places. Who would want to spend a few years as head of a Mafia family if it meant spending many decades, until one's death, in a bleak prison cell? The trade-off was not worth the millions of dollars and dictatorial power that one enjoyed for a brief time. Giuliani had taken a sledge hammer to the structure of the commission, the Mafia's board of directors. And for that, Carmine Persico and John Gotti had urged the commission members to order a hit on Giuliani; however, the commission rejected their plea. After their sentencing, the convicted bosses may have wished they had chosen to kill the man who brought about their downfall. Persico and Gotti's intention is reminiscent of Dutch "the Dutchman" Schultz's desire to kill District Attorney Thomas Dewey; Schultz's plan to kill Dewey was rejected by the National Crime Syndicate's members, many of whom Dewey subsequently prosecuted.

Several defendants avoided conviction in the Mafia Commission case: one was Rastelli because he had been kicked off the commission for his complicity in permitting FBI agent Joseph Pistone (aka Donnie Brasco) to become a member of the Bonanno crime family. Rastelli, however, didn't escape prosecution; he was indicted on separate labor racketeering charges and convicted. Castellano was assassinated on December 16, 1985; and Dellacroce died of cancer on December 2, 1985.

The seven defense attorneys had been faced with a seemingly insurmountable problem in dealing with the RICO charges. They had asked Giuliani if he would be willing to engage in plea bargaining; Giuliani said only if the defendants agreed to plead guilty to all charges. His position was non-negotiable. Other than having their clients plead guilty, the defense lawyers had no alternative but to go to trial.

The attorneys and Persico (who acted as his own attorney with the help of a legal advisor) decided to argue that membership in the Mafia and membership in the commission were not evidence of criminal activity. (Their opinion was confirmed to the jury of five men and seven women by Judge Richard

Owen who said that the mere fact that someone belonged to the Mafia was insufficient for a conviction. He would go on to instruct the jury that convicting a defendant required them to find that the Mafia Commission existed and that the defendants conducted its affairs in a pattern consisting of at least two acts of racketeering.) The bosses had initially refused to admit their membership in the Mafia because it would have obviated their code of omerta. However, the prosecution had hours of incriminating recordings that would prove otherwise. It would have been absurd to contradict what was apparent. So the bosses finally agreed to let their attorneys say that the Mafia existed, but their clients would not be called on to confirm the statements of their lawyers. The trial provided the first time when the very existence of the Mafia was affirmed by defense attorneys in a court.

On November 19, 1986, following 6 days of jury deliberations, the defendants were found guilty of all 151 indictments. It was a big win for the government and a shocking outcome for the Mob. There had never been anything like it in the history of organized crime and the judiciary. Less than 2 months later, on January 13, 1987, the bosses were sentenced to 100 years in prison. Indelicato got off with a less severe term of 44 years. Salerno, Corallo, Santoro, Furnari, Persico, Langella, and Scopo died in prison. In 2000, Indelicato was paroled from prison, but he was returned to prison for 8 months following a parole violation. Parole and a parole violation occurred again in 2004. His luck finally ran out on December 16, 2008, when Indelicato was convicted for the 2001 murder of Frank Santoro. He was sentenced to 20 years in prison.

Ralph Blumenthal in a *New York Times* article headlined, "Verdict is Termed a Blow to the Mafia," wrote,

> The guilty verdicts in the Mafia Commission trial yesterday will not by themselves put the mob out of business. . . .
> But [prosecutors] hailed the convictions as certain to disrupt long-entrenched patterns of criminal activity and to make it easier for authorities to fight racketeering in a host of industries long prey to traditional organized crime.[2]

While the trial proved to be a disaster for organized crime, it created a platform for Giuliani, who would use his newfound fame as a successful Mob prosecutor to run as mayor of New York City. Prosecutor Michael Chertoff went on to become US Secretary of Homeland Security.

Although many Mob observers say that the Mafia is in a state of decline, others say that it is thriving but simply operating in the shadows, maintaining a low profile so neither the media nor law enforcement will take notice of them. Those points of view are not contradictory because if the Mob is keeping a low profile, it may indeed seem to be in decline. And if it is thriving, then it better keep a low profile so that it can operate unhindered. Here are four estimations of the status of the Mafia and the changes that resulted from the RICO convictions from attorneys who have defended mobsters and those who prosecuted them:

Prominent attorney Jay Goldberg, author of *The Courtroom Is My Theater*, told the author,

> that early mob leaders, such as Meyer Lansky, Carlo Gambino, and Tony Salerno, were god-like figures. They exerted a level of control comparable to army generals. Prior to the RICO convictions in the Mafia Commission Trial, bosses were able to maintain the code of omerta amongst their capos, soldiers and associates. Following sentences of hundreds of years behind bars for the bosses of the various families, many mobsters chose to go into the Witness Protection Program rather than spend the rest of their lives in prison.

Joseph Giannini, an attorney who represented many wise guys from the Lucchese and Colombo crime families, told the author "the Mafia's power and reach has declined steadily for decades." He added, "that the effective use of RICO against Mafia bosses, the inter and intra family Mob Wars, and mob informers are the culprits."

Robert Santucci, former chief of the Rackets Bureau, Office of the District Attorney of Bronx County and Special Assistant for the Southern District of New York Public Corruption Unit stated that "the mob is in decline, but still active. Current mobsters are shadows of those who controlled organized crime decades ago. They are doing all that they can to avoid being arrested and sent to prison under the RICO law."

Michael Vecchione, former Chief of the Rackets Division of the Brooklyn District Attorney's office and coauthor of *Friends of the Family*, told the author,

> To paraphrase Mark Twain, the reports of the death of the American Mafia are greatly exaggerated. The mob is alive and well. It is as dangerous and profitable as it has always been. In my opinion, what has given the impression to mob observers that the Mafia is a thing of the past or a shell of itself, is the fact that there are no longer guys like "the Teflon Don" John Gotti, or "the Oddfather," Vincent "the Chin" Gigante, or Sammy "the Bull" Gravano, in the spotlight of the press. These guys were the headline makers, reporters' dreams and paparazzi followed them wherever they could. However, along with the spotlight came the searing interest of law enforcement, which was not good for business. The Mafia of today has learned a lesson from this past publicity and in many ways has gone back to the old style of flying under the radar. This allows them to do business and make money with little to no interruption. With the exception of an incident here or there that catches some agent's or reporter's eye, the American Mafia will likely remain in the shadows and thrive!

Numerous other criminal defense attorneys, former prosecutors, and police investigators have told the author that the Mafia, though a shadow of its former self, is still operating and raking in millions of dollars. It is particularly active in the drug trade, online gambling, stock fraud, and construction. Old standbys, such as loan-sharking and extortion, also contribute to Mafia coffers. The big difference between the old-time gangsters and today's gangsters is that the previous generations came from poverty and schemed to get themselves into positions of power. Many members of the contemporary generation are college graduates who never experienced the hardships of poverty and were handed their positions in the Mafia as if they were princes entitled to dynastic successions. Today's young gangster heirs keep low profiles as their various legal advisors help them avoid indictments and subsequent long jail terms that had condemned those convicted in the Mafia Commission Trial. The tradition of omerta has been gathering dust and been shelved along with the hierarchical discipline that enforced it.

Notes

Chapter 1

1. F. Scott Fitzgerald, *The Great Gatsby* (New York: Charles Scribner's Sons, 1953), 48.

2. Leo Katcher, *The Big Bankroll: The Life and Times of Arnold Rothstein* (New York: Da Capo, 1994), 22.

3. Jeffrey Sussman, *Boxing and the Mob: The Notorious History of the Sweet Science* (Lanham, MD: Rowman and Littlefield, 2019), 3.

4. David Pietrusza, *Rothstein: The Life, Times, and Murder of the Criminal Genius Who Fixed the 1919 World Series* (New York: Carroll & Graf, 2003), 235.

Chapter 2

1. "Bugsy Siegel Is the Most Charming Gangster in the History of Las Vegas." Available from: www.casinoz.club/content/bugsy-segel-the-most-charming-gangster-652.html (accessed 10 May 2019).

2. Nicholas Gage, "The Mafia at War," *New York Magazine* (July 10, 1972). (Accessed January 25, 2019.)

Chapter 3

1. David Critchley, *The Origin of Organized Crime in America: The New York City Mafia, 1891–1932* (New York: Routledge, 2009), 138.

Chapter 4

1. Anthony M. DeStefano, *Top Hoodlum: Frank Costello, Prime Minister of the Mafia* (New York: Citadel Press, 2018), 24.
2. Tim Newark, *Boardwalk Gangster: The Real Lucky Luciano* (New York: Thomas Dunne Books, Imprint of St. Martin's Press, 2010), 62–63.
3. Retired New York City Detective Sergeant Ralph Salerno interviewed by author in 1992.

Chapter 6

1. Carl Sifakis, *The Mafia Encyclopedia* (New York: Checkmark Books, an imprint of Facts on File, Inc., 1999), 332.
2. Sifakis, *The Mafia Encyclopedia*, 333.
3. Paul Sann, *Kill the Dutchman!* (New York: Da Capo Press, 1971), 137–138.
4. Sann, *Kill the Dutchman!*, 61–68.

Chapter 7

1. Paul R. Kavieff, *The Life and Times of Lepke Buchalter* (Fort Lee, NJ: Barricade Books, 2006), 45.
2. Kavieff, *The Life and Times of Lepke Buchalter*, 69.
3. Kavieff, *The Life and Times of Lepke Buchalter*, 105.
4. Kavieff, *The Life and Times of Lepke Buchalter*, 132.

Chapter 8

1. Allan R. May, *Gangland Gotham* (Santa Barbara, CA: Greenwood Press, 2009), 54.
2. *Schuster v. City of New York*, 5 N.Y.2d 75 (1958).
3. Carl Sifakis, *The Mafia Encyclopedia* (New York: Checkmark Books, an imprint of Facts on File, 1999), 11.
4. May, *Gangland Gotham*, 42–43.
5. Sifakis, *The Mafia Encyclopedia*, 14.

Chapter 9

1. Martin Gosch and Richard Hammer, *The Last Testament of Lucky Luciano* (Boston: Little, Brown and Company, 1974), 38.

2. Allan R. May, *Gangland Gotham* (Santa Barbara, CA: Greenwood Press 2009), 189.

3. J. Y. Smith, "Samuel Leibowitz, Noted Judge, Dies." *The Washington Post* (January 12, 1978). Available from: www.washingtonpost.com/archive/local/1978/01/12/samuel-leibowitz-noted-judge-dies/30cc052b-afa3-4b7c-9326-6838070eb364/?noredirect=on (accessed August 16, 2019).

4. Carl Sifakis, *The Mafia Encyclopedia* (New York: Checkmark Books, an Imprint of Facts on File, 1999), 19.

5. Sifakis, *The Mafia Encyclopedia*, 152.

6. Dennis Eisenberg, Uri Dan, and Eli Landau, *Meyer Lansky: Mogul of the Mob* (New York: Paddington Press, 1979), 248.

Chapter 10

1. Allan R. May, *Gangland Gotham* (Santa Barbara, CA: Greenwood Press, 2009), 161.

2. John H. Davis, *Mafia Dynasty* (New York: Harper Collins Publishers, 1993), 100.

3. Ed Magnuson, "The Assassination: Did the Mob Kill J.F.K.?" *Time* (June 21, 2007). Available from: content.time.com/time/magazine/article/0,9171,956397,00.html (accessed August 27, 2019).

4. Davis, *Mafia Dynasty*, 102.

5. "Joseph A. Colombo, 54, Paralyzed in Shooting in 1971 Rally, Dies; Some Progress in Condition. A Departure From the Usual. A Series of Arrests 'What's the Mafia?' *New York Times* (May 24, 1978), Section B, page 2. Available from: www.nytimes.com/1978/05/24/archives/joseph-a-colombo-sr-54-paralyzed-in-shooting-at-1971-rally-dies.html (accessed August 28, 2019).

6. Carl Sifakis, *The Mafia Encyclopedia* (New York: Checkmark Books, An Imprint of Facts on File, Inc.,1990), 147.

Chapter 11

1. Taped conversation with the author.

2. Selwyn Raab, *Five Families* (New York: Thomas Dunne Books, St. Martin's Press, 2016), 250.

3. John H. Davis, *Mafia Dynasty* (New York: Harper Collins Publishers, 1993), 155.

4. Davis, *Mafia Dynasty*, 214.

5. Davis, *Mafia Dynasty*, 206.

6. Richard Stengel, "The Passionate Prosecutor." *Time* (June 24, 2001). Available from: content.time.com/time/magazine/article/0,9171,1101860210-143096,00.html (accessed September 12, 2019).

7. Nick Squires, "Sicilian Mafia 'Plotted to Kill' Former New York Mayor Rudy Guiliani." *The Telegraph*. Available from: www.telegraph.co.uk/news/worldnews/europe/italy/10667504/Sicilian-mafia-plotted-to-kill-former-New-York-mayor-Rudy-Giuliani.html (accessed September 12, 2019).

Chapter 12

1. Nat Hendley, *American Gangsters, Then and Now* (Santa Barbara CA: ABC-CLIO, 2010), 83.

2. John H. Davis, *Mafia Dynasty: The Rise and Fall of the Gambino Crime Family* (New York: Harper Collins, 1993), 265–266.

3. Interview with Anthony Celano, former New York Police Department Squad Commander, Queens District Attorney's office, New York, October 1, 2019.

4. Selwyn Raab, *Five Families* (New York: Thomas Dunne Books, an imprint of St. Martin's Press, 2016), 442.

5. Raab, *Five Families*, 442.

Chapter 13

1. Peter Maas, *Underboss* (New York: Harper Collins Publishers, 1997), 50.

2. "Bruce Silverglade Discusses Sammy Gravano." Available from: www.youtube.com/watch?v=ao-vFXmAg7c (accessed 7 October 2019)

3. Maas, *Underboss*, 68.

4. Maas, *Underboss*, 78.

5. Maas, *Underboss*, 91.

6. Interview with Joseph Giannini, October 9, 2019.

7. Maas, *Underboss*, 135.

8. "Sammy Gravano Interview." Available from: www.youtube.com/watch?v=9cUdMbhzaNg (accessed October 10, 2019).

9. Richard Johnson, "Sammy the Bull Thinks the President Should Be a Mob Boss." *New York Post* (April 22, 2018). Available from: pagesix.com/2018/04/22/sammy-the-bull-thinks-the-president-should-be-a-mob-boss/ (accessed October 10, 2019).

10. Oliver Coleman and Dennis Slattery, "Sammy Gravano's Daughter Wants Father's Pal Trump for President, Hopes GOP Front-Runner Gives Mob Rat Pardon." *New York Daily News* (March 9, 2016). Available from: www.nydailynews.com/news/politics/sammy-gravano-daughter-dad-pal-trump-president-article-1.2557697 (accessed October 10, 2019).

11. Jay Goldberg with Alex S. Huot, *The Courtroom is My Theater* (New York: Post Hill Press, 2018), 247.

Chapter 14

1. Jennifer Redfearn, "Sins of the Father." *Village Voice* (January 16, 2007). Available from: www.villagevoice.com/2007/01/16/sins-of-the-father-3/ (accessed October 21, 2019).

2. Larry McShane, *Chin: The Life and Crime of Mafia Boss Vincent Gigante* (New York: Kensington Books, 2016), 89.

3. Selwyn Raab, *Five Families* (New York: Thomas Dunne Books, an imprint of St. Martin's Press, 2016), 569.

4. Raab, *Five Families*, 562.

5. Joseph P. Fried, "Peter Savino, Mafia Associate Who Became an Informer, 55." *The New York Times* (November 1, 1997). Available from: www.nytimes.com/1997/11/01/nyregion/peter-savino-mafia-associate-who-became-an-informer-55.html (accessed October 22, 2019).

Chapter 15

1. Anthony Varesi, *The Bob Dylan Albums* (Toronto, Ontario, Canada: Geurnica Editions, 2002), 131–133.

2. Carl Sifakis, *The Mafia Encyclopedia* (New York: Checkmark Books, an imprint of Facts on File, 1999), 149.

3. Interview with Anthony Colella, October 24, 2019.

4. Selwyn Raab, *Five Families* (New York: Thomas Dunne Books, an Imprint of St. Martin's Press, 2016), 197.

5. "Blood in the Streets: Subculture of Violence." *Time* (February 28, 2002). Available from: content.time.com/time/magazine/article/0,9171,213669,00.html (accessed October 26, 2019).

6. "Joey Gallo." *Mafia Wiki*. Available from: mafia.wikia.org/wiki/Joey_Gallo (accessed October 26, 2019).

Chapter 16

1. Michael Kaplan, "Rise & Fall of the Harlem Kingpin Who Took on the Mafia—and Won." *New York Post* (September 23, 2019). Available from: nypost.com/2019/09/23/rise-fall-of-chess-playing-gangster-who-ruled-as-harlem-godfather/ (accessed November 5, 2019).

2. Kaplan, "Rise & Fall of the Harlem Kingpin."

3. Marc Jacobsen, "The Return of Superfly." *New York Magazine* (August 14, 2000). Available from: nymag.com/nymag/features/3649/index.html (accessed November 5, 2019).

4. "The Nation: Bad, Bad Leroy Barnes." *Time* (December 12, 1977). Available from: content.time.com/time/magazine/article/0,9171,915810,00.html (accessed November 7, 2019).

5. "Telling Tales." *Time* (January 30, 1984). Available from: content.time.com/time/magazine/article/0,9171,954086,00.html (accessed November 7, 2019).

6. Sam Roberts, "Crime's 'Mr. Untouchable' Emerges from the Shadows." *New York Times* (March 4, 2007). Available from: www.nytimes.com/2007/03/04/nyregion/04nicky.html (accessed November 7, 2019).

Chapter 17

1. Jay Goldberg, *The Courtroom Is My Theater* (New York: Post Hill Press, 2018), 279.

2. Goldberg, *The Courtroom Is My Theater*, 281.

3. Selwyn Raab, *Five Families* (New York: Thomas Dunne Books, an Imprint of St. Martin's Press, 2016), 342.

4. "Greg Scarpa Interview with Harold Dow." Available from: www.youtube.com/watch?v=gfYXZuZ7qB4 (accessed November 25, 2019).

5. Selwyn Raab, *Five Families*, 342.

6. Frederic Dannen, "The G Men and the Hit Man." *New Yorker* (December 9, 1996). Available from: www.newyorker.com/magazine/1996/12/16/the-g-man-and-the-hit-man (accessed November 26, 2019).

7. Mary B. W. Tabor, "Settlement in Lawsuit on HIV-Tainted Blood." *The New York Times* (August 30, 1992). Available from: www.nytimes.com/1992/08/30/nyregion/settlement-in-lawsuit-on-hiv-tainted-blood.html (accessed November 21, 2019).

8. "Greg Scarpa Interview with Harold Dow."

Chapter 18

1. Tommy Dades and Michael Vecchione with David Fisher, *Friends of the Family* (New York: William Morrow, an Imprint of Harper Collins Publishers, 2009), 53.

2. Ed Shanahan, "Police Officer Found to be Hit Man for the Mob, Dies at 71," *New York Times,* November 8, 2019, B11.

3. Dades et al., *Friends of the Family*, 71.

4. Jimmy Breslin, *The Good Rat* (New York: ECCO, an imprint of Harper Collins Publishers, 2008,) 258.

5. Breslin, *The Good Rat*, 261.

Chapter 19

1. Alain Sanders and Priscilla Painton, "Law: Showdown at Gucci Gulch. Designed as a Mob buster, RICO has become a powerful catchall," *Time*, August 21, 1989, Vol. 134 Issue 8, 48.

2. Ralph Blumenthal, "Verdict Is Termed Blow to the Mafia," *New York Times*, November 20, 1986, B8.

Bibliography

Breslin, Jimmy. *The Good Rat*. New York: ECCO, An Imprint of Harper Collins, 2008.

Capeci, Jerry, and Tom Robbins. *Mob Boss*. New York: Thomas Dunne Books, St. Martin's Press, 2013.

Cawthorne, Nigel, and Colin Cawthorne, eds. *The Mammoth Book of the Mafia*. Philadelphia: Running Press, 2009.

Cohen, Rich. *Tough Jews*. New York: Simon and Schuster, 1998.

Critchley, David. *The Origin of Organized Crime in America, The New York City Mafia, 1891–1931*. New York: Routledge, 2009.

Dades, Tommy, and Michael Vecchione with David Fisher. *Friends of the Family*. New York: William Morrow, an Imprint of Harper Collins, 2009.

Davis, John H. *Mafia Dynasty: The Rise and Fall of the Gambino Crime Family*. New York: Harper Collins, 1993.

Destefano, Anthony M. *Top Hoodlum: Frank Costello, Prime Minister of the Mafia*. New York: Citadel Press, 2018.

Eisenberg, Dennis, Uri Dan, and Eli Landau, *Meyer Lansky: Mogul of the Mob*. New York: Paddington Press, 1979.

Feder, Sid, and Joachim Joesten. *The Luciano Story*. New York: DaCapo Press, 1994

Fitzgerald, F. Scott. *The Great Gatsby*. New York: Charles Scribner's Sons, 1953.

Fox, Stephen. *Blood and Power: Organized Crime in the 20th Century*. New York: Morrow, 1989.

Franceschini, Remo. *A Matter of Honor*. New York: Simon & Schuster, 1993.

Goldberg, Jay with Alex S. Huot. *The Courtroom Is My Theater*. New York: Post Hill Press, 2018.

Gosch, Martin, and Richard Hammer. *The Last Testament of Lucky Luciano*. Boston: Little, Brown and Company, 1974.

Hendley, Nat. *American Gangsters, Then and Now*. Santa Barbara, CA: ABC–CLIO, 2010.

Jacobs, James B, with Coleen Friel and Robert Radick. *Gotham Unbound: How New York City Was Liberated from the Grip of Organized Crime*. New York: New York University Press, 1999.

Jackson, Kenneth T. *The Encyclopedia of New York City*. New Haven, CT: Yale University Press, 1995.

Jennings, Dean. *We Only Kill Each Other*. New York: Fawcett Crest Books, 1968.

Katcher, Leo. *The Big Bankroll: The Life and Times of Arnold Rothstein*. New York: Da Capo, 1994.

Kavieff, Paul R. *The Life and Times of Lepke Buchalter*. Fort Lee, NJ: Barricade Books, 2006.

Kurtis, Bill. *Mafia: The History of the Mob in America*. New York: The Osterland Company and A & E Television Networks, 1993.

Lacey, Robert. *Little Man: Meyer Lansky and the Gangster Life*. Boston: Little Brown and Company, 1991.

Lance, Peter. *Deal With the Devil*. New York: William Morrow, An Imprint of Harper Collins 2013.

Lansky, Sandra. *Daughter of the King, Growing Up in Gangland*. New York: Weinstein Books, 2014.

Maas, Peter. *Underboss: Sammy "the Bull" Gravano's Story of Life in the Mafia*. New York: Harper Collins, 1997.

Maas, Peter. *The Valachi Papers*. New York: G P Putnam's Sons, 1968.

Martin, Raymond V. Martin, *Revolt in The Mafia*. New York: Duell, Sloan and Pearce, 1963.

May, Allan R. *Gangland Gotham*. Santa Barbara, CA: Greenwood Press, 2009.

McShane, Larry. *Chin: The Life and Crimes of Mafia Boss Vincent Gigante*. New York: Kensington Books, 2016.

Newark, Tim. *Boardwalk Gangster: The Real Lucky Luciano*. New York: Thomas Dunne Books, St. Martin's Press, 2010.

Pietrusza, David. *Rothstein: The Life, Times, and Murder of the Criminal Genius Who Fixed the 1919 World Series*. New York: Carroll & Graf, 2003.

Raab, Selwyn. *Five Families*. New York: Thomas Dunne Books, An imprint of St. Martin's Press, 2016.

Rockaway, Robert A. *But He Was Good to His Mother*. Jerusalem, Israel: Geffen Publishing Company, 2000.

Sann, Paul. *Kill The Dutchman! The Story of Dutch Schultz*. New York: A Da Capo Paperback, 1971.

Scarpa, Linda, with Linda Rosencrance. *The Mafia Hit Man's Daughter*. New York: Pinnacle Books, Kensington Publishing, Corp. 2016.

Sifakis, Carl. *The Mafia Encyclopedia*. New York: Checkmark Books, 1999.

Stuart, Mark A. *Gangster*. London: Star Book, division of W. H. Allen & Co, 1986.

Sussman, Jeffrey. *Boxing and the Mob: The Notorious History of the Sweet Science*. Lanham, MD: Rowman and Littlefield, 2019.

Turkus, Burton B., and Sid Feder. *Murder Inc*. New York: Da Capo Press, 1992.

Varesi, Anthony. *The Bob Dylan Albums.* Toronto, Ontario, Canada: Geurnica Editions, 2002.

Newspapers

New York Times
New York Daily News
New York Post
Newsday
Village Voice
Washington Post

Magazines

Time
Newsweek
New York Magazine
The New Yorker
People

Movies

Billy Bathgate
Bugsy
Eight Men Out
Goodfellas
Lepke
Murder Inc.
The Godfather
The Valachi Papers

Interviews

Anthony Celano (retired New York Police Department Detective Squad Commander)
Anthony Colella
Tommy Dades (retired New York Police Department organized crime detective)
Jerry Fiorenza (former undercover detective investigating Gambino crime family)
Remo Franceschini (former Queens District Attorney Squad Commander)
Chris Franzblau (former prosecutor and criminal defense attorney for alleged organized crime figures)

Joseph Giannini (criminal defense attorney)
Jay Goldberg (trial lawyer, criminal defense lawyer, and corporate lawyer)
Larry Lebowitz (former Assistant District Attorney)
Angelo Parisi (retired Washington DC detective)
Lou Piccolo
Ralph Salerno (former New York City Organized Crime Task Force detective)
Robert Santucci (former Chief of the Rackets Bureau, Office of the Bronx District Attorney and Special Assistant US Attorney for the Southern District of New York, Public Corruption Unit)
Michael Vecchione (former Chief of Rackets Division, Office of the Brooklyn District Attorney and coauthor of *Friends of the Family*)

Index